BEATING A RESTLESS DRUM

The Poetics of Kamau Brathwaite and Derek Walcott

June D. Bobb

Africa World Press, Inc.

P.O. Box 1892
Trenton, NJ 08607

P.O. Box 48
Asmara, ERITREA

Africa World Press, Inc.

P.O. Box 1892
Trenton, NJ 08607

P.O. Box 48
Asmara, ERITREA

Copyright © 1998 June D. Bobb

First Printing 1998

Cover design: Linda Nickens

Library of Congress Cataloging-in-Publication Data

Bobb, June.
    Beating a restless drum : the poetics of Kamau Brathwaite and
Derek Walcott / by June Bobb.
        p.   cm.
    Includes bibliographical references and index.
    ISBN 0-86543-599-5. – ISBN 0-86543-600-2 (pbk.)
    1. Brathwaite, Kamau, 1930- --Criticism and interpretation.
2. Caribbean poetry, English--History and criticism. 3. Caribbean
Area--Civilization--African influences. 4. Walcott, Derek-
-Criticism and interpretation. 5. Caribbean Area--In literature.
6. Poetics. I. Title.
PR9230.9.B68Z54 1998
811--dc21   98-6594
                                                            CIP

To

Melvin Dixon

and for

Sybil Doreen Clarke and Lynette deWeever Dolphin

Contents

Acknowledgements

This book has its origins in 1990 when a Magnet Fellowship from the Graduate Center of the City University of New York enabled me to travel to collections in the Caribbean and to interview many of the poets and scholars whose own work has influenced my own. Kamau Brathwaite has encouraged and supported this project from its inception, and I thank him. Bob Stewart read an earlier version of this book, and it has benefitted from his comments. In Trinidad, Gordon Rohlehr offered support, and led me to the Walcott papers, not catalogued at that time, and housed in the West Indian collection of the University. I want also to acknowledge J. Edward Chamberlain's fine study of Caribbean poetry published in 1993, and to thank him for the particular assistance he offered. For making my research trips productive and memorable, I want to thank Hazel and Bentley Gibbs and Crystal and Winston Pitt in Barbados, and Maureen and Allan Winter in St. Lucia.

In its various manifestations this work has taken shape and been guided by the suggestions of many friends and colleagues at the City University of New York who, in spite of the volume of their own work, took the time to read various sections of the book, commented critically or offered their technological expertise. They are: Ali Ahmed, Phyllis Cannon-Pitts, Valli Cook, Jacqueline deWeever, Joan Grant-Boyd, Joyce Harte, Gale Jackson, Steve Kruger, Marybeth McMahon, Joan Nestle, Lindsay Patterson, Amy Tucker and Barbara Webb. I thank them all sincerely.

Over the years that this project has taken to come into being, I have had the pleasure of working with Juan Collado, Ferentz Lafargue and Isabelle Pierre-Rollin, Mellon fellows at Queens College, who have been my research assistants at various stages of this project. I am indebted to them not only for their meticulous research, but also for their goodwill and enthusiasm. For galvanizing me into action two years ago when the end of this book seemed to be ever elusive, even illusory, I owe a debt of gratitude to Karen Gravelle and Sylvian Diouf-Kamara.

My editor, Patricia Allen at Africa World Press has saved the work from many infelicities, and I thank her. I also thank Kassahun Checole, the publisher and Wanjiku Ngugi, the editorial coordinator for their graciousness and patience as I tried to navigate the formidable world of computer technology. In this endeavor, I shall be eternally grateful to Helene Guidice, Reese Harris and Alain Sanon, and to Alexis Mulman-Cajou who simply took over and made it possible.

That I survived the rigors of this past semester is entirely due to the cheerful and efficient assistance of the following students: Karen Alston, Oeklen Kenol, Jacqueline Marquez-Duprey and Sabrina Nakhwattie Lauhar.

Finally, I owe this book to Robert and Kamau Bobb who have lived with it for a long time, yet continued to offer love, support and encouragement. For this I am truly grateful.

Introduction

I looked for some ancestral, tribal country

—Walcott, *Another Life*

Kamau Brathwaite, winner of the 1994 Neustadt International Prize for Literature, and Derek Walcott, winner of the 1992 Nobel Prize for Literature, are the Caribbean's most prominent poets. Walcott has received more international recognition, perhaps because in his poetic world he does not excavate past and present catastrophes in as relentlessly graphic a manner as Brathwaite does. Walcott's work has a certain gentility and accommodation that is not in Brathwaite's. Walcott estab- lishes poetic distance between historical and contemporary catastrophes and his own creative involvement. This distancing creates a safe space where past and present disharmonies are acted out. Thus, the devastation of the historical past and the dispossession of the present are filtered through Walcott's active intervention. While his critique of past European and current Caribbean political systems is harsh, it does not appear as confrontational as Brathwaite's.

Brathwaite, on the other hand, descends into the darkness of the Caribbean's fragmented psyche searching always for "the nature & complexity . often complicity . of the BROKEN dispossessed sometimes alienated GROUND on which we at 'first' find ourselves."[1] Very often Brathwaite is attacked for "celebrating endlessly the purgatorial experience of black people." He is also accused, as one critic puts it, of "ranting at the world for its refusal to be properly ashamed of slavery."[2] Such an accusation trivializes the searing power of memory and history and the poet's real work in historical and cultural rehabilitation.

Walcott, too, is engaged in historical and cultural rehabilitation. For Walcott, "Antillean art is this restoration of our shattered histories, our shards of vocabulary, our archipelago becoming a synonym for pieces broken off from the original continent."[3] Both poets journey back to the past through memory, and each, in his unique way, brings to the surface of Caribbean consciousness a history too traumatic to forget. Toni Morrison describes this journey as "a kind of literary archeology" to a site to see what remains were left behind and to reconstruct the world that these remains imply."[4] Both Kamau Brathwaite and Derek Walcott have embarked on this artistic mission. Their divergent approaches to historical and cultural excavations highlight the complexity of the imaginative journey, one further complicated by the Caribbean's disruption from origins and its attendant sense

of loss. Each poet's sense of personal disruption has its ori-
gins in the historical world of the Caribbean, a world of tur-
moil and torture.

In the West Indies, Columbus met an indigenous culture
that did not long survive the alien presence of Europeans. Like
travellers who had preceded him and those who followed, he
was enchanted by the islands he came upon, and, writing to
his sovereign from Cuba, he noted:

> The banks of the rivers are embellished with lofty palm
> trees, whose shade gives a delicious freshness to the air, and
> the birds and the flowers are uncommon and beautiful. I was
> so delighted with the scene, that I had almost come to the
> resolution of staying here for the remainder of my days; for
> believe me Sire, these countries far surpass all the rest of the
> world in beauty and conveniency.[5]

Travellers, ancient and modern, have been attracted to the
majestic beauty of the region. But writers and poets con-
tinue to be confronted by the region's central paradox; the
intrusion of the machinery of slavery and colonization onto
a world of such lyrical beauty. From the beginning, European
explorations into the Caribbean were motivated by econom-
ics and greed. Eric Williams describes Columbus' voyage as
the "first gold rush in history," and he quotes from Columbus'
journal to substantiate his statement:

> Without doubt, there is in these lands a vast quantity of gold,
> and the Indians I have on board do not speak without rea-
> son when they say that in these islands there are places
> where they dig out gold, and wear it on their necks, ears,
> arms and legs, the rings being very large.[6]

The presence of Columbus in the New World initiated relentless battles between the European powers concerning ownership of the region. The Portuguese and the Spanish appealed to the Pope, who, in 1493, declared that the East belonged to Portugal and the West to Spain. This did not prevent other contenders from joining in the scramble for colonial possessions. The French, the English and the Dutch competed in the race for new possessions. There was even a Danish and a Swedish presence in the Caribbean. Denmark ruled the Virgin Islands before they were sold to the United States in 1917, and Sweden ruled the island of St. Barthelemy from 1784 to 1877.[7]

Thus, it can be seen that the European presence has long been visible in the Caribbean. Having eliminated the indigenous peoples from their own soil shortly after "discovery," the Europeans found it necessary to provide a substitute people to fill the labor force for the sugar plantations. This is the origin of the African presence in the region. As Williams puts it, "the Negro...was to have his place, though he did not ask for it: it was the broiling sun of the sugar, tobacco and cotton plantations of the New World."[8] Africans were transported to the Caribbean to work as laborers. The European slavers pillaged the coasts of Guinea in their relentless pursuit of a work force. After rounding up their African cargo, the slavers led the Africans to seaports where they were inspected by potential buyers. On the slave ships, they were "packed in the hold on galleries one above the other." Slaves were chained to each other, and, during the long voyage to the Caribbean, the hatches were firmly secured; "in the close and loathsome darkness they were hurled from one side to another by the heaving vessel, held in position by the chains on their bleeding flesh."[9] Africans, stolen from various tribal communities and speaking many different languages, were thus violently uprooted from their history and culture and forced into a completely alien world, a world in which they were brutalized and dehumanized. Exiled from home and homeland, culture and the richness of their past, the Africans developed strategies of resistance in this new world. The Africa of their past became preserved in the world of their imagination, and the oral tradition became the agent of its transmission from generation to generation. In this way, Africa, both real and mythic, inspirited and actively transformed New World encounters between European colonizers and Africans, encounters in which, initially, the Africans were passive and powerless.

While the Abolition of the Slave Trade Act in the British Empire was passed in 1807, slavery continued until the passage of the Act of Emancipation in 1834, which officially ended the practice of slavery in the English-speaking colonies of the Caribbean. Although slavery was abolished, the European forces maintained their presence as controllers and the governors of the region's destiny. The abolition of slavery did not result in any major improvement in the social and economic conditions of the Caribbean's black inhabitants. Etched in the memory of these displaced Africans were the horrors of the Middle Passage journey and the degradation of their lives on the sugar plantations of the Caribbean.

After Emancipation, the mass exodus of Africans from the plantations made survival precarious. When the Caribbean plantation system collapsed and the privileged status of the investors no longer existed, Europeans immediately abandoned the Caribbean and searched for more profitable havens in other parts of the world, a pattern of colonial rule from the early days of the European-Caribbean relationship through the period of pre, and post independence.

Further complicating the Caribbean's turbulent history was the presence of other ethnic groups bent on maintaining a separate and unequal relationship with the region's recently freed black population. After the abolition of slavery and the mass exodus of Africans from the plantations, it became increasingly necessary to find other sources of cheap labor for the region's sugar plantations. Thus, prominent planters turned to India and China for the importation of cheap laborers. These laborers were not slaves but indentured servants, contracted to work for approximately five years, after which they were free to return to their homelands. In addition, they were provided with housing, free medical attention, and a fixed wage "of 1s 6d a day (the equivalent of 20 cents US) for a specific number of days in each year."[10] Though considerably better off than slaves, the living conditions of the indentured servants left much to be desired. At this time, range or barrack houses came into existence as the crude domicile of indentured servants. In describing range yards in Guyana, Walter Rodney writes: "[They] were unventilated, the water supply was polluted and lavatory facilities nonexistent...disease outbreaks tended to assume epidemic proportions."[11]

Immigrant labor in the Caribbean was also augmented by the presence of the Portuguese. In Guyana, immigrants from Madeira, (an island off the coast of Portugal), arrived in 1835. These immigrants were supposed to be examples, to the Africans, of the dignity of hard work: "The character of the Free Labourer cannot but be raised in his own estimation, and in that of the Negroes generally when they witness free White Men willingly submit to the same employment."[12] This was the beginning of the region's ethnic conflicts. Each group of immigrants came to the region with its culture intact, in spite of the horrendous living conditions, maintaining their religious practices and the rituals and customs of their cultures. There was little or no crossculturization between the Indian (from India), Chinese, or Portuguese and the African population. Africans viewed these groups as separatists, a view compounded by the fact that even after their time of indenture expired, these immigrants entered the fields of commerce maintaining businesses in which only members of their own ethnic groups were hired.

With this new hierarchy, blacks were confronted not only by their demeaning relationship with their European "masters," (a relationship governed not only by annihilating mental and physical violence and the intention to annihilate the black self), but they were also confronted by the corrosive separatist attitudes of the new immigrants to the region. Given the nature of these realities, it is not surprising that black Caribbeans remain conscious of the dark days of slavery and colonization, of their resulting psychic fragmentation, and of their position as the region's powerless and damned. Such intense awareness of private and public chaos, of destruction and creation, of life and death is poignantly captured in "After One Year" by the Guyanese poet, Martin Carter:

> Old hanging ground is still green playing field.
> Smooth cemetery proud garden of tall flowers.
> But in your secret gables real bats fly
> mocking great dreams that give the soul no peace, and everywhere wrong deeds are being done.

Carter's acknowledgment of possibility at the center of destruction and the restlessness of the artist's quest for transformation increases the pathos of his final truth: "Men murder men, as men must murder men, / to build their shining governments of the damned."[13] Carter, in his modernist framework, is very much aware of the alienation of the artist and of the artist's attempt to re-create the world by bringing into existence the forbidden and the neglected, thus challenging the complacency and the politics of a Caribbean government steeped in the ideology of its colonial masters. It is at this cusp of a Caribbean modernist movement that the poetry of Brathwaite and Walcott must be positioned.

Kamau Brathwaite and Derek Walcott, both born in 1930, grew up in a Caribbean world where there were visible manifestations and tangible vestiges of an oppressive colonial presence. The intent of their islands' official educational policy was to create a new breed of colonials in blackface. This new breed was educated to think and behave in mimicry, following the established pattern of its colonial masters. Although Brathwaite was given a colonial education, he came to transcend that paradigm.

Kamau Brathwaite was born in Bridgetown, Barbados. After graduating from Harrison College, he won an island scholarship and, in 1950, left for Cambridge University in England where he studied history. Between 1955 and 1962, Brathwaite taught in Ghana. These early years of Ghana's independence, under the leadership of Kwame Nkrumah, were inspirational and empowering for a Caribbean man who had grown up in colonial society, and, as Brathwaite writes in "Timehri," he was moved to acknowledge and explore his African ancestry:

> Slowly, ever so slowly...I was coming to an awareness...of cultural wholeness, of the place of the individual within the tribe. Slowly, ever so slowly, I came to a sense of iden-

tification with these people, my living diviners. I came to connect my history with theirs, the bridge of my mind was linking Atlantic and ancestor, homeland and heartland.

This reaching out for "cultural wholeness" was also fermenting in the Caribbean, and Brathwaite's yearnings for African groundings were inspired by the 1953 publication of George Lamming's *In the Castle of My Skin*. Brathwaite, with clear reference to Lamming, writes: "Here breathing to me from every pore of line and page, was the Barbados I had lived. The words, the rhythms, the cadences, the scenes, the people, their predicament. They all came back. They were possible."[14] In addition to his years in Barbados, Brathwaite spent several years in Jamaica. In 1980, he was named Professor of History at the University of the West Indies. His theoretical explorations of Caribbean culture were strongly influenced not only by his early years in Barbados, but also by Jamaican culture and the personal and political violence that was so much a part of daily life there.[15] Since 1991, Brathwaite has been Professor of Comparative Literature at New York University.

Derek Walcott was born in Castries, St. Lucia. He graduated from St. Mary's College, a high school for boys. In 1950, he left the island to attend the University College of the West Indies in Jamaica on a British Colonial Development and Welfare Scholarship. Walcott graduated three years later with a B.A. in English, French, and Latin. In 1959 he moved to Trinidad, his home for twenty-two years, where he established the Trinidad Theatre Workshop. Although Walcott has been teaching creative writing at Boston University since 1981, he often returns to the Caribbean, particularly to St. Lucia, the island of his poetic inspiration. Walcott, in the international literary world, has been adopted as an English

poet who happens to come from the Caribbean. This desig-
nation diminishes his essentially Caribbean sensibility. He,
like Brathwaite, is a product of a Caribbean world steeped in
the realities of the colonial and slave experiences. The work
of both poets is informed by the totality of their obsession
with the Caribbean's historical and cultural experience. Such
an obsession drives them to explore the submerged violence,
terror, and chaos existing beneath the startling beauty and
apparent placidity of Caribbean life.

In his latest work on Edouard Glissant, J. Michael Dash
makes the following observation: "[Glissant's] vision of opac-
ity, disorder, chaos and infinite profusion, so confusing
before, now seems to offer new insights into the exclusive
complexity of the Caribbean experience."[16] It is in Brathwaite's
disorderly and chaotic poetic world that the "complexity of
the Caribbean experience" is always fully explored. Antonio
Benítez-Rojo, recognizing the chaotic nature of the Caribbean
experience, describes Caribbean society as one that "origi-
nated in the most violent currents and eddies of modern
history where sexual and class differences are overlaid with
differences of an ethnographic nature."[17] The "violent currents
and eddies of modern history" inform Brathwaite's public
and private relationships. This repetitive pattern of frag-
mentation, disruption and violence characterizes the nature
of Caribbean experience and, paradoxically, imposes upon it
its own order. As Brathwaite describes it: "The history of cat-
astrophe . . . requires a literature of catastrophe to hold a bro-
ken mirror up to broken nature."[18] But Brathwaite's engage-
ment with the Caribbean experience is multilayered. In his
early writings (*The Arrivants*,[19] *Mother Poem*,[20] *Sun Poem*,[21] and
X/Self[22]) Brathwaite explores Caribbean alienation and dis-
possession while confronting the dread of history in an

attempt to refashion Caribbean identity. In his later works *The Zea Mexican Diary*,[23] *Barabajan Poems*,[24] and *DreamStories*[25]—there is a futuristic leap into a postmodern world, where the poet subverts ways of thinking and experience and even language itself as he eliminates existing barriers, gives face to new oppressors, and remaps old boundaries between oppressor and oppressed. In fact, Brathwaite's latest poetry does what he claims Caribbean literature, with the exception of Wilson Harris' work, has not done. It "act[s] itself out—as omens of catastrophe."[26] Brathwaite moves to another level. With the mastery of what he deems his "video style," chaos visibly enters his visionary world. Once it does, he can move on to the next step—redemption. His vision moves beyond the insular to the global, thus hinting at the possibility of unity in diversity, with the Caribbean as the crucible for such experimentation. Frederick Buell suggests that such an "exploration of global interactiveness...is a means of revising [the dominant] picture of the past."[27] Brathwaite achieves more than a simple "revision." His recognition that the history of the New World was never whole demands an identification of its fragments; for the fragments were initially part of a cultural and historical totality.

Derek Walcott, in his life and work, is consumed by the forces of history, yet at times he displays an ambivalence toward the past:

> I say to the ancestor who sold me, and to the ancestor who bought me I have no father, I want no such father, although I can understand you, black ghost, white ghost, when you both whisper "history," for if I attempt to forgive you both I am falling into your idea of history which justifies and explains and expiates, and it is not mine to forgive, my

memory cannot summon any filial love, since your features
are anonymous and erased and I have no wish and no power
to pardon.[28]

Walcott constantly struggles to bring to life the phantoms
of the ancestral past. He confronts the history of the "white
ghost," and, as he rewrites this history, he struggles to restore
the "features" of his black ancestors. Unlike Brathwaite,
Walcott withdraws from open confrontation as he struggles
for this restoration; restoration is achieved only in his artis-
tic world. Brathwaite, the poet of confrontation and experi-
mentation, is constantly exploding frontiers of form and lan-
guage. Walcott, on the other hand, the poet of accommoda-
tion, well-versed in Prospero's language, utilizes this lan-
guage to explore the nuances of the Caribbean experience. In
putting this experience into words, there are times when the
experience fits uncomfortably. Yet, he brings life to the past,
creating a space in which the world is reshaped and a new
artistic and moral truth revealed. The distinction between
poets is perhaps inevitable. While both poets are from the
Caribbean, each is shaped by his peculiar circumstances and
his individual imagination.

Brathwaite, in Barbados, was strongly subjected to the
British influence while Walcott, in St. Lucia, was enveloped by
both the British and the French colonial presence. In addition,
there existed in the Caribbean the remnants of the civiliza-
tion of the region's indigenous people as well as survivals of
African culture, a legacy of the region's contact with the insti-
tution of slavery. From this region of varied cultural influences
emerges the poetic vision of these two men. Each poet, in his
own way, reacts to the destruction of self and society that is
an expression of the realities of slavery and colonization. The

task of each poet becomes the rewriting of history, a kind of cultural mythmaking, the purpose of which is to reconnect the severed parts of the Caribbean psyche, or as Brathwaite puts it: "To make the fragments whole." For Brathwaite, this means a reconnection to an African past with an understanding of the vitality of the rituals and history of the African people. It is in such a reconnection, transposed upon a Caribbean world inhabited by the region's many peoples, that he sees the possibility of Caribbean survival and a reaffirmation of a Caribbean sensibility.

Walcott, on the other hand, while recognizing the African presence and its Caribbean manifestations, does not look solely to Africa for sustenance and survival; he wants to recognize all the ancestors simultaneously:

> I give the strange and bitter and yet ennobling thanks for the monumental groaning and soldering of two great worlds, like the halves of a fruit seamed by its own bitter juice, that exiled from your own Edens you have placed me in the wonder of another, and that was my inheritance and your gift.[29]

While there is a difference in absorption of the region's diverse cultural makeup, both poets share a similarity of vision. Each is concerned with molding a Caribbean sensibility rooted in an awareness of its tortured past, a past grounded in the violence of slavery and colonization and the torment of its struggles for freedom and independence. At the same time, each poet celebrates the present and the vibrant spirit of the New World and sings of the pain as well as the joy of the Caribbean and its people. In their revisioning of the historical past, both poets create a present in which the region and its folk become towering symbols of endurance and survival.

This revisioning is, however, on a mythic level. In addition, the killing legacy of the past is explored in the real world of the Caribbean, a world of violence and of new and vicious colonial masters not as easily recognizable as before. In such a world, where the fragmentation and destruction of the past collide with the fragmentation and destruction of the present, Kamau Brathwaite and Derek Walcott have adopted the Herculean task of recreating a mythic Caribbean territory. Upon this territory, both old and contemporary wounds will be exposed and cleansed, paving the way for the creation of a psychic space where the true identity of the Caribbean will be inscribed.

To accomplish this task, both poets draw upon the vernacular tradition so much a part of the reality of the region. Out of this tradition emerge the literary techniques that enable Kamau Brathwaite and Derek Walcott to reclaim history and memory. A reclamation of the past facilitates the re-creation of a Caribbean universe. Existing at the center of this new universe are the Caribbean people—reshaped and revitalized, no longer aliens in their homeland. This act of re-creation, by its very nature is political and becomes the conscious "soldering" of myth and history resulting in the remaking of the Caribbean world, the reclamation of tradition and the renewal of faith:

> For on this ground
> trampled with the bull's swathe of whips
> where the slave at the crossroads was a red anthill
> eaten by the moonbeams, by the holy ghosts
> of his wounds
>
> the Word becomes
> again a god and walks among us...[30]

Notes

1. Kamau Brathwaite, "A Post Cautionary Tale of the Helen of Our Wars," *Wasafiri* 22 (Autumn 1995): 75.
2. Robert Skidelsky, "A Song of Lost Islands," *The Economist* (10 December 1994): 93.
3. Derek Walcott, "The Antilles: Fragments of Epic Memory," *The Nobel Lecture* (New York: Farrar, Straus, Giroux, 1993) 9.
4. Toni Morrison, "The Site of Memory," in *Inventing the Truth: the Art and Craft of Memoir,* ed. William Zinsser (Boston: Houghton Mifflin, 1987) 112.
5. J.H. Parry and Philip Sherlock, *A Short History of the West Indies* (London: Macmillan, 1971) 3.
6. Eric Williams, *From Columbus to Castro* (New York: Vintage, 1984) 23.
7. Gordon K. Lewis, *The Growth of the Modern West Indies* (New York: Monthly Review, 1968) 48.
8. Eric Williams, *Capitalism and Slavery* (New York: Putnam, 1966) 4.
9. C.L.R. James, *The Black Jacobins* (New York: Vintage, 1963) 8.
10. Williams, *From Columbus to Castro* 352.
11. Walter Rodney, *A History of the Guyanese Working People, 1881-1905* (Baltimore: Johns Hopkins UP, 1981) 37.
12. Mary Noel Menezes, *Scenes from the History of the Portuguese in Guyana* (Surrey, England: Victoria, 1986) 20.
13. Martin Carter, "After One Year," *Selected Poems: Martin Carter* (Georgetown, Guyana: Demerara, 1989) 83.
14. Kamau Brathwaite, "Timehri," Is Massa Day Dead? *Black Moods in the Caribbean,* ed. Orde Coombs (New York: Anchor, 1974) 32-33.
15. See Brathwaite's poetic account of his personal confrontation with Jamaican violence in *Trench Town Rock* (Providence: Lost Roads, 1994) No. 40.
16. J. Michael Dash, *Edouard Glissant* (Cambridge: Cambridge UP, 1995) 25.
17. Antonio Benítez-Rojo, *The Repeating Island: The Caribbean and the Postmodern Perspective,* trans. James E. Maraniss (Durham: Duke UP, 1992) 27.
18. Kamau Brathwaite, "Metaphors of Underdevelopment: A Proem for Hernan Cortez," in *The Art of Kamau Brathwaite,* ed. Stewart Brown (Plantin, Wales: Cromwell, 1995) 235.
19. Kamau Brathwaite, *The Arrivants: A New World Trilogy* (London: Oxford UP, 1973).
20. Kamau Brathwaite, *Mother Poem* (Oxford: Oxford UP, 1977).
21. Kamau Brathwaite, *Sun Poem* (Oxford: Oxford UP, 1982).

22. Kamau Brathwaite, *X/Self* (Oxford: Oxford UP, 1987).
23. Kamau Brathwaite, *The Zea Mexican Diary* (Madison: U of Wisconsin P, 1993).
24. Kamau Brathwaite, *Barabajan Poems* (Kingston & New York: Savacou North, 1994).
25. Kamau Brathwaite, *DreamStories,* Essex: Longman, 1994.
26. Brathwaite, "Metaphors of Underdevelopment" 235.
27. Frederick Buell, *National Culture and the New Global System* (Baltimore: Johns Hopkins UP, 1994) 343.
28. Derek Walcott, "The Muse of History," *Is Massa Day Dead?,* ed. Orde Coombs (New York: Anchor, 1974) 27.
29. Walcott, "The Muse of History" 27.
30. Brathwaite, "Vèvè," *The Arrivants* 263.

Chapter 1

Reconceiving Self and World

I wear this
past I borrowed; his-
tory bleeds
behind my hollowed eyes;

—Brathwaite, "Sunsum," *The Arrivants*

Historically, the Caribbean world has been seared by the fires of slavery and colonization. The result is a peculiar fragmentation of the psyche of its people. This debilitating fragmentation permeates the life and the literature of the region and may be traced to the racist, paternalistic attitudes and practices of the early colonists, slave holders, and historians. From its very beginnings, Caribbean poetry has engaged the chaos and violence of the history that has given it birth, and the poetry of Kamau Brathwaite and Derek Walcott emerges from that space of violence and chaos. Both poets confront the trauma of the historical misrepresentation of the Caribbean and its people, and each develops a poetics of resistance as an antidote to personal and communal pain. For these poets the poetic act is political. It is a weapon central to the process of the reclamation of self and world. The imaginary landscapes created by Kamau Brathwaite and Derek Walcott offer healing spaces from which the debasement and humiliation of the past are expelled.

From the time they landed on Caribbean soil, the captured Africans faced humiliation. Kenneth Kiple describes the process to which the slaves were subjected at ports of entry:

> [Their] skins were rubbed with oil to make them shine, rum was administered to clear the eyes and brighten the countenance, sores were covered with iron rust and gunpowder, lesions closed, and even anuses corked to prevent the telltale leakage of the flux.[1]

Once they were sold to various plantations and estates, slaves were branded, generally on their shoulders, as a means of identification.[2] Such physical violation was institutionalized in the Code Noir—laws affecting the slaves of the island of Jamaica—a collection of the most dehumanizing and cruel restrictions and punishments guaranteed to reduce human beings to the level of bestiality. According to the Code, pregnant female slaves convicted of breaking the law would not be executed until after their delivery. A slave convicted of receiving stolen goods was punished by death, dismemberment or transportation to a remote part of the island.[3] In addition to laws that demoralized and dehumanized the slave population, the cycle of their daily lives was just as inhumane. Slaves working on sugar estates were "expected to open at least one hundred cane holes a day and failure to do so was punished by whipping." The exceedingly strenuous nature of this work drove the overseers to hire "jobbing gangs." These gangs were composed of slaves owned by small businessmen who then hired them out to work on various sugar estates. In addition to digging cane holes, they were hired to "make and repair roads, clear forests, and...to do the most arduous work on the estates." Gangs had no fixed living quarters and slept wherever the night found them. Gang members lived at most seven years from their impressment.[4]

More than the actual physical battering the slaves were subjected to, there was also a history of psychological attacks against their perception of self. As early as 1774, Edward Long suggested that some Africans were more closely related to the orangutan than to the white race of men, and that Africans or imported Negroes were addicted to the "most bestial vices."[5] Bryan Edwards in 1793 viewed Africa as uncivilized and Africans as savages.[6] Thomas Carlyle, in "Occasional Discourse on the Nigger Question," published in 1849, saw the West Indian as an "idle Black gentleman, with his rum-bottle in his hand, no breeches on his body, pumpkin at discretion, and the fruitfulest region of the earth going back to jungle round him."[7] Anthony Trollope, too, in 1859, presents the world of the West Indies as exotic and its black inhabitants as carefree and simple:

> He lies under his mango-tree and eats the luscious fruit in the sun; he sends his black urchin up for a breadfruit, and behold the family table is spread. He pierces a cocoa-nut, and, lo! there is his beverage. He lies on the grass surrounded by oranges, bananas and pineapples.[8]

Added to these views, James Anthony Froude, in 1888, suggests that West Indians lack intellect and are incapable of governing themselves and even asserts that slavery is liberating for the West Indian:

> The negroes of the West Indies are children, and not yet dis-
> obedient children. They have their dreams, but for the pre-
> sent they are dreams only. If you enforce self-government
> upon them when they are not asking for it, you may turn the
> dream into a reality, and willfully drive them back into the
> condition of their ancestors, from which the slave trade was
> the beginning of their emancipation.[9]

Throughout the eras of slavery, colonization, preindepen-
dence and beyond, these perceptions of the West Indies and
West Indians remain dominant and are etched into the con-
sciousness of the people with devastating effects. Out of this his-
torical climate emerges the West Indian's tendency to denigrate
things West Indian and to idolize things European.

After Emancipation in 1838, Lord Grey, the Secretary of State
for the Colonies, suggested to the Governor of Trinidad that the
freed slaves should "look to labour on the estates as their main
dependence." He also suggested that schools should be estab-
lished to "encourage a love of employment."[10] The newly freed
slaves did not experience a startling difference in the quality of
their lives. The colonial powers had maintained a presence in the
region since the fifteenth century, and while the abolition of slav-
ery ended the practice of white masters owning black slaves, abo-
lition was purely a technicality. White masters merely continued
to subjugate the black work force as they exploited the resources
of the region for the benefit of their various motherlands. Thus,
when Lord Grey advocated the "encourage[ment] of a love of
employment" on the part of the newly freed slave, it was politically
a cosmetic exercise, for in the colonial context both education and
employment were restricted. Employment meant the careful cul-

tivation of workers who had been educated into believing that only things European and capitalist were of value. As Walter Rodney puts it: "Colonial schooling was education for subordination, exploitation, the creation of mental confusion and the development of underdevelopment."[11] Such "schooling" also encouraged the divisiveness of class. The vast black population was seen as a source of cheap labor, and no attempt was made under colonial rule to provide an adequate education for the masses. Blacks and coloreds of middleclass standing and aspirations, were educated with local whites according to the English public school system. C.L.R. James describes his belated understanding of his colonial education:

> It was only long years after that I understood the limitation on spirit, vision and self-respect which was imposed on us by the fact that our masters, our curriculum, our code of morals, everything began from the basis that Britain was the source of all light and learning, and our business was to admire, wonder, imitate, learn; our criterion of success was to have succeeded in approaching that distant ideal—to attain it was, of course, impossible. Both masters and boys accepted it as in the very nature of things.[12]

It is no accident that in the schools no attempt was made to include the study of African and Caribbean history and literature. Therefore, generations of West Indians emerged and continue to emerge with ambivalent attitudes about race, and very often with distinctly anti-West Indian, anti-black sentiments. Léon Damas, the poet from French Guiana, captures the resulting sense of mimicry and the element of caricature:

> I feel ridiculous
> in their shoes

their dinner jackets
their starched shirts
and detachable collars
their monocles and
their bowler hats

I feel ridiculous
my toes not made
to sweat from morning until night's relief
from this swaddling that impedes my limbs
and deprives my body of the beauty of its hidden
sex.[13]

It is this caricature of the West Indian, fitting uncomfortably into a mold created by colonizers, that Caribbean people struggle against. One of the earliest voices raised in opposition to this negative stereotyping is the Trinidadian, J.J. Thomas, who in 1889, published in London a response to J.A. Froude's *The English in the West Indies* or *The Bow of Ulysses*. The original title of Thomas' work was Froude's *Fables on the Negro in the West Indies*.[14] According to Thomas, Froude's immediate purpose was to present "the dark outlines of a scheme to thwart political aspiration in the Antilles."[15] Froude's basic position was that blacks in the West Indies were inferior to whites and lacked political skills and social graces. In spite of his grudging admiration for the women—"they might serve as sculptors' models"—he remained convinced that blacks were totally incapable of governing themselves. In his repudiation of *The English in the West Indies,* Thomas attempts to assert Caribbean selfhood. He recognizes the colonial outsider's intent to present the world of the colony as "other," maintaining a construct of difference based upon claims of intellectual and moral superiority.

Froudacity becomes an important text in the development of Caribbean literary resistance. As Terry Eagleton suggests, "nobody can live in perpetual deferment of their sense of selfhood, or free themselves from bondage without a strongly affirmative consciousness of who they are."[16]

Early in the nineteenth century, Caribbean poetry underwent a shift in subject matter. Poets began to explore the local landscape. This shift begins to manifest itself in the collection of Guyanese poetry edited by Norman Cameron.[17] In Cameron's collection the poet, Leo, moves from a celebration of Queen Victoria's Jubilee: "Let Britain close / Far-reaching wings and strong / O'er her colonial throng" (108), to singing the beauty of the local sorrel tree (82). W. McA. Lawrence sings of Guyana's mighty waterfall, Kaiteur: "And falling in splendour sheer down from the height / that should gladden the heart of an eagle to scan, / That lend to the towering forest beside thee / the semblance of shrubs trimmed and tended by man" (81). The turn of the early poets' gaze inward to focus on the local flora and fauna signals a rebellion against the imposition of an alien construction of identity.

In the islands of the Caribbean and in Guyana, national and colonial identities have confronted each other as a result of the reality of geography and the accident of history. Very early in the eighteenth century the Jamaican poet, Francis Williams recognized that "every island's but a prison / Strongly guarded by the sea / Kings and princes for that reason / Prisonner's are as Well as We."[18] Because of the region's confinement, it is not surprising that early poetic voices were largely imitative. Williams, in 1759, in "An Ode" to George Haldane, a governor of Jamaica, utilizes the conventions of the Latin panegyric:

> Oh! *Muse,* of blackest tint, why shrinks thy breast,
> Why fears t' approach the *Caesar* of the West!

Dispel thy doubts, with confidence ascend
The regal dome, and hail him for thy friend:
Nor blush, altho' in garb funereal drest,
Thy body's white, tho' clad in sable vest.[19]

Williams is the "muse of blackest tint." Describing himself as a white man in a black skin, he expresses his awe in the presence of a representative of the British empire. While the reverence for things British continued, there were dissenting voices. Vivian Vertue from Jamaica celebrates the beauty and the lushness of the Jamaican landscape:

I have seen March within the ebony break
In golden fire of fragrance unsuppressed;
And April bring the lignum-vitae dressed
In dusty purple; known pale rust awake
The mango's boughs; the poinciana take
Immortal wound of summer. I have pressed
The cassia's spendthrift yellow to my breast:
I could love earth for one tree's royal sake.[20]

The roots of a poetry of national awareness lie in Vertue's celebration of the Caribbean landscape. Vere T. Daly in Guyana expresses a longing to be free from colonial constraints:

We are weary of searching for hope who should not be
hopeless,
We whose faith did not fail with the failing years;
It is better by far to be wild, free men than the
scopeless / And prince-governed men of tears.[21]

A. J. Seymour hears the drums of Africa: "The white hair like a snow cap on his head / That thin old negro had beat the rhythm for years / The Ibu rhythm, learnt in African forests / From hands as proud and serpent-veined as his."[22]

While many Caribbean poets saw themselves as inheritors of a European tradition, other voices emerged firmly rooted in a vernacular tradition. Because of the intermingling presence of Africans, Chinese, Indians, and Portuguese in the Caribbean, the vernacular tradition manifested itself in various forms: legends, folk tales and songs, proverbs, and Anansi stories. Each of these groups contributed to the richness of the vernacular tradition in the Caribbean, a tradition that continues to be a source of both inspiration and material for the region's artists.

Out of this vernacular tradition, the works of poets such as Claude McKay, Evan Jones, Louise Bennett, and later Kamau Brathwaite and Derek Walcott emerge. The vernacular tradition presents the Caribbean poet with a visionary world that is distinctive. As O.R. Dathorne has noted, "The dialect verse of Claude McKay and Louise Bennett could not have been written without this folk-tradition which [involves] a new way of seeing as well as of hearing."[23] The world of the vernacular provides a source of ideas, symbols, and imagery that informs the art of poets and writers. As a result, their visionary worlds are imbued with the beauty and magic of ancient belief and rituals. The presence of the vernacular tradition also adds a sense of wholeness and an appreciation of earth, labor, and the simple folk from which modern society often distances itself.

Claude McKay, in his Preface to the *Constab Ballads*, discusses the "rubs" of daily life and the "rebellion" that was always in his heart.[24] The honor of work is the theme of "Bumming": "Our trouble is dat those above / Do oftentimes oppress; / But we'll laugh at or pity dem, / Or hate dem mo' or less."[25] McKay writes about the experiences of the masses, their pain and oppression in the language of their daily lives. Evan Jones, in "The Song of the Banana Man," captures the feeling for the land, the appreciation of the value of labor and the dignity and selfhood of the ordinary folk, and he does this in their unique voice:

> I leave m'yard early-mornin time
> An set m'foot to de mountain climb,
> I ben m'back to de hot-sun toil,
> An m'cutlass rings on de stony soil,
> Ploughin an weedin, diggin an plantin
> Till Massa Sun drop back o John Crow mountain,
> Den home again in cool evenin time,
> Perhaps whistling dis likkle rhyme,
> Praise God an m'big right han
> I will live an die a banana man.[26]

Louise Bennett follows in the direct literary footsteps of Claude McKay. Bennett was strongly influenced by the culture of rural Jamaica and concerned herself with the influences of colonization on the minds and lives of the common folk, their daily struggle for survival, and the business of politics. "Independance" discusses Jamaica's direct departure from British rule, and the attitude of the ordinary man to the imminent changes in the society:

> She hope dem caution worl-map
> Fe stop draw Jamaica small
> For de lickle speck cyaan show
> We independantniss at all!
> Morsomover we mus tell map dat
> We doan like we position
> Please kindly tek we out a sea
> An draw we in de ocean.[27]

Martin Carter, like Louise Bennett, is in the front line of literary resistance to oppression established by the earlier poets. *Poems of Resistance* is his reaction to the particularly deadening climate of the 1950s in Guyana: the general unrest and violence, the presence of the British occupation forces, and the experience of a people under siege:

> This is the dark time, my love.
> It is the season of oppression, dark metal, and
>   tears.
> It is the festival of guns, the carnival of misery. Everywhere the
> faces of men are strained and
>   anxious.[28]

Out of these internal and external forces—the battle for recognition of an indigenous voice, the struggle against the annihilation of the mind that is the legacy of colonialism, and an innate response to the vernacular tradition—emerge the poetic sensibilities of Edward Kamau Brathwaite and Derek Walcott. Both poets challenge the stereotypical presentation of Caribbean people and their identity; both poets return to an African past and new world beginnings to reenvision the present Caribbean reality.

The internalization of the negative attitudes and images that Brathwaite and Walcott attempt to erase from the Caribbean consciousness has resulted at times in a denial of the Caribbean's African connections and the emergence of a literature of negation. V.S. Naipaul, for example, claimed brazenly: "History is built around achievement and creation; and nothing was created in the West Indies."[29] Naipaul's acceptance of a cultural and historical void accounts for the sense of displacement often found in the life and literature of the region. In an attempt to reclaim the past of his ancestors, Naipaul returned to Trinidad in his forties. In questioning his mother about the form his father's madness took, she said: "He looked in the mirror one day and couldn't see himself. And he began to scream."[30] His father's scream might well be Naipaul's own scream of disinheritance and displacement, which symbolizes his lack of connection to a cultural imagination. Brathwaite and Walcott are connected to a cultural imagination informed by an ancestral past. In the imaginary landscapes they create, this past enters into present history.

Their mission is an important one, for very often critics and theorists, convinced of the superiority of Western literature, and awed by the sanctity of Western literary traditions, impose upon non-European literatures a tradition of Western aesthetics. In addition, in Caribbean discourse, the Western critic at times is shrouded in a mantle of omniscience that results in closed readings of Caribbean texts. Helen Vendler, in commenting on Walcott's use of Creole states that "a macaronic aesthetic, using two or more languages at once, has never yet been sustained in poetry at any length."[31] Vendler's criticism points to the very real need of the critic to be aware of the tradition out of which these poets emerge. Vendler's point is not accurate, for Walcott has complete control of the English language as well as French and English Creole. Fredric Jameson recognizes such critical omniscience as a struggle for power and the preservation of certain Western world views:

> ...to read [the third world] text adequately—we would have to give up a great deal that is individually precious to us and acknowledge an existence and a situation unfamiliar and therefore frightening—one that we do not know and prefer not to know.[32]

An unwillingness to explore or attempt to understand the "unfamiliar" results in the colonization of Caribbean texts. Critical neglect as well as misreadings are part of this process of colonization. Edward Said not only acknowledges the realities of "power and authority," he also acknowledges the resistance mounted by communal movements and national organizations and the role they play in bringing texts into existence:

> The realities of power and authority—as well as the resistance offered by men, women, and social movements to institutions, authorities, and orthodoxies—are the realities that make texts possible, that deliver them to their readers, that solicit the attention of critics. I propose that these realities are what should be taken account of by criticism and the critical consciousness.[33]

George Lamming, the Barbadian novelist, aware of the "realities of power and authority" in the colonial Caribbean, discusses domination and authority in terms of the relationship between Caliban and Prospero. Lamming is the first writer in the English-speaking Caribbean to identify the colonial in the Caribbean with Shakespeare's Caliban. He reads the Shakespearian relationship between Prospero and Caliban as analogous to the relationship between colonizer and colonized in the Caribbean. Prospero gives to Caliban language and its transforming power. Language, as Lamming uses the word, means not only "English," but "speech...as a way, a method, a necessary avenue towards areas of the self which could not be reached in any other way."[34] This gift of language can, however, also be the vehicle of imprisonment, and it poses a dilemma in the Caribbean. Caribbean people (while they speak various Creole languages, depending upon the language of their particular colonizers), in order to enter the arena of debate with their colonizers employ the language of the colonizer. Brathwaite and Walcott, like Lamming, realize the ambivalence inherent in this situation. They see the need to return to a pre-European historical era. They acknowledge that the Caribbean's transplanted Calibans entered the New World with their own speech before Europeans imposed the mixed blessing of their language.

A recognition of an existence, history and culture before the European presence in the region negates the theory of the void, that is, the colonial view that the region has no history. The ambiguous relationship between the colonizing agent and the colonial subject is analyzed by Aimé Césaire, who sees the relationship as one that transforms "the colonizing man into a classroom monitor, an army sergeant, a prison guard, a slave driver, and the indigenous man into an instrument of production." Furthermore, he notes that the colonial relationship is governed by suspicion and domination. It results in "societies drained of their essence, cultures trampled underfoot, institutions undermined, lands confiscated, religions smashed, magnificent artistic creations destroyed, extraordinary *possibilities* wiped out."[35] In colonial societies and societies subjected to political and cultural domination and violence, artists adopt the responsibility of upholding and preserving the national culture. National culture, as defined by Fanon, is "the whole body of efforts made by a people in the sphere of thought to describe, justify, and praise the action through which that people has created itself and keeps itself in existence."[36]

It is through the vision of Brathwaite and Walcott that past history is interpreted and filtered, and that present realities of colonial and postindependence existence are brought to the forefront of the public consciousness. They are consumed by the writer's responsibility in a world where imagination is often buried under the expedient, and the world of the material is sacred. In an attempt to destroy the gods of materialism and return their people to a world in which the human spirit is valued and individual and communal possibilities cherished, these poets present both the terror and the beauty of society. This sensitivity to past and present and the ability to interpret history and to rewrite it give the poet his godlike place in society; for as Chinua Achebe puts it:

> The writer cannot expect to be excused from the task of re-education and regeneration that must be done. In fact he should march right in front. For he is after all...the sensitive point of his community.[37]

Ranging from *The Arrivants* to *X/Self*, Brathwaite focuses on the nurturing and cultivating of community; his celebration of the customs and rituals of the African ancestors is an integral part of the struggle for liberation in which he is engaged. He envisions a Caribbean world at the center of which lie the life-affirming principles and philosophies of the African ancestors. In articulating a theory of Caribbean aesthetics, Brathwaite recognizes that at the heart of Caribbean literature is the presence of the vernacular traditions of the region. The colonial presence eroded almost all aspects of the lives and personalities of those it dominated, and the culture of the region was forced underground. Brathwaite brings this vernacular culture to the surface of Caribbean consciousness in the process of reshaping Caribbean identity. But this identity is not always at home in a region where colonial masters and New World colonists celebrate conformity and denigrate difference—a difference which Eagleton recognizes "must pass through identity if it is to come into its own."[38]

The Caribbean landscape becomes the inspiriting source of

this creation of identity. Brathwaite's carefully crafted language, amalgam of customs, rituals, and music are the instruments he utilizes to recarve the story of his land and his people. For him, "the basis of culture lies in the folk." Brathwaite celebrates "not in-culturated, static groups, giving little; but a people who, from the centre of an oppressive system have been able to survive, adapt, recreate."[39] Brathwaite's poetics is one of community. For him, the region's survival depends upon the individual's ability to merge self into a collective consciousness, a consciousness deeply rooted in the memory of Africa. Out of this knowledge of an ancestral culture, Brathwaite reclaims lost rights and rites and acknowledges an enduring Caribbean tradition. The dispossessed and alienated enter history:

> Should you
> shatter the door
> and walk
> in the morning
> fully aware
> of the future
> to come?
> There is no
> turning back.[40]

Caribbean writers are very much aware of this state of inevitability and implosion. Unlike many of their white Western counterparts, they do not have the luxury of distance and distancing. They exist at the cutting edge of societies and are close to the power of the government and the poverty of the masses. While many Caribbean writers who live and write in the region complain of being marginalized, this feeling of marginalization is a matter of their perception of the distance between the artistic imagination and the pragmatism of government. They attempt to lessen the distance between the powerful and the powerless. In Guyana, in the flush of the postindependence movement to close gaps and to expand horizons and possibilities and to ensure that, in Guyanese parlance, "the small man is the real man," the vision of Carifesta became a reality in 1972. The theme of this festival of the arts was the role of the artist in Third World societies. Brathwaite views this as an important moment of recognition in the Caribbean. People from all parts of the region came together in celebration and discovered their "common Caribbean style."[41] There was also the recognition of the crucial role of the artist in the building of the nation and the initiation of change. As Edouard Glissant states: "...cultural activism must lead to political activism."[42] In the convergence of artist and society lies the ideal union that Brathwaite envisions. Through the sacred space of his imagination, the poet filters the triumphs and horrors of the historical past. This union of past memory and present history informs the region's future, and has always been a part of the region's literary vision. Vera Bell, a precursor of Brathwaite, displays the same vision of a present world intimately connected to and rising from history's pain:

Ancestor on the auction block
Across the years
I look
I see you sweating, toiling, suffering
Within your loins I see the seed
Of multitudes
From your labour
Grow roads, aqueducts, cultivation

A new country is born

Yours was the task to clear the ground
Mine be the task to build.[43]

Brathwaite, like Bell, clearly recognizes the nature and scope of the poet's "task" to build a region's psychological and spiritual identity.

While Brathwaite's muse celebrates community, Walcott's muse celebrates the individual. This difference may be attributed to each poet's peculiar vision of the role of history in the development of a poetic consciousness. For Brathwaite, the poet's racial memory is the key to his understanding and interpretation of history, and while the remembered past is filled with historical horrors, at the same time the poet's imagination leaps beyond the boundaries of the region's actual history to an African golden age:

city of gold,
paved with silver,
ivory altars,
tables of horn,
the morn-
ing sun of
seven hills
greets you best,
knows you blessed.[44]

Derek Walcott, in "The Muse of History," appears to be sharply critical of Brathwaite's reverence for and celebration of an African golden age: "This shame and awe of history possess poets of the Third World who think of language as enslavement and who, in a rage for identity, respect only incoherence or nostalgia."[45] But Walcott's appraisal lacks conviction and undermines his own reading of the past. He is concerned with the ambivalence of history and, in an attempt at reconciliation, consciously utilizes the persona of the alienated artist battling the dualities of the past in order to refashion a future. Walcott's past, however, is problematic. He conceives of a personal past inhabited by his ancestors, both European and African, and a regional mythic past inhabited by the presence of all the region's peoples. In a society that has always been ravaged by divisions of race, such all-inclusiveness is appealing. But, in spite of his good intentions, the public Walcott cannot be all races, and in a society where racial identification has always been dominant, he cannot escape his African ancestry. As he himself has noted: "The sense of history in poets lives rawly along their nerves."[46] In the process of rewriting history, Walcott creates in his poetic world, a number of concentric worlds, each one devoted to some aspect of his Caribbean world picture. He focuses on the rituals and customs of the folk, religion and its Caribbean transformations, and on the appropriation and rewriting of the language of the colonizer. His poetry, as it ranges from the tentative explorations of self and landscape in *25 Poems*,[47] to the pain of a divided consciousness in *In a Green Night*[48] and *The Castaway*,[49] and the autobiographical power of *Another Life*,[50] is a pilgrimage of reconnection to a mythic memory. At the same time, Walcott is very much a part of a Caribbean sensibility, and his work is grounded in a celebration of the St. Lucian folk and, by extension, the folk of the region. This all coalesces in his most recent work, *Omeros*, which is, in spite of Walcott's denial, his appropriation and reinvention of the epic form transposed to the Caribbean landscape.

Testifying to the complexity of the Caribbean's cultural heritage, Walcott's theorizing is not always at one with his actual poetic explorations and experimentations. He rails against the "apotheosis[ing] [of] the folk form,"[51] yet he is constantly reshaping forms and reworking rituals in the process of creating a Caribbean aesthetic expansive enough to accommodate the clashes and conflicts constantly at work in his poetic imagination.[52] For example, in his play *Dream on Monkey Mountain* he has several vernacular forms: proverbs, folk tales, and the rituals and performance of African religious ceremonies. *Ti-Jean and His Brothers,* another play also demonstrates Walcott's skill at integrating St. Lucian folk tale, fable and street performance into his work.[53] He is well aware of the African tradition of camouflaging for survival, discussing this once again in "The Muse of History": "What seemed to be surrender was redemption. What seemed the loss of tradition was its renewal. What seemed the death of faith was its rebirth."[54] Walcott comes to terms with the issues of history and ancestral memory, more comfortably in the medium of the drama than he does in his poetry. In the theater of drama, Walcott in his role as director successfully masks the personal, and from this artistic distance safely descends into the world of folk culture. Unlike Brathwaite, who clearly articulates his position and does not hesitate to point out that Africa informs his poetic vision and his theory of Caribbean aesthetics, Walcott is not as declarative. In the created space of his imagination, Walcott invents a self that, theoretically, can fit more easily into the Caribbean landscape. The process of invention in which Walcott utilizes elements of a self both real and created, is explored in his autobiographical work, *Another Life.*

In its opening section, "The Divided Child," the poet presents a cast of characters mythic and folkloric: "Berthilia / the frog-like, crippled crone," "Emanuel / Auguste, out in the harbour, lone Odysseus," "Helen? / Janie, the town's one clear-complexioned whore" (18-19). As the poet explores the personal landscape of his development in St. Lucia, he imposes his own order on assorted memories of people and place. This imposition becomes a conscious act of recovery. Walcott fights against the reality of rootlessness and submission to the colonial will. This historical submission fosters feelings of self-destruction and nothingness in the Caribbean mind. The poet, in the space between these extremes, creates a sacred place where recovery can continue. At times, the process of creation battles the forces of destruction, and this struggle permeates Walcott's poetic world. It accounts for the tortured consciousness of *In a Green Night* and *The Castaway,* and the pain of Walcott's most quoted lines from "A Far Cry from Africa":

> I who am poisoned with the blood of both,
> Where shall I turn, divided to the vein?
> I who have cursed
> The drunken officer of British rule, how choose
> Between this Africa and the English tongue I love?
> Betray them both, or give back what they give?
> How can I face such slaughter and be cool?
> How can I turn from Africa and live?[55]

These lines have locked critics into characterizing Walcott as a poet and a person, that is, as artist and man torn apart by divisions of self and world. In fact, according to Robert Hamner,

> ...since [Walcott] is descended from a white grandfather and
> a black grandmother on both the paternal and maternal sides,
> he is a living example of the divided loyalties and hatreds that
> keep his society suspended between two worlds.[56]

Lloyd Brown suggests that the poet "is repelled by both the barbaric colonizer and the violent rebellion of the African; the poet is paralyzed by the feeling that he is 'poisoned' with the blood of both sides."[57] While focussing on the poet's tortured consciousness and personal pain, critics lose sight of the wider implications of Walcott's lines and the poet's conscious recreation of the universal struggle between possessor and possessed.

This struggle does not result in paralysis, however, for the poet attempts to impose an order on his world, an order denied by the forces of colonization; for a recognition of an ordered Caribbean society would mean a shattering of the mental imprisonment instituted and perpetuated by the colonial powers. For Walcott, the questions raised in "A Far Cry from Africa" are rhetorical; while he agonizes over the possibility of submitting to the forces of destruction, he is at the same time already at work reinventing a Caribbean identity that would purge these negative forces and restore order in the Caribbean world.

Walcott and Brathwaite constantly journey back into the past in search of origins that may order the present and create a future of possibility. Toni Morrison, in her essay "The Site of Memory," explains the writer's obsession with the past and the need to journey back to a place of origins: "...the route back to our original place...is emotional memory—what the nerves and the skin remember as well as how it appeared."[58] The act of re(member)ing addresses the African's violent separation from the original body. It also addresses the New World need for reconnection to the original body and the creation of an identity out of the ruins of the past. This new identity—as it is forged by Brathwaite and Walcott, with its grounding in the past—will be validated in the New World society.

In St. Lucia, Walcott is confronted by visible remnants of the past. The ruins of The Morne and Vigie are ever present reminders of the English and French presence on the island:

That was Vigie, and when

The sea still beats against the aging wall,
And the stone turrets filled with shaken leaves
When the wind brings the harbour rain in sheaves,
The yellow fort looks from the historic hill,
(As it were Poussin, or fragment from Bellini)
Its racial quarrels blown like smoke to sea
From all that sorrow, beauty is our gain,
Though it may not seem so
To an old fisherman rowing home in the rain.[59]

Ruins are a visible part of the poet's present reality, and a metaphor for journey, struggle, and survival. They are always at the center of his imaginary landscape. Walcott's fisherman, against the backdrop of ruins, connects past and present in an unusual moment of tranquility. Yet, even at this moment the memory of Africa is present:

There must be even in a legendary sense, a reflection of Africa...in the details of a lot of things quite apart from the language and the way of life. [For example], the activity of fishing becomes more than a simple activity, to me in a way it becomes something legendary.[60]

Walcott adopts the persona of an island fisherman. Through this persona, he parts the waves of memory in order to commune with ancestral presences buried at the bottom of the sea of language. He is the keeper of history, and the interpreter of the absolute power of "nouns":

But, line, live in the sounds
that ignorant shallows use;
then throw the silvery nouns

to open-mouthed canoes.[61]

Walcott is obsessed with "words" and the writer's craft. History is the skeleton upon which he builds the future. His poetic vision bridges the gap separating past and present, and projects a future in which the "myths" and "fables" of his people, instead of being viewed as halting inarticulations of the simple, will be granted their rightful place in the world of literature: "These fables of the backward and the poor / marbled by moonlight, will grow white and richer. / Our myths are ignorance, theirs are literature."[62]

Myths and folktales are a part of the collective consciousness. They are a tribute to endurance and the subversive power of the vernacular tradition. The experience of Caribbean people has been built on suppression and silence, but a silence under which the "word" was carefully preserved. Walcott is obsessed with this contradiction. He views the mission of the poet as a sacred one, the giving of life to the experience and to the word. He believes, like Edouard Glissant, in the subversive power of the vernacular tradition:

> ...myth consecrates the word and prepares the way for writing; on this level, the folktale proceeds by means of a sacrilegious approach. So what is attacked is from the outset the sacred status of the written word. The Caribbean folktale focuses on an experience suppressed by decree or the law. It is antidecree and antilaw, that is to say, antiwriting.[63]

The concept of "antiwriting" is central to the development of Caribbean poetry. Brathwaite is very much aware of the subversive power of the vernacular tradition, its hidden texts and coded messages. Violently opposed to attempts to force the tradition underground, he is engaged in the process of bringing this tradition to life by naming its elements and forcing a rebirth that will grant meaning and endurance in time:

How then shall we
succeed?

The eye must heed
the meaning

the eye must be free
seeing.

What is a word
to the eye?

Meaning.[64]

Given the colonial sensibility of the Caribbean of Brathwaite's time, his poetic purpose is revolutionary and reinforced by his conscious intention to create and identify a Caribbean aesthetic:

...my own aesthetic formulation for ourselves begins with rhythm: survival rhythm, emancipation rhythm, transfiguration rhythms; and how the one, the ego, comes to this, comes out of this, relates to this and us and others.[65]

This is Brathwaite's manifesto. He engages the rhythms of Africa, the Caribbean, and black America against the backdrop of European conquest in a symphony epitomizing struggle, survival and enormous strength of will. He celebrates hope and possibility and the indestructibility of community, while being very much aware of the poet's individual responsibility:

> We must therefore work to discover ourselves, to excavate
> from memory,...Then we must...begin the process of edu-
> cation, redefinition, re-discovery and re-assessment.[66]

Brathwaite's voice rings with the power of the African griot and the Old Testament prophet. This combination of powers is a reflection of the society at large, where practitioners of African religions see no contradiction in the merging of African and Christian rituals. What is important about Brathwaite's work is the unity of theory and practice that he achieves. *The Arrivants* is the map of his grand design, an attempt to redefine, rediscover, and reassess the history and reality of the Caribbean people. It is also a celebration of the simple ordinary lives of the Caribbean masses, their creativity and power. But Brathwaite is a realist, and while Walcott remains attracted to and in awe of European and classical traditions, it is the underside of these traditions with which Brathwaite concerns himself. The nostalgia for European culture that surfaces in the form and content of Walcott's work is absent from Brathwaite's poetic world.

Brathwaite confronts the region's history directly; he attacks the European legislators of slavery and colonization, and does not romanticize the poverty of the region. He focuses on the mental, spiritual and economic devastation that is the result of the colonial presence in the Caribbean. He is concerned with the European's constant quest for power and control and the attempt to strip the colonized of all sense of self and identity. His poetry moves, however, beyond the desperation and violence of *Third World Poems*[67] to the acts of reconstruction that occur in *Mother Poem*[68] and *Sun Poem*,[69] where the island becomes the source of a people's renewal and revitalization. These themes are further developed in *X/Self.* Here, even as the persona spirals into confusion and negation, there is a flowering of selfhood in community. The self is inspirited by ancestral voices offering healing and benediction:

> touch
> him
> he will heal
>
> you
>
> word
> and balm
> and water
>
> flow
>
> embrace
> him
>
> he will shatter outwards to your light and calm and history
>
> your thunder has come home[70]

It is inevitable that slavery, emancipation, and the mythic vision of Africa should be such a vital part of the Caribbean literary imagination. This clearly manifests itself in Brathwaite's work, but is not as visible in Walcott's. In fact, layers of doubt and hereditary ambivalence must be removed before Walcott's intrinsic connections to Africa are revealed. He adds to the complication by not being a very reliable commentator on either his theory or practice. While there is no tension in Brathwaite's work between theory and practice, with Walcott there is always tension and a peculiar straining as the poet struggles to come to terms with both Africa and Europe. This tension is most obvious when the poet confronts the history of slavery:

> In the New World servitude to the muse of history has produced a literature of recrimination and despair, a literature of revenge written by the descendants of slaves or a literature of remorse written by the descendants of masters....The truly tough aesthetic of the New World neither explains nor forgives history.[71]

The Caribbean situation, by the very nature of its historical experience, does not lend itself to such stark polarization. An example of this blurring of identity is illustrated in the following excerpt from Louise Bennett's "Back to Africa":

> Me know say dat you great great great
> Granma was African,
> But Mattie, doan you great great great
> Granpa was Englishman?
>
> Den you great granmader fader
> By you fader side was Jew?
> An you granpa by you mader side
> Was Frenchie parlez-vous?
>
> But de balance a you family,
> You whole generation,
> Oonoo all barn dung a Bun Grung?
> Oonoo all is Jamaican![72]

Michael Gilkes, too, captures this blurring of racial identity:

Doan tell me 'bout Guyana.

I barn deh in t'irty-t'ree.

Meh great-gran'fadda wuz a black man

grandmudda wuz a puttagee.

Meh gran'fadda wuz a coolie: ah draw Buck, white an'

Chinee.

Deh call it 'land of six peoples'

but is seven, 'less you doan count me.[73]

In life as well as in history there has been a forced merging of the African and European worlds, further complicated by the Caribbean's Asian connections. The African experience is the dominant one by virtue of the enormous weight of slavery, but the powerful influence of European forces so engulfs the Caribbean psyche that Walcott can still present such disparate categories and not acknowledge the existence of a tradition of literary resistance in the Caribbean. Such a refusal denies not only Walcott's own attempts at resistance (for in spite of what he says, he does resist), but also the resistance of Brathwaite and other poets who attempt to rewrite the language of the Caribbean in the rhythms and speech patterns of the region.

The Caribbean poets' conscious and unconscious obsession with language is a part of the engagement with the theoretical concerns of their art, and the need to acknowledge its place in a distinctly Caribbean aesthetic tradition. Kamau Brathwaite and Derek Walcott identify with the familiar world of the Caribbean. The identity they forge is rooted in the realities of the Caribbean's historical and cultural past. Brathwaite, more than Walcott, has leaped beyond modernist concerns of alienation and loss and postmodernist concerns of void or nothingness. Brathwaite has reached a point in his literary development where, in the process of reclaiming identity, he has developed a style and form that transform the marginality of the past into a centralizing force.

For Brathwaite and Walcott, their islands are symbolic and real, liberating and imprisoning. At the center of these oppositions is the poetic imagination that forges out of these contradictions a place where the self is inviolate and the community sacrosanct. To reach this place, Brathwaite and Walcott journey back to a history and a past they refuse to relinquish. According to Brathwaite, this tortured positioning is a "movement of possession into present and future."[74] Possessed by the past and history, Kamau Brathwaite and Derek Walcott reclaim and rewrite the history of the Caribbean, giving voice and identity to its people.

Notes

1. Kenneth Kiple, *The Caribbean Slaves: A Biological History* (London: Cambridge UP, 1984) 57.
2. Today, on the Worthy Park estate in Jamaica, the same brand that once marked slaves is used to identify the estate's cattle. See Orlando Patterson, *Slavery and Social Death: A Comparative Study* (Cambridge: Harvard UP, 1982) 59.
3. Edward Long, *The History of Jamaica,* vol. 2 (London: 1774) 485-490.
4. Orlando Patterson, *The Sociology of Slavery* (New Jersey: Fairleigh Dickinson UP, 1967) 65-66.
5. Long, *The History of Jamaica* 409.
6. Bryan Edwards, *The History, Civil and Commercial, of the British West Indies 1773* (New York: AMS, 1966), vol. 2:4, chap. 3.
7. Thomas Carlyle, "Occasional Discourse on the Nigger Question," *English and Other Critical Essays, 1849* (New York: Dutton, 1925) 310.
8. Anthony Trollope, *The West Indies and the Spanish Main* (New York: Hippocrene, 1985) 83.
9. James Anthony Froude, *The English in the West Indies or The Bow of Ulysses* (London: Longmans, 1909) 208.
10. J.H. Parry and Philip Sherlock, *A Short History of the West Indies* (London: Macmillan, 1971) 247.

11. Walter Rodney, *How Europe Underdeveloped Africa* (London: Bogle L'Overture, 1972) 264.
12. C.L.R. James, *Beyond a Boundary* (London: Stanley Paul, 1990) 38-39.
13. Léon Damas, "Sell Out," *The Negritude Poets: An Anthology of Translations from the French,* ed. Ellen Conroy Kennedy (New York: Thunder's Mouth, 1975) 50-51.
14. This title was amended to *Froudacity: West Indian Fables by James Anthony Froude explained by J.J. Thomas.*
15. J.J. Thomas, *Froudacity* (London: New Beacon, 1969) 51.
16. Terry Eagleton, *Nationalism, Irony and Commitment,* Derry, Ireland, Field Day Pamphlet 13 (1988): 16.
17. Norman Cameron, ed. *Guianese Poetry: 1831-1931* (British Guiana: Argosy, 1931).
18. Francis Williams, "A Double Exile," *Voices in Exile,* eds. Jean D'Costa and Barbara Lalla (Tuscaloosa: Alabama UP, 1989) 12.
19. Williams 11.
20. Vivian Vertue, "I Have Seen March," *Caribbean Voices,* vol. 2, ed. John Figueroa (London: Evans, 1972) 141.
21. Vere T. Daly, "The Song of Young Guiana," *Guianese Poetry,* ed. Norman Cameron (Guiana: Argosy, 1931) 111.
22. A.J. Seymour, "Drums," *The Guiana Book* (Guiana: Argosy, 1948) 9.
23. O.R. Dathorne, ed. introduction, Caribbean Verse (London: Heinemann, 1967) 3.
24. Claude McKay, preface vol. II, *The Constab Ballads: The Dialect Poetry of Claude McKay,* 2 vols. (Salem, New Hampshire: Ayer, 1987) 7.
25. McKay, "Constab Ballads," vol. 2: 35.
26. Evan Jones, "The Song of the Banana Man," *The Penguin Book of Caribbean Verse in English,* ed. Paula Burnett (London: Penguin, 1988) 223.
27. Louise Bennett, "Independance," *The Penguin Book of Caribbean Verse in English,* ed. Paula Burnett (London: Penguin, 1988) 36.
28. Martin Carter, "This Is the Dark Time My Love," *Poems of Resistance* (Georgetown: Guyana UP, 1964) 17.
29. V.S. Naipaul, The Middle Passage (Middlesex: Penguin, 1969) 29.
30. V.S. Naipaul, "Prologue to an Autobiography," *Finding the Center* (New York: Vintage, 1986) 70.
31. Helen Vendler, "Poet of Two Worlds," *The New York Review* (4 March 1982): 26.
32. Fredric Jameson, "Third World Literature in the Era of Multinational Capitalism," *Social Text* 15 (Fall 1986): 66.

33. Edward Said, *The World, the Text and the Critic* (Cambridge: Harvard UP, 1983) 5.
34. George Lamming, *The Pleasures of Exile* (London: Allison & Busby, 1984) 109.
35. Aimé Césaire, *Discourse on Colonialism* (New York: Monthly Review, 1972) 21.
36. Frantz Fanon, *The Wretched of the Earth* (New York: Grove, 1963) 233.
37. Chinua Achebe, "The Novelist as Teacher," *Morning Yet on Creation Day* (New York: Anchor, 1976) 59.
38. Terry Eagleton, *The Ideology of the Aesthetic* (Oxford: Blackwell, 1990) 4.
39. Kamau Brathwaite, *Contradictory Omens: Cultural Diversity and Integration in the Caribbean* (Mona, Jamaica: Savacou, 1974) 64.
40. Brathwaite, "Epilogue," *The Arrivants: A New World Trilogy* (London, Oxford UP, 1973) 81.
41. Brathwaite, at the launching of the new edition of *Black + Blues,* New York, 24 April, 1996.
42. Edouard Glissant, *Caribbean Discourse,* trans. Michael Dash (Charlottesville: Virginia UP, 1989) 253.
43. Vera Bell, "Ancestor on the Auction Block," *Caribbean Verse,* ed. O.R. Dathorne (London: Heinemann, 1967) 18-19.
44. Brathwaite, "Kumasi," *The Arrivants* 138.
45. Derek Walcott, "The Muse of History," *Is Massa Day Dead? Black Moods in the Caribbean,* ed. Orde Coombs (New York: Anchor, 1974) 2.
46. Walcott, "The Muse of History" 5.
47. Walcott, *25 Poems* (Bridgetown, Barbados: Advocate, 1949).
48. Walcott, *In a Green Night* (London: Cape, 1969).
49. Walcott, *The Castaway* (London: Cape, 1969).
50. Walcott, *Another Life* (Washington: Three Continents, 1982).
51. Walcott, "What the Twilight Says: An Overture," *Dream on Monkey Mountain and Other Plays* (New York: Noonday, 1989) 34-35.
52. Gordon Rohlehr, "The Problem of the Problem of Form," *The Shape of That Hurt* (Trinidad: Longman, 1992) 1-65. Here Rohlehr explores Walcott's ambivalence toward Caribbean folk forms, demonstrating how, in his own work, Walcott refashions these forms in spite of publicly negating them.
53. Walcott, "Ti-Jean and His Brothers," *Dream on Monkey Mountain and Other Plays* 81-166.
54. Walcott, "The Muse of History" 7.
55. Walcott, "A Far Cry from Africa," *In a Green Night* 18.
56. Robert D. Hamner, *Derek Walcott* (Boston: Twayne, 1981) 22.

57. Lloyd Brown, *West Indian Poetry* (London: Heinemann, 1984) 124.
58. Toni Morrison, "The Site of Memory," *Inventing the Truth: The Art and Craft of Memoir,* ed. William Zinsser (Boston: Houghton Mifflin, 1987) 119.
59. Walcott, "Roots," *In a Green Night* 60.
60. Interview, Melvin Bragg, *The South Bank Show, London Weekend Television,* November 2, 1988.
61. Walcott, "Night fishing," *The Arkansas Testament* (New York: Farrar, 1987) 56.
62. Walcott, "White Magic," *The Arkansas Testament* 38.
63. Edouard Glissant, *Caribbean Discourse* 84.
64. Brathwaite, "Naming," *The Arrivants* 217.
65. Brathwaite, "The Love Axe/1," *Bim* 16:61 (June 1977): 65.
66. Brathwaite, "The Love Axe/1" 65.
67. Kamau Brathwaite, *Third World Poems* (Essex: Longman, 1983).
68. Brathwaite, *Mother Poem* (Oxford: Oxford UP, 1975).
69. Brathwaite, *Sun Poem* (Oxford: Oxford UP, 1982).
70. Brathwaite, "Xango," *X/Self* (Oxford, Oxford UP, 1987) 111.
71. Walcott, "The Muse of History" 2.
72. Louise Bennett, "Back to Africa," *The Penguin Book of Caribbean Verse,* ed. Paula Burnett (London: Penguin, 1986) 31.
73. Michael Gilkes, "Son of Guyana," *Voice Print,* eds. Stewart Brown et al. (Essex: Longman, 1989) 241.
74. Brathwaite, "Timehri," *Is Massa Day Dead? Black Moods in the Caribbean,* ed. Orde Coombs (New York: Anchor, 1974) 42.

Chapter 2

Africa and the Poetic Imagination

I sing
I shout
I groan
I dream
about
Dust glass grit
the pebbles of the desert

—Brathwaite "Prelude," *The Arrivants*

In his essay entitled "Interior of the Novel: Amerindian/ European/African Relations," Guyanese novelist Wilson Harris tells the story of a meeting between Mahanarva, an Amerindian chief, and the English governor of Demerara and Essequibo, two counties in British Guiana, now Guyana.[1] From the earliest days of colonial occupation, Amerindians had been used to capture runaway slaves and to stall slave revolts. In this incident, Mahanarva appears before the English governor to claim compensation for using his forces to aid the British. However, the governor has discovered that Mahanarva had not told the truth, and that no Amerindian forces were under his command. Harris describes this meeting between them as "painful revelation, on one hand, unmasking, on the other." He continues to characterize this meeting further as

> one of those peculiar *'holes'* within the body of history—through which one may detect something of the psychological womb and climate of a new creative necessity in that one begins to move through and beyond a formal ground of relations—sovereign Governor on one hand, shaman or trickster on the other—towards a new subconscious alliance within a chasm of proportions belonging to the past, present and future.   [11]

The process of "revelation" and "unmasking" is at the heart of the relationship between colonizer and colonized in the Caribbean, and the "psychological womb" is the space inhabited by all New World peoples. For both Kamau Brathwaite and Derek Walcott the memory of Africa is nurtured in this space. Here, each poet creates strategies of resistance and survival in an attempt to eliminate the boundaries separating the powerful and the powerless, and to restructure the nature of the relationship between them.

The memory of Africa has always haunted the Caribbean imagination, but because the New World was created out of the bones of history, the vision of Africa has been an ambivalent one. Interwoven with dreams of the glory of its ancient civilizations is the pain of the Africans' involuntary journey to the New World.

The Caribbean poets' engagement with Africa has been both tragic and romantic. The poetic landscape has been informed by past glory, the degradation of the Middle Passage, the legacy of slavery, and a people's desire to survive. An early anonymous poem, "Jamaica, a Poem in Three Parts, Written in That Island in the Year 1776," epitomizes the pain of enslavement and the longing for freedom as well as the attempt, often visible in Caribbean poetry, to fuse African sensibility and European form:

> Here sable Caesars feel the christian rod;
> There Afric Platos, tortur'd, hope a God:
> While jetty Brutus for his country sighs,
> And sooty Cato with his freedom dies![2]

The anonymous poet, on a quest for identity, places Africans in Africa and in a classical tradition to validate the African experience. This need to locate the Caribbean experience solely in Africa continues in the early twentieth century with Harold M. Telemanque's celebration of ancestral achievements:

> To those
> Who lifted into shape
> The huge stones of the pyramid;
> Who formed the Sphinx in the desert...
> Who walked lithely
> On the banks of the Congo....[3]

He pays tribute to a glorious African past celebrating artistic vision as well as physical grace, but the celebrated ancestors remain firmly on African territory. However, Eric Roach transports Canga, a hero in African folklore, to the Caribbean and celebrates his wiles in the "Ballad of Canga":

He is a old Ashantee man
Full of wickedness;
Bring obeah straight from Africa;
What he curse don't bless.[4]

Caribbean poets have continued to be attracted to a vision of Africa that is tragic, romantic, and magical. Kamau Brathwaite and Derek Walcott share this attraction. Brathwaite journeys back to an edenic Africa, where people were close to their gods, and their customs and rituals brought order and ceremony into their daily lives. In this transportation of people, customs, and rituals to the New World, Brathwaite sees the humanizing influences that inform Caribbean identity. But Africa, in Walcott's poetic world does not have the same all-consuming power of anchorage and homing that it has for Brathwaite. There is always a sense of uncertainty, a longing for revelation, and the hope that somehow he can reconcile his African and European heritages. While there are internal contradictions in Walcott's statements about his cultural positioning in the world, these are constantly negated by the metaphors of his text. Walcott cannot escape the shaping presence of Africa and its concrete manifestations in daily Caribbean existence. As Walcott journeys towards reconciliation between Africa and Europe, he explores the nature of Caribbean identity and the role of the artist in carving out this identity. In spite of the different locations of Africa in their visionary worlds, at the center of both worlds are edenic Africa, the Middle Passage journey, slavery and the colonial Caribbean experience. Caribbean identity emerges out of this convergence of African history and New World circumstance.

Africa assumes several symbolic levels in Brathwaite's poetry. When opposed to the hell of the New World plantations, it is a paradise for those whose ties to Africa were involuntarily severed, a longed-for symbol of rootedness and homeland; it is a motherland of safety and plenty. In *Masks*, the poem "Prelude" provides an introduction to this compression of symbols. Africa leaps into history in the splendor of its kingdoms: Mali, Chad, Timbuktu. At the same time, the ritual music of the drums signals a moment of birth and beginnings:

> Beat heaven
> of the drum, beat
> the dark leaven
> of the dungeon
> ground where buds are wrapped
> twist-
> ed round dancing roots...

Brathwaite also recalls ancient religious rites: "take the blood of the fowl / drink."[5] Africa is source, bursting with vibrancy, vitality and promise. The New World poet, cut off for so long from Africa, attempts to write himself into this historical time. The poet pays tribute to "Asase Yaa, Mother of Earth" and consecrates the tools of his craft to Mother Africa. Africa is both place and person. It is also a symbol of paradise. Brathwaite's persona is inspired by the beauty and splendor of Africa as well as by the vastness of its possibilities. In this paradise, he is transformed, and Africa is personified as the muse of his inspiration and the force informing his creativity:

> And may the year
> this year of all years
> be fruitful
> beyond the fruit of your labor:
> shoots faithful to tip

juice to stem
leaves to green...

But as the speaker bridges the expanse between past and present, he is confronted with the very real fears of the present moment:

and may the knife
or the cut-
lass not cut
me; roots blunt,
shoots break,
green wither...   [92]

Africa, in memory, retains its idyllic intensity, but the real world of the Caribbean can be a dangerous one, and the poet fears not only the violence of his time but also personal violence if he is no longer able to create. These are the forces tearing the poet apart. As he tries to integrate the vision of Africa as paradise into his rewriting of Caribbean identity, he is constantly battling past and present inhumanities.

These forces explode in "Kingston in the Kingdom of This World."[6] Brathwaite superimposes the dangers, the violence and the barren ground of Kingston onto an African landscape that is paradisal. In the African world, his words and actions have ancestral power. The ground is sacred and blessed by the performance of ancient rituals and celebrations:

my authority was foot stamp upon the ground
    the curves the palms the dancers
my authority was nyambura: inching closer
    embroideries of fingers silver earrings:
    balancers...

In spite of the powerful presence of Africa, the poet in present time experiences a reduction of self:

> i am reduced
> i am reduced
> i am reduced
> to these black eyes
> this beaten face
> these bleaching lips blearing obscenities...   [55]

Yet Brathwaite presents the evils of present circumstances as a transient condition, for he is secure in the sense of change and possibility that his belief in the force of Africa brings. At the heart of this belief is the concept of Nam, which he describes in an essay as:

> ...the word we give to the indestructible and atomic core of man's culture. It is the kernel of his name, his nature of immanence, man in extremis, extremest nativeness, disguised backward (nam/X\man). It is the essence of our culture in the sense that culture is the essence what man eat (nyam, yam); and the power and the glory out of that: nyame, onyame, dynamo.[7]

In addition to the tangible survivals of African culture that outlasted the Middle Passage journey, Brathwaite recognizes a more subtle connection. It is an intuitive force, inescapably African that is an integral part of the Caribbean identity he creates.

The perpetuation of the myth of Africa is essential in a contemporary Caribbean world wracked by violence, where locally bred colonials contribute to the real and psychic destruction of a people. In this situation, myth is the catalyst for change. Mythical and historical connections are integral elements of national consciousness, assuming heroic proportions in times of violence and unrest. The awareness of a motherland becomes particularly important, offering ancestral ties to a people experiencing the discontinuities of history. "Springblade," from Brathwaite's collection *Black + Blues,* explores the tension between a past that goes unacknowledged in spite of a recognition of its healing properties and a present in which the evils of a slave/colonial history is reenacted. In this poem, Brathwaite amasses stark images of devastation and of physical and spiritual impoverishment: "eyes fragmented by louvres / vision corrupted by crevices"; "hungry belly flattens the faeces / the milk blackens in the bread / of breasts"; "the floorboards widen / and are full of mice"; "the mattress with its history of sweat, of some- / times sweetest slavery: in- / cinerated cemeteries of sperm..." (47-48). He presents a dire picture of a country, and a region that has severed ties to its ancestral past. Motherland becomes a barren concept, and motherhood is unproductive. The lack of creativity, the stultifying atmosphere of the private world, and the death of the individual mirror the decay and devastation of the larger community. This destruction of self and world is linked to the dark days of slavery in the New World after the African's violent separation from Africa. Brathwaite is sharply aware of what is lacking in his society:

> We could have rendered them [these children] painfully,
> respecting themselves through their fathers, surrendering
> themselves to their grandmothers'
> > visions
> through the tales of their ancestors
>
> they would have understood the meaning of ships
> heraldic whip and armoured scar

how hostile slavery ushered in
the medieval age of the african....[8]

New World children, having lost their African connections, do not understand the powerful history of their past. Yet, out of the recalling of the past, the cultivation of the "tales of their ancestors," will come the creation of tradition and the salvation of spirit, self, and community:

spirit of the blaze
red river of reflection
vermilion dancer out of the antelope

i summon you from trees
from ancient memories
from the uncurling ashes of the dead
that we may all be cleansed....[9]

In his essay "The African Presence in Caribbean Literature," Brathwaite identifies four categories of literature connected to the African experience. The first he describes as "rhetorical." Here, the author knows very little of Africa and uses Africa as a "mask" or "dream." The second is "the literature of African survival." The literature in this category is an examination of African survivals in the Caribbean, but the author does not try to create a linkage between discovered survivals (remnants of African languages, rituals, and customs) and "the great tradition of Africa." The third category is "the literature of African expression," which explores the transformation of vernacular material into "literary experiment." The final category is "the literature of reconnection," which is written by Caribbean writers who have actually lived in Africa and, as a result, try to connect African and New World experiences. According to Brathwaite, these writers "consciously reach...out to rebridge the gap with the spiritual heartland."[10] This essay can be read as Brathwaite's personal manifesto. More than any other Caribbean artist, he is possessed by the spirit and spirits of Africa and consciously attempts to make connections with an African experience that would explain and give validity and meaning to a Caribbean identity. In fact, in his own work, the four categories he has identified never appear as distinct and separate. They are integral parts of his poetic vision and necessary steps in the movement towards reconnection.

Brathwaite does not limit the attempt at reconnection to the Caribbean. He envisions a diasporic connection; thus in "Blues for Billie Holiday," he links the African-American experience to Africa:

> she travels far back . ex
> plores ruins . touches on old immemorial legends
> everyone but herself has forgotten . she
> becomes warrior and queen and keeper of the
>
> tribe . there is no fear
> where she walks....[11]

In black America as in the Caribbean this knowledge of Africa, direct or subcutaneous, is powerful and creative and has the additional force of protection, the protection of self and identity. In black America as in the Caribbean, the colonizing process has distorted and at times eliminated self and identity. The chasm between black America, the Caribbean, and Africa must be bridged; the "ruins" explored and reconstructed in order to bring into being the New World self and identity. Brathwaite's conscious intention is to rebuild the ruins. Interestingly, the pain, terror, and disintegration that would result if this mission were not accomplished are clearly illustrated in Orlando Patterson's novel *An Absence of Ruins.* The protagonist, Alexander Blackman, searches for a past: "There is a past here. There must be a past here" (104). But he remains a man without connections, totally alienated from self and society:

> I cannot say whether I am civilized or savage, standing as I do outside of race, outside of culture, outside of history.... I am busy going nowhere, but I must keep up the appearance of going in order to forget that I am not.[12]

Brathwaite is concerned with this warped perception of Caribbean people, as existing outside of "race," "culture," and "history." Such a perception, based upon a denial of the African experience, reinforces the position that the black person in the Caribbean is without history and ancestral roots. Realizing this, Brathwaite places Africa where it legitimately belongs, at the center of the aesthetic principles and cultural mythology he is developing. He reclaims the links and refashions the connections between Africa and the Caribbean. He would transform Blackman's tentative gropings through the historical past into an active pilgrimage of rediscovery, a movement from negation to affirmation; for Alexander Blackman is aware, on some level, that there is a buried history waiting to be excavated, a history that goes beyond "twisted bones of crippled, mutilated black slaves":

> One day I shall destroy those evil institutes with their corridors and shelves of lies, and I shall burn them to the ground. I, Alexander Blackman, shall redeem the truth of my heritage, of my great past, that lies hidden somewhere.
>
> [104-105]

Blackman's tragedy, and, as Patterson suggests, the tragedy of Caribbean people, lies in this ambivalence, the desire to know and the fear of knowing; for knowing brings with it not only entrance into a hallowed community of ancestors, but also a confrontation with ancestral dread, the violent passage into the New World and the alienating experience of plantation existence. The historical journey must be made, however, in order to integrate the ancestral experience into the community. Brathwaite's cultivation of the myth of an African motherland offers spiritual unity and self-realization.

In cultivating this myth, Brathwaite confronts the pain of the Middle Passage and slavery's tortured reality of dispossession. But attempts at dispossession were not entirely successful. Instead of the total destruction of African culture, there was a camouflage and burial of African traditions and rituals. In "Prelude," the opening poem of his *Rights of Passage,* Brathwaite ranges from the Caribbean's plantation existence, to life in the early glorious kingdoms of Africa, to African slavery and the journey to the New World. In "Epilogue," the closing poem, the persona undergoes a magnitude of experiences as he journeys from the Caribbean to Paris, Brixton, London, New York, and Rome. In the persona's consciousness there is a peculiar merger of a pristine lyrical world and the everyday world of endless toil; hope is ephemeral, but the struggle continues:

> but my people
> know
> that the hot
> day will be over
> soon
> that the star
> that dies

the flamboyant car-
cass that rots
in the road
in the gutter
will rise...
in the butter-
flies of a new
and another morning   [81-82]

To arrive at this "new morning," the experience of slavery has to
be recalled; a denial of this experience results in spiritual and
intellectual death. Harold Telemanque, in his poem, "In Our
Land," shies away from naming this experience, merely alluding
to the sunken "stain":

In our land
The ugly stain
That blotted Eden garden
Is sunk deep only.[13]

Brathwaite would argue that the "stain" of slavery is an integral
part of the Caribbean's collective consciousness, and must be
named. It is an always present reminder of separation, disloca-
tion, and isolation. Orlando Patterson, in *Slavery and Social
Death,* discusses the slave's complete isolation in society. The
slave suffered a dual isolation: from his ancestors and their
"social heritage" and from his community. There was no overt
body of experience or knowledge to "anchor the living present
in any conscious community of memory."[14] Brathwaite sees this
reclamation of communal memory as his literary and spiritual
task. He must dig deeply within the Caribbean existence and con-
sciousness to recover the past; his imagination is the medium

through which this past is reclaimed and transcended. Out of the reclamation of knowledge, the understanding of the past and the transcendence of its evils will come the new Caribbean identity.

This is the poetic achievement of Brathwaite's trilogy, *Mother Poem*,[15] *Sun Poem*[16] and *X/Self*.[17] The poet consciously interweaves the Caribbean, African, and colonial histories together with its contemporary neocolonial political experiences. In his preface to *Mother Poem,* Brathwaite states: "This poem is about porous limestone: my mother, Barbados: most English of West Indian islands, but at the same time nearest, as the slaves fly, to Africa." *Mother Poem* is a distillation of female essences and principles. "Mother" is Africa and Barbados and the women of the island as they struggle to survive and to maintain ancestral connections. The persona, mother, speaks in many voices, public and oratorical, private and personal. "Alpha," the poem introducing the volume, is a gathering-up of forces, a celebration of strength and survival, a praise-song to mother, mother country, and ancestral mother. At work here is Brathwaite's theory of "tidalectics." A "tidal dialectic moves outward from the center to circumference and back again."[18] The poem, dedicated to Barbados, cannot possibly escape this association. In an endless tidal pattern, the poet returns to sources and remembered places. He recalls the slaves' journey to the New World and the colonial plantations even as he goes back in time to "ancient watercourses" linked to ancestral memory.

These experiences converge in the inspiriting presence of the mother who "rains upon the island with her loud voices / with her grey hairs / with her green love" (3). She sings of wisdom and hope and connections that make possible the survival of the father who "swims through the noise / through the blankets of jute on his lungs" (4). The mother and father are the spirits of creation out of whose union a new order will emerge. But before this can happen, there are many battles to be fought, and at the heart of the turbulence is the mother icon with powers of consecration and damnation, a composite of ambiguities. In "Hex," she "sings," "quarrels," "rattles," and "shakes." These actions signify her many roles as historian, warrior, keeper of the dead and preserver of religious ceremony and rituals. In her public role as mother/island/home, she guards and maintains the connections with history past and present:

> she will remember the floorboards of a cabin
> how there was a grave there
> where she buried her children
> their skin drilled to screams....   [47]

Further:

> she wears on her wrist the shadow of the chain
> history of the flesh
> written by whip of torture
> legacy of bribe....   [47]

Mother is also healer, diviner and arbiter:

> from the sicknesses of the plantation
> she gathers sticks
> gutters them to fashion pipes flutes siphons
> rambles of herbs she touches and sniffs
>
> offering them prayers and names:
> mint nunu kema-weed shamar
> pem-pem piaba fall-down-bush
> and she crumples words into curses....   [47]

While this mother is guardian of history and protector of culture, she is confronted by the rape and devastation of the island mother, Barbados. On the plantations of the present, there is a negation of the region's history: "They learn to smile with keats and milton ... / but know nothing of the men who marched / from congo rock / from belleplaine / from boscobelle..." (50). At the heart of this bombardment the mother remains bent on her mission of preservation. In his personal wasteland the narrator struggles for wholeness and survival:

> for the mind is dry
> where there are no rivers
>
> the sky of hope shines high with barren metal
> where there are no watercourses
>
> i struggle through the silver thorn
> and cannot find the pool   [51]

But the mother will lead the narrator back to "ancient watercourses" and "rivers," to the circle of the "pool." This movement away from the metallic to the circular is central to the poet's thought. Brathwaite views the metallic and the circular as oppositions identifying essential differences between African and European cultures. He employs the symbols of missile and capsule to epitomize these differences. The metallic is linked to the missilic, representing technology, profit, and aggression; while the circular is aligned with the capsulic, representing the preservation and containment of culture. According to Brathwaite, "We came across the Atlantic in this space capsule within the missile of the Europeans, and...we enshrined our memories, our rituals, our histories within this life-supporting schema." A space capsule thus becomes the symbol for Caribbean history, both past and present:

> ...our history was carried to us by our conquistadores, by the people who came to possess us all, by Columbus, Drake, Raleigh, and all of those who came afterwards, by the educators and the missionaries...the ship was a form of missile and...our own experience was the space capsule within the missile.[19]

The history of the "space capsule" continues to be one of bombardment in time and, in *Mother Poem,* it is the mission of the mother/priestess as symbol, as icon, to maintain the culture intact. In "Nametracks," the conflict is between colonizer, symbolized by O'Grady, and the colonized, symbolized by the voice of the narrator. In the deceptive world of a childhood game familiar to Caribbean children, the poet locates this battle for identity. O'Grady, with the force of the colonizing power, insists that the narrator "say name." But in African culture, the name is sacred. In *Muntu,* Janheinz Jahn quotes from the Yoruba priests: "There is nothing that there is not; whatever we have a name for, that is."[20] The act of naming, of breathing life into words, is a creative act and becomes linked to the preservation of culture:

> she lisper to me dat me name what me name
> dat me name is me main an it am is me own an lion eye
> mane / dat whinner men tek you an ame, dem is /
> nomminit diff'rent an nan / so mandingo she yessper /
> you nam   [62]

The mother speaks for cultural preservation and history in the language of the Caribbean which is rooted in Africa. The child must acknowledge his cultural history and name his Caribbean experiences and their connection to the ancestral experiences if he is to refashion the history of the doomed:

> the child
> is born to splinters
>
> broken islands
> broken homes   ["Mid/Life," 108]

While *Mother Poem* feminizes Brathwaite's imaginative world with its emphasis on protection and nurture, and the mother speaks in the voice of priestess, provider and guardian of the African past, in *Sun Poem,* the male principles emerge. But "sun" is also "son" of "the dark muse his mother," and, as a result, inherits her intuitive qualities and is drawn into the past and ancient African memories in an attempt to understand the present condition in which he finds himself. The introductory poem to the volume, "Red Rising," goes back to origins in a powerful mixture of the African and the Caribbean. Mount Soufriere is paired with Kilimanjaro; Jah and Isis and the father/narrator/persona offer a lyrical song in the voice of a griot who sings of beginnings and possibilities:

> and the trees on the mountain be-
> come mine: living eye of my branches
> of bone; flute
> where is my hope hope where is my psalter
>
> my children wear masks dancing towards me the mews of their
> their origen earth   [1]

The mood soon changes in spite of the idyllic setting in which the poet places the central character, Adam. His battle with Batto the bully hints at the existence of other evils. The sea becomes a source of memory and pain. Adam attempts to escape from Batto as they struggle in the sea. In the consciousness of Adam's sister, fishes are transformed into birds "trying to leave the dark heavy water dragging the links of the chains of the water," but they are unable to leave the "prisoner sea." Present is the memory of the Barbadian plantations where black people struggled for survival: "the sons of the earth working in long rows / in long chains / in long queues" (37).

On a quest for identity and to move his people beyond pain, Brathwaite reverses the Middle Passage journey. In "The Crossing," as Adam goes on a Sunday school excursion to Cattlewash, the poet rewrites history in the song that the children sing:

> we're going to a won der ful place
> we're going to a wonder full place
> over the hills and far away
> we're going to a wonderful place   [40]

As the bus slowly winds its way up Hearse Hill, Adam is filled with terror, fearing that the bus will "slip-back-down-to-the-gully," but it reaches the top, and "below...was the promised land." But the promise remains unfulfilled, and in "Noom," Adam is confronted with the story of slavery's beginnings on his island. At the same time, the poet introduces Adam's sources of liberation: the African gods and the warrior/hero Bussa. He meets Legba, the go-between and the interpreter of the gods. He is also introduced to Shango, the warrior god of thunder and Ogoun, the god of war and metals. Brathwaite carefully introduces the

African gods as he charts the route to Caribbean salvation and wholeness. The self/son he creates, however, is fragile; the forces of history overpowering. The journey to salvation is full of obstructions, not the least being the perversion of relationships and the impotence of black men in a society where they have no visible power except over their women and children. Adam is faced with this reality: "But our heroes were in books / and few of our fathers were heroes" ("Noom" 61). In fact, Brathwaite provides a catalogue of fatherly and husbandly deficiencies in a world of unfaithfulness and child neglect. For example, the Christian father is described in this way:

> temperate discrete ruthless perhaps at noon with naomi
> but all between the four white walls of moderation
> and not squeezed in against the backseat igloo roof of the
> toyola /   ["Clips," 67]

Brathwaite paints a dire picture of a bleak and apparently hopeless Caribbean landscape: "a man cyan be / faddah to faddah if e nevvah get chance to be son/light" (71). Bleakness also permeates what initially appears to be a lyrical, playful interlude between Adam and Esse. She is wreathed in sunlight and "son" light and perched in a "duncks" tree; they are playing the game of flirtation, but very soon the mood is transformed from the playful to the malevolent. First, she pricks her hand on a "pimpler" or thorn; then, the poet uses the mechanized image of driving a lorry to describe their attempts at a sexual encounter and its possible consequences: "an aftha yu finish drive bout like yu like.../ an fuhget bout de bill when a / accident come an de lorry dey pun de dump/heap" (79). Esse's youthful world of innocence and sexual initiation is threatened by worldly realities of accidents and despair. Ultimately, she is sacrificed at the

altar of male pleasure. Lovers vanish; her husband "died in his
testicles," and she is left to sing "the hymn without tune with-
out words" (84). Esse's future is tied to the endless numbers of
women singing the song of broken promises.

However, inherent in this landscape of pain, is a female
source of consolation and renewal:

> for mothers stood in the light of the door
> way mothers stood at the end of the yard
>
> mothers were loa were stone crabs were fish traps of no
> they were pebbles of sound down the floor of a well.   [77]

The image of mothers as loa offers the possibility of unity and
recovery. Possessed by the spirits of the gods, these women
can recharter their lives and rewrite their history. Her flirta-
tiousness and sensuality link Esse to the loa/goddess of love,
Erzulie. In this guise love can remain the game Adam wants to
play, and Esse can remain distant and in control. But this, too,
remains a promise.

Ultimately, Brathwaite returns to the purity of beginnings.
In the final poem of this volume, "Son," Brathwaite returns to
beginnings. Out of the nothingness, the darkness and the silence
before creation, "came nam / nameless dark horse of devouring
morning." This essence, "nam," which the poet has described as
source or essence or "the indestructible and atomic core of
man's culture," is personified, transfigured, and associated with
the thunder of Shango. There is a mighty gathering of the forces
of light and darkness and thunder and a lyrical description of the
origin of things:

> with a slow rising light of leviathan

with a thunder called firmament

and the salt became stars
they say

and the light grew

and opened the eye of its flower   [97]

In this world, created by new and powerful Gods, the new
Caribbean self will come into being:

and my thrill-
dren are coming up coming up coming up
and the sun

new   [97]

But this new being, the Caribbean self that Brathwaite
reshapes and brings to life, is extremely fragile and struggles to
survive in a Caribbean landscape where the forces of history are
constantly warring, where the Babylons of poverty and oppres-
sion are deeply rooted and, in the words of Bob Marley, there
is a movement toward "total destruction." In the epigraph to
X/Self, the poet asks: "without reason, all you hope gone / ev'ry-
thing look like it comin out wrong. / Why is dat? What it mean?"[21]
The poet's unconscious task is to reorder the elements of
consciousness and to make meaning, to propose an alternative
to destruction, to replace despair with hope. As "Salt" opens,
"Rome burns / and our slavery begins." The pain of the enslaved
is expressed in a communal roar embracing all of history's slaves:

the slaves groan

cerements of bone
and alabaster

rises in hellelluia   [7]

The poet sets the stage for the vast sweep of history upon
which his sight will rest. He captures eternities of pain. In *X/Self*
this ranges from the destruction of the Roman Empire, the begin-
ning of Western civilization, and the origins of slavery to present-
day revisions of slavery and colonization:

there is a crack within the uttar stone of ethiopia
watch where the mediterranean sea comes seeking through

where cleopat unmummied peachskin coloured chick
floating to harvest in her berth of hippo milk
loves anthony her sallow diver of the olive groves
the widowed nipples of her breasts pout north to slavery

["Edge of the Desert," 11]

Embarking on a journey from slavery's past to present, the poet
examines the various historical influences that chip away at the
self. But even as he breaks this self apart, he hints at strategies
of survival and salvation. "Phalos" calls for the abandonment of
materialistic European values and a return to the religious beliefs
of ancestral gods and the wisdom and cultural practices of the
elders, a movement back to a knowledge of "herbs" and "naked
saviours" (16).

Brathwaite speaks for the oppressed of all humanity. In
"Dies irie," the poet's voice thunders the message of destruction
and violence; his personal apocalyptic vision includes the vio-
lence of both nature and man. The poet, as the voice of the rebel

who represents the people's desire for change and a new order, will attempt to reorder society by the power of the "word":

> day of thunder day of hunger
> bring me solace bring me fire
> give me penance bring me power
> grant me vengeance with thy word   [39]

"Word," in this context, is imbued with the special spiritual qualities of the African "Nommo." In his discussion of the concept of Nommo, Janheinz Jahn writes: "All magic is word magic, incantation and exorcism, blessing and curse. Through Nommo, the word, man establishes his mastery over things."[22] Brathwaite constantly returns to ancestral sources for the inspiration and power to transform his society and to exorcise the evils that plague it. To achieve this transformation, from which new meaning will come, the poet creates symbols that speak to the experience of the Caribbean people, and that attempt to make sense out of the clash of the African and European worlds. This is the achievement of *X/Self*, where the poem, "The visibility trigger" explores this cataclysmic confrontation in history: "i offered you a kola nut / ...and you broke it into gunfire" (48). At the heart of this poem, which explores the violence of conquest, Brathwaite goes back to precolonial time, creating a moment that he hopes to recapture in present history:

> and unprepared and venerable i was dreaming mighty wind in
> trees / our circles talismans round hut round village cooking
> pots
> the world was round and we the spices in it
> time wheeled around our memories like stars...
> and i beheld the cotton tree

guardian of graves rise upward
from its monument of grass   [49]

It is in such a circle, a spot sacred to the ancestors, that
the self which the poet is so carefully nurturing can be made
whole. Here, under the protection of the silk cotton tree, a
tree sacred to the ancestors, the wisdom of the Gods will be
made manifest. In Africa and the lands of the diaspora, the silk
cotton tree is revered as a place where ancestral spirits feel an
affinity. It is never tampered with or cut down without special
rituals and prayer. In Guyana, it is also a reminder of the hor-
rors of slavery, for the Dutch masters would bury their treasure
under the silk cotton tree, afterwards killing a slave and leav-
ing his spirit to protect the treasure. In the poet's revisioning,
this tree, "our great odoum," witness to the lamentations of the
past, becomes the "nam," symbolizing, simultaneously, the
eternal African spirits and new Caribbean beginnings and thus
allowing for the rewriting and validation of the Caribbean's
cultural history:

and our great odoum
triggered at last by the ancestors into your visibility crashed
into history   [50]

Violent beginnings and continuities permeate the poetic land-
scape of "Nam." The tortured South African blacks and the
oppressed Rastafarians of the Caribbean are linked in their
struggle for liberation. Here, in the rhythms of the Caribbean,
Brathwaite's narrator gives voice to the "dread" experienced by
the Rastafarians. "Dread," as Gordon Rohlehr describes it, is
"the image of naked elemental survival and the mythical sense
of Apocalypse with which the Rastafarian lives day after day."[23]

The experience of "dread," and its resulting tortured fragmentation and disintegration, is at the center of "*X/Self*'s Xth Letters from the Thirteen Provinces." In a space that is almost overpowered by a modern sense of imminent destruction, and a realization that the Calibans of the world remain dispossessed, X/Self attempts to write the Caribbean self into history. The landscape of the poem is broken and disjointed, but X/Self struggles to write and be right:

> a fine
> a cyaan get nutten
>
> write
>
> a cyaan get nutten really
> rite
>
> while a stannin up here in me years & like I inside a me shadow
> like de man still mekkin i walk up de slope dat e slide
> in black down de whole curve a de arch
>
> i
>
> pell
>
> ago   [86]

At this point, the self that the poet describes is a mixture of resilience and fragility, and the fragmentation of words reflects that of the community which the poet fights against. He tries to understand the Caribbean predicament and its meaning and returns to the questions posed in the epigraph:

why is

dat?

what it

mean?

To answer these questions, the poet introduces Caribbean heroes,
African gods, and sacred places into the imaginary landscape.
In "Stone," the Maroon town of Palmares is such a place. Palmares,
led by the legendary hero, Zambi, was established by runaway
slaves in the seventeenth century and survived against attack
for more than sixty years.[24] In the poet's imagination, Palmares
is transformed into a mythic homeland, a timeless symbol of free-
dom and achievement: "everything looks inwards to this centre"
(93). Brathwaite suggests a kind of cultural self-exploration, and
he erects signposts that would guide the self to recognition and
awareness.

Palmares, like Accompong, the Maroon village in Jamaica,
is an important site for Brathwaite on his exploratory journeys
in time. He rebuilds these landmarks linguistically, and, in them,
he locates truths relevant to today's Caribbean society. He recon-
structs a place and a history that would offer hope and a sense
of wholeness to a people not at home in their homeland. For
example, in the contemporary Caribbean, island people are odd-
ities to tourists. The plantations of slavery have shifted to North
and South American cities:

tourists let inwards by the sweeper at the market gate
rush in and shoot us with their latest nikons and many of
our men / are lured away to work at chipping ice in sin
cinnati cutting the canal at christopher
columbus place in panama....   ["Stone," 94]

Accompanying this panoramic sweep of history is the refrain
"runagate / runagate," from Robert Hayden's poem of the same
name. This is another return, a return to the African-American
experience of "dread." But, the poet suggests that such "dread" can
be overcome and freedom achieved. His recreation of Palmares
is ceremonial and ordered and the effect is very powerful:

> High up in this littered world of rock. stone...
>
> wind we know always sharp slant sleet howl but warm
> as your lips and gentle as a mother with her baby cheek
> to cheek misty mornings high noons spectacular sunsets
>
> at the bottom of this high world high above it all we
> draw / the lion.   ["Stone," 93]

Palmares, filtered through the poet's imagination, becomes a cel-
ebration of community. It appears to be impregnable, a haven of
the spirit surrounded by the evil forces of man and nature.
Again, for the poet, salvation comes in the recovery of ancestry
as he returns to the past and the Lion of Judah, Haile Selassie,
Emperor of Ethiopia. Brathwaite captures the essence of Palmares
in a merger of language and spirit. This reaching back into the
past brings the fragile self at the heart of *X/Self* out of a troubled
privacy and into a beautifully ordered community life.

"Xango," the final poem in *X/Self*, is a song of praise to
Shango, the African warrior god of fire, thunder, and lightning.
He represents power over enemies and opposing forces. He is a
magician/king. The landscape of *X/Self* is a mixture of "dread"
in various forms, as it exists on the world's islands and conti-
nents. It is peopled by heroes as well as the hopeless and those
struggling to survive, the inhabitants of the Trench towns of the

Caribbean and the Americas. The unknown self of the Caribbean, the self struggling to discover its sources, must negotiate this dangerous landscape that threatens to devour it. It is not surprising, then, that the poet calls upon Shango the magician/king to offer possibility and hope. In his notes to *X/Self*, Brathwaite describes the "dub riddims and nation language and calibanisms" as his "magical realism" (113). This gathering together of the religious and the profane, the invocation of ancient African gods and the spirit of Bob Marley, achieves a peculiar harmony; for it is out of the assimilation of these elements that the Caribbean identity will emerge, accepting its tortured past and present reality. Shango offers reconciliation and healing:

>   touch
>   him
>   he will heal
>   you
>
>   word
>   and balm
>   and water
>   flow
>
>   embrace
>   him
>   he will shatter outwards to your light and calm and history
>
>   your thunder has come home   [111]

In rewriting the Caribbean's history and restoring its gods, heroes, and sacred places, Brathwaite anchors and protects the renewed self as it struggles to emerge and ultimately participate in community, a community symbolizing achievement. In this way, Brathwaite refutes entrenched theories of the region's presumed existence in a state of void and historical nothingness.

Brathwaite and Walcott epitomize the duality of the region's relationship to Africa. Brathwaite, having lived in Africa, not only comes into contact with its history, but experiences the civilizing grandeur of its ceremonies and rituals. For the poet to have embraced Africa so entirely was a courageous and sometimes painful act for a man of his time in Caribbean society, a society deeply enamored of all things European, and, as Gordon Lewis describes it, a society in which the average Caribbean person is "the uneasy possessor of a pseudo-European culture in an Afro-Asian environment."[25]

Compared with Brathwaite's celebration of the glory of Africa and the transformative power of its rituals, Walcott distances himself from the splendors of the African past. Walcott is drawn to the dark side of Africa and the pain of being faced with dehumanizing European myths, and while he experiences no epiphany, he comes to a gradual awareness of Africa's place in the Caribbean world that he is inventing. This vision of Africa is one dominated by the trauma of the Middle Passage and the resulting enslavement of African peoples and their descendants. As he recreates a history for his people, he comes to an awareness of the ennobling power of Africa in his visionary world and in the Caribbean he is refashioning.

In his early poetry Walcott's voice is one of separation and alienation: "For these lands belong to no one but the luckless; / (Not to the conquering teeth of foreign engines) / to lost red and black tribes...." Also, "Black and White live apart." Yet, the poet prays: "...might God and His wise machines elect to cross / With a shower of blossoms, and make if no Eden / Then such peace as traveller expects of islands."[26] But the poet is a long way from achieving "peace." Peace is granted to strangers to the islands who are entranced by their beauty and oblivious to the dread underlying their edenic appearance. Continuing to haunt Walcott's visionary world are the monumental tragedies of the destruction of the Amerindians and the destruction and enslavement of the Africans:

> Long, long before us,
> those hot jaws like an oven
> steaming, were open
> to genocide; they devoured
> two minor yellow races, and
> half of a black....[27]

"Ruins of a Great House" couples this sense of destruction with an awareness of creativity.[28] Decay and degeneration have enveloped what was once a monument to human accomplishment and elegant living, but achieved at the expense of the lives of slaves:

> A spade below dead leaves will ring the bone
> Of some dead animal or human thing
> Fallen from evil days, from evil times.   [19]

Walcott juxtaposes the pain of "exiled craftsmen" and the conquest of "ancestral murderers," for example, Hawkins, Raleigh, and Drake. This dual relationship resonates in the Caribbean literary imagination:

> The world's green age then was a rotting lime
> Whose stench became the charnel galleon's text.
> The rot remains with us, the men are gone.   [20]

Walcott rewrites this text. He is driven by a sense of loss for an

African past often distorted or omitted from history. Out of this past the spirit of struggle and survival is distilled; it is located in ancestral memory and is at the center of Walcott's rewriting of history. Before Africa can be rewritten into the new text, Walcott has to destroy the myths of darkness, ignorance, and excessive sexuality—myths perpetuated by Europeans and Caribbeans alike. "Goats and Monkeys" is an attempt at such destruction. Walcott's source is Othello:

> ...His earthen bulk
> buries her bosom in its slow eclipse.
> His smokey hand has charred
> that marble throat. Bent to her lips,
> he is Africa, a vast, sidling shadow
> that halves your world with doubt.   [27]

Walcott appropriates the narrative of Othello and interprets it as a narrative of colonization. Othello is Africa; he is also the enslaved and the colonized. In reinforcing the terrors of these conditions, Walcott creates a surrealistic world where racism and sexuality, coupled with the horror of miscegenation, become palpable fears. In this world, where apprehensions of the "other" loom larger than existence itself, colonial fears are transformed into irrational and ludicrous actions, "a bestial, comic agony" (28). Walcott confronts and alleviates this agony by demystifying Africa and the colonized Caribbean world. He peels away the layers of terror and the fascination with which Africa has been shrouded in the European and Caribbean imagination to expose the simple reality: "this mythical, horned beast who's no more / monstrous for being black" (28).

Africa, however, is not always buried in myth and mystery; its soul is made manifest in the Caribbean, "this further shore of

Africa." The poet moves beyond apparent nothingness, "There's nothing here / ...no visible history," to an intricately woven tale of existence and vitality. What is visible in the Caribbean is the obvious colonial heritage, but as the poet realizes, vibrant African ties exist beneath the surface. Almond trees are transformed into slaves: "their writhing trunks... / Their bodies fiercely shine! / ...they endured their furnace." Superimposed on this history, is the superficial picture in present time of "the forked limbs of girls toasting their flesh / in scarves, sunglasses, Pompeian bikinis." The poet journeys back in time to other "limbs," the limbs of slaves "lashed raw ...washed / out with salt and fire-dried."[29] Because of their survival, the soul of Africa is reborn in the Caribbean strengthened by the crucible of the Middle Passage.

The Middle Passage as symbolic of endurance and the transmission of history is central to the poet's thought. This history is a mixed one, a combination of the exhilaration that comes from a grounding in African custom and rituals and the painful reality of slavery and plantation life. "Laventville" is a meditation on the Middle Passage.[30] As the poet climbs a hill to attend a christening, he is surrounded by deprivation:

we climbed...

where the inheritors of the middle passage stewed
five to a room, still clamped below their hatch,
breeding like felonies....   [32]

The confines of the slave ship have been exchanged for the desperate poverty of the tenement. In these dismal surroundings a child is baptized. On the surface, there is no sign of hope or vitality or future promise; but what links slave ship and tenement is the presence of the "hot, corrugated iron sea / whose horrors we all / shared…" (33). Again, the poet finds strength in the slaves' survival and suggests that this is a fitting gift for the newborn as he enters the collective memory of the race. The sea, peopled by the bones of the ancestors, makes the connection between the violent African exodus and this life in the New World. As a result, the sea is a symbol of the ancestral memory, and it becomes a matter of spiritual survival to explore its depths to recover "customs and gods that are not born again" (35). Walcott suggests that Caribbean people are faced with a choice; they can be imprisoned or liberated by the sea of memory. African customs and gods cannot survive in their initial purity, for they have been affected by the movement from the Old to the New World. However, in their new forms they inhabit the Caribbean world and are an integral part of the movement of liberation.

It is these new forms that concern the poet; forms that have their origins "where Africa began: / in the body's memory."[31] *Another Life,* Walcott's autobiographical work, explores the poet's journey of artistic awareness and his "re-searching of the personal history for an idea of human destiny, an order of truth."[32] At the same time, it is a probing exploration of the poet's attempt to realize the ineluctable memories of an ancestral African past. Walcott recognizes the legacy of this past in the folk culture of St. Lucia. It is a culture threatened by the cynicism of the middle and upper classes who associate folk customs and rituals with country folk and the poor and see the obeahman as a collaborator of the devil. Walcott's mentor, Harold Simmons, was very much aware of this reality. According to Simmons, expressions of Caribbean folk tradition are "at variance with established authority, orthodox religion, upper class morality, law, and other cultural forms having the sanction of authority."[33] But it is in the folk culture of St. Lucia, rooted in its African past, that Walcott finds the human-

izing graces of the Caribbean that are so necessary to the iden-
tity he is engaged in refashioning.

In *Another Life,* Walcott carefully nurtures and protects this
identity he is bringing into existence. He goes back in time to an
African past of lyrical beauty and vitality, and this past speaks
to him clearly:

> I looked for some ancestral, tribal country,
> I heard its clear tongue over the clean stones
> of the river....   [41]

The poet's sense of rootlessness does not lead him to a state
of total alienation and despair. He channels these feelings into
the positive effort of reconstruction in which he is engaged. It
is this focus on rebuilding and reconstruction that Walcott's
friends and contemporaries Dunstan St. Omer, the St. Lucian
painter, and George Odlum both admire. In fact, Odlum believes
that a constant critical focus on Walcott's "divided self" denies
the development of the poet and his efforts to transform the
"dross" of street and country life in St. Lucia into the "vivid
tableau" that emerges in the landscape of his poetic world.[34] St.
Omer sees Walcott as St.Lucia's "foremost national hero" who
"holds up the spirit of St. Lucia to the world."[35] Both men recog-
nize the poet's mission as the refashioner of his island's reality.

Walcott gives voice to this mission in "Homage to Gregorias";
Gregorias is his name for Dunstan St. Omer. He identifies their
common purpose: "we would never leave the island / until we had
put down, in paint, in words, / ... all of its sunken, leafchoked
ravines, / every neglected, self-pitying inlet / muttering in brack-
ish dialect..." (50). To accomplish this mission, the poet returns
to the island's African connections. He delves beneath the sur-
face of things to discover hidden realities and truths. On this

journey underground, he conquers "history thickening with amnesia" (51). Walcott views this "amnesia" as the "true history of the New World" to which "the slave surrendered." The result of this was a "tribal memory...salted with the bitter memory of migration."[36] Walcott's task becomes that of moving back in time beyond the confinement of the Middle Passage to an African tribal existence:

> so that a man's branched, naked trunk,
> its roots crusted with dirt,
> swayed where it stopped, remembering another name;
> breaking a lime leaf,
> cracking an acrid ginger-root,
> a smell of tribal medicine stained the mind...
> here was a life older than geography....   [51]

Walcott's concern here is not with a glorious epic of the Africa of conquest and tragedy; instead, he focuses on the Africa of folklore and farmers and on the preservation of culture and customs and their transmission and transformation in the Caribbean. The memory of the past is used to inform and shape present Caribbean history.

In *Sea Grapes,* Walcott penetrates the heart of history to forge a connection to a past that will offer rootedness and hope for Caribbean people, particularly the poor and the dispossessed.[37] Rastafarians are living manifestations of the poverty and dispossession of the region's black masses in contemporary postindependence times. The Rastafarian presence in Jamaica in particular, and in the Caribbean in general, is a visible reminder of the pull of the forces of exile and return that exist, acknowledged or not, in the Caribbean soul. The alienation of the Rastafarians in Jamaican society, and their desire to return to

Africa, literally, is an example of this duality. Rastafarian beliefs are grounded in their interpretation of the scripture. Therefore, African slavery and the horrors of plantation life are analogous to the "Scattering of the twelve tribes of Israel and the Exile in Babylonian captivity." The Jews' return to the Promised Land is analogous to the Rastafarians' wish to return to Africa.[38] At the center of Rastafarian theology is the "experience of dread," which Joseph Owens characterizes as "the awesome, fearful confrontation of a people with a primordial but historically denied racial selfhood."[39] The Rastafarian's relationship to Africa—Africa as myth, religious center, and geographical place—epitomizes the subconscious longing of the Caribbean's black people for cultural wholeness and the recognition that Africa, not its physical presence but its visionary form, exists at the sensitive point of Caribbean existence:

> This Africa is a presence, a dialectically given existential presence. And this Africa in a white racist colonial era became the burden and the possibility of black manhood. The absence of Africa became the presence of Africa. A persistent, nagging, aching possibility.[40]

Walcott's "Dread Song" captures, on the one hand, the essence of Rastafarian existence, the purity of belief: "Forged from the fire of Exodus / the iron of the tribe"; and, on the other hand, "the dreams and the lies." The poet confronts the ambivalence of the Rastafarian existence, an ambivalence that embraces the exodus from Africa as well as its economic justification:

> Economics and Exodus,
>
> embrace us within

bracket and parenthesis

their snake arms of brotherhood
(the brackets of the bribe).   [25]

The microcosmic world of the Rastafarian intensifies and mirrors
the larger black Caribbean world complete with its contradictions.
Here, Walcott speaks out against separation, "bracket and paren-
thesis," and suggests a "brotherhood" that, while rooted in past
mythology and history, at the same time reflects this past in the
actuality of the Caribbean.

Walcott calls for the end of superficiality at all levels of soci-
ety, advocating a depth of "vision" and a return of "faith": not
blind faith, but a faith based on the knowledge of the region's
fragmented history and the belief that it can be made whole. He
recognizes that a symbolic return to Africa does have its place;
for such a reversal of the original journey would be an exploration
and an excavation of history, a recognition that the region is an
historical entity, and not a "mimicry" of European societies.
Such "mimicry" in colonial and postcolonial societies, Homi K.
Bhabha believes, "conceals no presence or identity behind its
mask."[41] Walcott sees the necessity for cementing form and con-
tent, destroying the mask and revealing the recreated history of
the region. He is well aware of the Caribbean's obsession with "the
loss of history, the amnesia of the races." Imagination replaces
"loss" and "amnesia."[42] Imagination is creative and inventive.

Walcott recognizes these dual acts of destruction and cre-
ation in the work of Eric Roach, the poet from Trinidad and
Tobago, and celebrates Roach's achievement in a lyrical tribute,
"The Wind in the Dooryard."[43] In 1974, Roach committed suicide
by drowning. In an amazing poem, "I am the Archipelago," Roach
compresses the story of the region's past and present history. But

even as he presents the region's convulsive periods of slavery and colonization, his vision of the region is one of reconstruction and hope: "I am the archipelago hope / Would mould into dominion...." Moving from this grand and prophetic opening statement that asserts a future for the region, Roach then descends to the depths of the region's suffering and expands the circle to include the world's dispossessed ranging from the shanty towns of the Caribbean to the shanty towns of Africa and America:

> ...And now
> My language, history and my names are dead
> And buried with my tribal soul. And now
> I drown in the groundswell of poverty
> No love will quell. I am the shanty town.
> Banana, sugarcane and cotton man;
> Economies are soldered with my sweat
> Here, everywhere; in hate's dominion;
> In Congo, Kenya, in free, unfree America.

He exhumes the "tribal soul" and, later, acknowledges the power of his New World religion, not only to unify the disparate elements of his ancestry, African and Caribbean, but also to provide salvation in present history and release in time:

> The cock, the totem of his craft, his luck,
> The obeahman infects me to my heart
> Although I wear my Jesus on my breast
> And burn a holy candle for my saint.
> I am a shaker and a shouter and a myal man;
> My voodoo passion swings sweet chariots low.[44]

What the obeahman, the shaker, the shouter and the myal man

have in common is the incorporation, into their religious prac-
tices, of some of the elements of traditional African beliefs and
customs.[45] The "sweet chariots" of the Negro spiritual are not
"coming to take [him] home" in the traditional Christian sense,
for "home" here is Africa. His inherent "voodoo passion" draws
him home to Africa. This celebration of Roach's ancestry and New
World creativity blends the essences of his dual existence, African
and Caribbean, and out of this mixture forms a Caribbean indi-
viduality that Derek Walcott acknowledges in "The Wind in the
Dooryard."

"The Wind in the Dooryard," while it confronts Roach's
tragic death even as it celebrates his life, explores Walcott's own
journey toward an understanding of the region's complex history.
Initially, he confronts and dismisses the grotesqueries of suicide:

> I didn't want this poem to come
> from the torn mouth,
> I didn't want this poem to come
> from his salt body....   [58]

Next, Walcott creates a beautiful myth to explain the poet's
death:

> He went swimming to Africa,
> but he felt tired;
> he chose that way
> to reach his ancestors.   [58]

The despair of suicide and its lack of control is transformed into
a moment of conscious choice, a renunciation of pain and an affir-
mation of ancestral life and history. The unity of death and life,
escape and return, body and spirit leads to peace and a home-

coming. Walcott puts his myth to work as a vehicle of salvation. In the process of naming this "home" and the return journey, the "stone barracoons" and the grinding poverty of peasant existence are transcended, thus offering hope and the "freshness of life" (60).

The sea is the central symbol linking Walcott's exploration of these journeys of death and rebirth. It is the keeper and guardian of the ancestral memory. In *Caribbean Discourse,* Edouard Glissant, discussing Caribbean history, quotes the phrase "the unity is submarine" with which Kamau Brathwaite concludes his study on "Cultural diversity and integration" in the Caribbean.[46] Glissant explains Brathwaite's phrase in this way:

> To my mind, the expression can only evoke all those Africans weighed down with ball and chain and thrown overboard whenever a slave ship was pursued by enemy vessels and felt too weak to put up a fight. They sowed in the depths the seeds of an invisible presence.[47]

It is this "invisible presence," for which Brathwaite uses the term "submarine," that dominates Walcott's collection, *The Star-Apple Kingdom:*

> Where are your monuments, your battles, martyrs?
> Where is your tribal memory? Sirs,
> in that grey vault. The sea. The sea
> has locked them up. The sea is History.[48]

The poet must open the "vault," make history visible, and point out its relevance to the New World, as a result, healing and creating an identity steeped in the region's history. In this poem, Walcott embarks on a submarine journey. It is interesting that Walcott, like Brathwaite, actually uses the term "submarine." When the persona is asked: "But where is your Renaissance?", he replies:

> Sir, it is locked in them sea sands
> out there past the reef's moiling shelf,
> where the men-o'-war floated down:
>
> strop on these goggles, I'll guide you there myself.
> It's all subtle and submarine,
> through colonnades of coral,
>
> past the gothic windows of sea fans
> to where the crusty grouper, onyx-eyed,
> blinks, weighed by its jewels, like a bald queen;
>
> and these groined caves with barnacles
> pitted like stone
> are our cathedrals,
>
> and the furnace before the hurricanes:
> Gomorrah. Bones ground by windmills
> into marl and cornmeal....   [26-27]

To answer the question posed, Walcott creates an underwater world of enchantment which lulls the reader and questioner into a feeling of well-being until suddenly faced with "bones ground." The periods of history do not get any pleasanter, for with emancipation comes the "congealing into towns"; the "white sisters," dispensers of charity and faith, are the legacy of colonization, and independence brings its own horrors in the shape of politicians who mimic colonial powers. But, in spite of the dismal landscape, the poet continues with his submarine explorations; for there is hope in his rereading of his text, the sea. In discussing the role of the artist in our time, Robert Elliot Fox writes: "Whereas, in the past, the artist was a kind of priest, today's artist is something like an archeologist of the soul, uncovering lost or hidden meanings."[49]

This statement quite clearly describes Walcott's role as New World poet. He retraces the steps of history, moving beyond present and past times of turbulence to discover;

...in the dark ears of ferns

and in the salt chuckle of rocks
with their sea pools, there was the sound
like a rumor without any echo
of History, really beginning.   [28]

The "rumor" Walcott hears is of the existence of Africa in both the real and the symbolic landscapes of the Caribbean. D.S. Izevbaye suggests that "Walcott's interpretation of the West Indian experience emphasizes the termination of the African phase at the time of the slave-ship."[50] Such a reading denies the poet's clear obsession with the sea as memory and cultural receptacle and his constant desire to salvage the legacy of the Middle Passage and transform it to fit its New World home. While his focus is on the journey of the Middle Passage, the slave ship becomes in his imagination not only a source of separation and pain but also the means of transporting and preserving the culture of Africa.

It is not by chance then that Shabine, the persona of *The Star-Apple Kingdom,* embarks on a journey across the Caribbean sea. Lloyd Brown describes this journey as "a kind of spiritual odyssey, one in which [Shabine] rediscovers history in memories of the middle passage and in which he recounts the history of the Caribbean

from the slave trade to the new nationhood."[51] In the opening lines
of "The Schooner Flight," the poet creates a haunting feeling of
timelessness. At the same time he creates the sense of the end-
ing of a personal existence and the beginning of a mythical one:

> In idle August, while the sea soft,
> and leaves of brown islands stick to the rim
> of this Caribbean, I blow out the light
> by the dreamless face of Maria Concepcion
> to ship as a seaman on the schooner Flight.   [3]

Shabine, the seaman, describes himself as a "red nigger" who
"have Dutch, nigger, and English in me, / and either I'm nobody,
or I'm a nation" (4). Confronted by the disparate elements of
Caribbean ethnicity, the horrors of existence in "the Limers'
Republic," Trinidad, and his descent into madness, Shabine
escapes to the sea to find his "harbor" and "the window [he] can
look from that frames [his] life" (8). This is a "window" into the
past, and Shabine is pulled into the world of "great admirals" and
"sailors before [him]" (11). But Walcott is not bent on celebrating
early Caribbean sea journeys or the courage of adventurers and
conquerors. Instead, he sweeps aside the glamour and the lust
for adventure, and Shabine, who lightly dismisses his identity,
is faced with the truth of his ancestry. However, this truth poses
another problem. In the multiethnic mixture that is the Caribbean,
racial divisions are not always clear-cut; and in true colonial style
the tendency exists to create as much distance as possible from
the Caribbean's African roots. At this stage, Shabine's journey is
not complete, and he lightly dismisses this moment that could
have been a moment of psychic awareness:

> Next we pass slave ships. Flags of all nations,

our fathers below deck too deep, I suppose,
to hear us shouting. So we stop shouting. Who knows
who his grandfather is, much less his name?   [11]

The posing of this question implies that to Shabine the answer
is not of much importance. Such a response is typical of the col-
onized mind bent on the erasure of memory and the adoption
of names granted by the colonial powers:

but we live like our names and you would have
to be colonial to know the difference,
to know the pain of history words contain...
if we live like the names our masters please,
by careful mimicry might become men.   [12]

It is this "mimicry" that must be rejected. At the center of
Walcott's visionary world lies a passion of resistance to such
"mimicry." Mimicry assumes the existence of a void, the delib-
erate donning of a mask to hide emptiness and a lack of history.
Walcott in his role as guardian of the region's history insists upon
a return to origins; "history is memory."[52] Walcott's obsession with
origins, the role of history in the struggle to establish a Caribbean
identity, and the liberating power of ancestral memory in the
poetic imagination, facilitated by the presence of New World gods,
all come together in his play, *Dream on Monkey Mountain*.[53]
     Handwritten in Walcott's Trinidad Theatre Workshop's copy
of Dream is the following statement:

Our stage technique must create magic, power, tricks hal-
lucinations—Remember the visual theme of the play—smoke,
mist, fire, coal, fog, heat, coal. Now link these metaphors—
perhaps cloud, mist at the base of the mountain—or actual

smoke—perhaps these could be linked by images that are the play's (poem's) beginning.[54]

His insistence on "magic" and "power," as well as a sense of the amorphous allow the poet a certain indefinite quality of time and space in which to work his own magic of transformation and, as a result, liberation. *Dream* can be read as a narrative poem that fits Patrick Taylor's definition of a "liberating narrative":

> It lifts human agents out of their closed realms to bring them into universal history, insisting on the fundamental unity, even in diversity, of all humanity. Any attempt to deny or negate human possibility, slavery and racism being primary Caribbean examples of such denial, is rejected by liberating narrative.[55]

Together, these two statements suggest a way of entering into the strangely haunting dream world of Walcott's play. His emphasis on magic, hallucination, smoke, fog, and mist creates an atmosphere beyond rational comprehension. Walcott's use of these theatrical conventions of smoke, mist, and fog is a physical manifestation of his own possession by the forces of history. In the imaginary world of the theater, where participants in the drama can leave the world of reality behind and enter the realm of imagination, Walcott is liberated, able to engage—vicariously—through his character, Makak, in the ritual of possession. He is possessed by history and historical forces; therefore, it is not surprising that hovering over this play and entering Makak's subconscious are the gods of Africa and the loas of the New World.

Makak, the protagonist, is a coal-burner, ugly, old and black, who lives on Monkey Mountain. Lloyd Brown makes the connection between monkeys and ugliness, blacks and ugliness, and blacks and monkeys.[56] Jan Uhrbach, too, views the connection as "dehumanizing": "Makak becomes macaque, a monkey of the genus macacus, originally including a large number of African and Asian species....In the European context, he is simply "an African monkey."[57] Such reductionist interpretations sever the African connections Walcott is emphasizing. Henry Louis Gates, in *The Signifying Monkey,* tells of the Fon myth where Legba, the Creator, becomes the father of the monkey.[58] This is the monkey who crosses the Atlantic and surfaces in the folk tales of the Caribbean. The Fon Legba is both creator and trickster. He is also the "protector of crossroads and doors, the protector of the herd....he is the interpreter of the gods, who translates the requests and prayers of men into their language." In Haiti, he is a crippled old man with a cane.[59]

Walcott's characters are wonderful mixtures of both worlds, reflecting the New World history that he is engaged in rewriting. Moustique the cripple is not only Makak's friend; in some ways he is an extension of Makak as archetypical Legba, embodying the trickster element. Makak links the worlds of the rational and the imaginary. Wakened one morning by Moustique, Makak tells of a dream in which a beautiful white woman appears to him. She advises him to change his way of living for he "comes from the family of lions and kings" (236). She is Erzulie, the "mother of man's myth of life—its meaning."[60] She is the vodoun goddess of love, beauty and the world of dreams:

> She is the dream impaled eternally upon the cosmic
> cross/roads where the world of men and the world of divin-
> ity meet, and it is through her pierced heart that "man
> ascends and the gods descend."[61]

In pictures, according to Janheinz Jahn, she appears "as a

white woman...and is identified with the Blessed Virgin."[62] But to Alfred Métraux, "She has all the characteristics of a pretty mulatto."[63] Milo Rigaud describes her "as a dark-skinned Ethiopian woman." Rigaud also stresses the relationship between Legba and Erzulie. Legba is the "male prototype" and Erzulie, the "female prototype" of vodoun. He is the "Christ," and she is the "Virgin."[64]

Walcott plays on all of these elements and characteristics as he delineates the relationship between Makak and the woman who appears to him. In this way, Walcott presents the Caribbean's deep-seated obsession with race and color. He transforms this obsession into a ritual of possession through which it will be eliminated. Makak symbolizes the dispossessed of the Caribbean who see no hope in the present world. The apparition lures him into a dream world of possibility, where achieving a place in a symbolic Africa and being given identifiable and regal ancestors are the initial steps in healing his tortured being. But Makak does not fully understand the apparition's message. In his simple, childlike approach to the world around him, he interprets the message literally and embarks on a personal idealistic quest that is thoroughly at odds with the society in which he lives. Makak mounts his horse and, together with Moustique, sets out on his journey to Africa. Soon they encounter a community of wailing people. At the center of the group is a sick man being carried by four men and accompanied by Basil, a "tall frock-coated man in [a] black silk hat, his face halved by white make-up" (243). He is "the carpenter, and cabinetmaker" and by implication the coffin maker (246).

Basil is a manifestation of Baron Samedi, ruler of the cemetery and the crossroads. He is a symbol of life as well as death, facilitating entry into the immortal life or the crossing over from one state of being into another. At Makak's intercession the sick man is healed. Basil is present in the background hovering over the ritual of healing. The sick man is the epitome of the evils afflicting society's masses. In this encounter between evil and good, Makak is the instrument through which this element of society is healed. Walcott suggests that healing comes through the understanding of and the identification with the gods and the ancient rituals that remain alive in the memory of a people. When the rituals are warped and used in the service of false gods, communities are destroyed and death results. Moustique, in his capacity as trickster, pretends to be Makak the healer and is unmasked by Basil. He is beaten to death by the crowd.

As the play begins, Makak is in jail in a cell with two thieves, Souris and Tigre. He was put there for "drunk and disorderly" behavior by Corporal Lestrade, a mulatto; he "mash up Alcindor cafe" (215). Corporal Lestrade attempts to place himself in a white world even as he denigrates the black world. He laughs at Makak's vision of himself as a "King of Africa" (214), and refers sarcastically to him as "the Lion of Judah" (217). In Lestrade's mind Makak, because he is black and poor, is no more than an animal. This diminishment of self and race occurs at all levels of the society; for example, the thieves pretend to believe in Makak's aberrations in order to gain access to his money. Makak in his simplicity cannot see through the mask of corruption enveloping the thieves, for he is still possessed by his vision: "I feel I was God self, walking through cloud. In the heaven on my mind" (227). Lestrade views Makak's possession as "the rage for whiteness that does drive niggers mad" (228).

But Makak's possession allows him to enter another world to escape the world of poverty and deprivation he knows only too well. He becomes a god. Métraux, in discussing the transformative power of possession, mentions the new role of the possessed person as advisor, healer, and foreteller of the future. The possessed person also advises himself.[65] Makak, in his role as god/loa, will reorder the world around him and rewrite the history of his people. To achieve this, Walcott returns Makak to the world of dreams where, accompanied by the two thieves, Lestrade is overcome and wounded, and, as the trio escapes, he says: "[They are] attempting to escape from the prison of their lives. That's the most dangerous crime. It brings about revolution" (287).

Walcott utilizes vodoun's power of religious possession to facilitate the mental and psychological liberation of the Caribbean people. He also inscribes in their memory revisions of their New World history. Religious possession, because of its transformative powers, becomes the ideal spiritual medium for accomplishing change. This is particularly important as the "function and purpose of [the] divine manifestation [during possession] is the reassurance and the instruction of the community."[66]

Walcott hopes to rid his community of the effects of a total acceptance of colonial history, a history that views Caribbean people as colonial imitators who, in such roles, dismiss their ancestral heritage and perpetuate the divisions of race, color, and class etched into their consciousness by their European masters. New World religious possession, crafted by the poet as a means of repossessing the region's history, is the source of knowledge, healing and reconciliation. Harold Courlander, discussing the phenomenon of possession, suggests that people possessed by loas "may talk about...community ancestors, about intimate affairs of the community, or about how things are going back in Africa. Sometimes they utter words or phrases recognized as 'African language.'"[67] This language of religious possession would be described as "nation language" by Kamau Brathwaite. Nation language is that aspect of Caribbean language informed by the African experience. The language of possession allows this "submerged, surrealist experience and sensibility" to come to the surface of consciousness.[68] It is essentially an African experience emanating from the vernacular tradition, a tradition in which sound and movement and the collective ancestral experience envelop the members of a community making them conscious of the individual's place in the continuity of the communal experience.

Makak's possession functions in all of these ways. He is transported to Africa, discovers ancestors, and becomes the voice of the community of the dispossessed. All this occurs in the play's second dream vision. Makak stabs Corporal Lestrade and, with his jail companions Souris and Tigre, finds himself in Africa. The journey becomes for Souris and Tigre a journey of discovery. For Souris, away from Africa he exists in "darkness" and "God was like a big white man, a big white man [he] was afraid of" (290). In the African Eden of Makak's imagination, Souris will lose his fear and emerge out of the darkness of ignorance and into the light of knowledge. The experience is a mystic one:

> ...after many moons, after many songs, we will see Africa,
> the golden sand, the rivers where lions come down to drink,
> lapping at the water with their red tongues, then the vil-
> lagers, the birds, the sound of flutes.   [291]

In this idyllic setting, Souris is possessed by the myth of Africa and is transformed. He exclaims: "Yes, yes, I see it. I see it"! Makak replies: "When your eyes open, you will be transformed, as if you have eaten a magic root" (291). While Walcott does not advocate the acceptance of mythic Africa in isolation from a New World past, he does realize its importance as the inspiriting force in the Caribbean imagination.

This is a necessary stage in Caribbean historical recovery. In this stage, believers are possessed by the myth of Africa, and this results in a new level of consciousness. They regain a sense of self and of possibility and are able to embark on the journey of recovery and psychic healing. Makak, the poor, ugly charcoal burner, is transfigured. Through his mouth, the loa of New World history speaks: "Makak will destroy" (295). What Makak destroys is the paralyzing hatred of self and of race and the belief, literally and figuratively, in white gods. Recovery is made possible.

Presiding over the process of recovery is none other than Baron Samedi in the form of Basil. This is a highly appropriate setting for the Baron's appearance, for he usually appears to his followers in a dream.[69] Baron Samedi possesses powers of healing and is the "last recourse against death."[70] Walcott brings Makak to this awareness: "Death is the last shadow I have made. The carpenter is waiting" (304). The fact that Basil as representative of Baron Samedi hovers over the proceedings leading up to and culminating in Makak's transfiguration is no surprise. Walcott identifies this section of the play as an "apotheosis."[71] Here, Makak is exalted to divine rank. Such a monumental change, a leap into history, has to be approved by the loa of the crossroads. This scene, Scene Three, is one of unfolding splendor and ceremony. There is a procession of warriors and chiefs and the stately roll of drums. Makak appears in regal glory as the leader and protector of his people and of old world history and culture. But, Walcott's purpose is to make the connection to current time; therefore, the recreating and mythologizing of the African past has its relevance for present Caribbean times. Corporal Lestrade now sees Makak as the "inventor of history" (311). This is the realization that the poet wants to achieve. He recognizes the importance of the African past as an integral element in the shaping of Caribbean history.

At the heart of such recognition and its transformation of the self is the awareness of a personal identity. The individual secure in self-knowledge is of value to his society. But Makak still wavers. He sees himself as a "shadow," a "hollow God," and a "phantom" (311). However, he is urged by Corporal Lestrade to right the wrongs of past and present history. He is presented with a list of offenders to be hanged, ranging from Noah and Abraham Lincoln to Sir Cecil Rhodes and Horatio Nelson (312). Moustique, already dead, is also presented for hanging. In addition, the white woman, who initially appeared to Makak, is a member of this society of the doomed.

The act of execution introduces a peculiar twist in the poet's working out of the themes of regeneration and reconciliation. Patrick Taylor believes that Baron Samedi, "as healer and giver of life," presides over the death of the apparition and ensures that "death is transformed into life," and this death results in Makak's "renewal of life." Baron Samedi becomes a "symbol of liberation."[72] Taylor's interpretation of Makak's act of execution is an idealistic one, for Makak actually kills his dream. The apparition, as a manifestation of the loa, Erzulie, is the loa of "impossible perfection."[73] However, Makak's ritual execution of the personalities representing society's evils cannot eliminate evil from his world. The execution of the apparition forces Makak to return to the world of the present and to recognize his own name: "My name is Felix Hobain..." (321).

To Robert Hamner, with the act of execution Makak is "finally free to be himself. The visionary goddess may have been white, but the inspiration she brought of African identity was as inauthentic and limiting as the one she was replacing."[74] Hamner's analysis, too, is limiting. Makak's confrontation of the past, his meting out of justice to historical figures opposed to the concept of black survival and self-knowledge, is analogous to Fola's examination of the past initiated by the Ceremony of Souls in George Lamming's *Season of Adventure*.[75] Both Fola and Makak come to accept past terrors and reenter present time free from the constraints of the past.

In *The Pleasures of Exile,* Lamming writes of the role of the living in the Ceremony of Souls:

> The living demand to hear whether there is any forgiveness, for redemption; whether, in fact, there may be any guide which may help them towards reforming their present conditions....They are interested in their Future.[76]

Walcott and Lamming transport Makak and Fola into a redemptive future. This redemption is possible when Africa finds its inevitable location at the center of Caribbean history and culture. The apparition, the bringer of the message, is executed, but the message survives. It is this message that will bring Corporal Lestrade out of his prison life and will ensure Makak eternal life in "the dream of his people":

> Let me be swallowed up in mist again, and let me be forgotten, so that when the mist open, men can look up, at some small clearing with a hut, with a small signal of smoke, and say, "Makak lives where he has always lived, in the dream of his people."   [326]

Walcott's Makak epitomizes the dreams of the dispossessed. In his psyche, the myth of Africa is united with the development of New World history. It offers to Caribbean people a new reading of this history together with a knowledge of an actual African past and its informing and inspiriting presence in today's Caribbean society.

In *Dream on Monkey Mountain,* the vision of Derek Walcott and Kamau Brathwaite converge. Here, Walcott brings together Africa and the Caribbean, and in this union offers to Caribbean society a history peopled with Old and New World ancestors. In spite of his denials, Walcott liberates the ancient gods and anchors them in Caribbean soil: "I am pounding the faces of gods back into the red clay."[77] This is the vision Derek Walcott and Kamau Brathwaite share.

Notes

1. Wilson Harris, "Interior of the Novel: Amerindian/European/ African Relations," *Explorations* (Denmark: Dangaroo, 1981) 11.
2. Paula Burnett, *The Penguin Book of Caribbean Verse in English* (Middlesex: Penguin, 1988) 111.
3. Harold Telemanque, "Poem," *Caribbean Verse,* ed. O.R. Dathorne (London: Heinemann, 1967) 73.
4. Dathorne, *Caribbean Verse* 57.
5. Kamau Brathwaite, "Prelude," *The Arrivants: A New World Trilogy* (London: Oxford UP) 91.
6. Brathwaite, "Kingston in the kingdom of this world," *Third World Poems* (Essex: Longman, 1983) 53-56.
7. Brathwaite, "Gods of the Middle Passage: A Tennament," *Caribbean Review,* vol. XI.4 (1982): 18.
8. Brathwaite, "Springblade," *Black + Blues* (Cuba: Casa de las Américas, 1986) 51-52.
9. Brathwaite, "Sun Song," *Black + Blues* 57.
10. Brathwaite, "The African Presence in Caribbean Literature," *Roots* (Havana: Casa de las Américas, 1986) 212.
11. Brathwaite, *Jah Music* (Jamaica: Savacou, 1986) 11.
12. Orlando Patterson, *An Absence of Ruins* (London: Hutchinson, 1967) 160.
13. Kenneth Ramchand and Cecil Gray, *West Indian Poetry* (Essex: Longman, 1989) 2.
14. Patterson, *Slavery and Social Death: A Comparative Study* (Cambridge, Harvard UP, 1982) 5.
15. Brathwaite, *Mother Poem* (Oxford: Oxford UP, 1977).
16. Brathwaite, *Sun Poem* (Oxford: Oxford UP, 1982).
17. Brathwaite, *X/Self* (Oxford: Oxford UP, 1987).
18. Brathwaite, "Caribbean Culture: Two Paradigms," *Missile and Capsule,* ed. Jurgen Martini (Bremen: n.p. 1983) 42.
19. Brathwaite, "History, the Caribbean Writer and X/Self," *Crisis and Creativity in the New Literatures in English,* eds. Geoffrey V. Davis and Hena Maes-Jelinek (Amsterdam: Rodopi, 1990) 32-33.

20. Janheinz Jahn, *Muntu,* trans. Marjorie Grene (New York: Grove, 1961) 133.
21. Brathwaite, preface, *X/Self* (Oxford: Oxford UP, 1987).
22. Jahn, *Muntu* 132.
23. Gordon Rohlehr, "West Indian Poetry: Some Problems of Assessment," *Bim* 14.55 (July-Dec. 1972): 134.
24. R.K. Kent, "Palmares: An African State in Brazil," *Maroon Societies,* ed. Richard Price (Baltimore: Johns Hopkins UP, 1979) 170-190.
25. Gordon K. Lewis, "The Caribbean: Colonization and Culture," *Studies on the Left,* vol. II.I. (1961): 40.
26. Derek Walcott, "Travelogue," *25 Poems* (Barbados: Advocate, 1949) 17.
27. Walcott, "Air," *The Gulf* (New York: Farrar, 1970) 69.
28. Walcott, "Ruins of a Great House," *In a Green Night* (London: Cape, 1969).
29. Walcott, "The Almond Trees," *The Castaway* (London: Cape, 1969) 36-37.
30. Walcott, "Laventville," *The Castaway* 32-35.
31. Walcott, *Another Life* (Washington, D.C.: Three Continents (1982) 24.
32. Patricia Ismond, "Another Life: Autobiography as Alternate History," *Journal of West Indian Literature* 4.1 (January 1990): 41.
33. Harold Simmons, "Notes on Folklore in St. Lucia," *Iouanaloa,* ed. Kamau Brathwaite (St. Lucia: n.p., 1963) 41.
34. Critical discussion of Walcott's poetry often focuses on his fragmented consciousness. To support this position critics refer to the poem "A Far Cry from Africa" in the collection *In a Green Night.* They fail to realize that the poem's final question is rhetorical and emphasizes the inescapable power of Africa in the poet's imagination. See Lloyd Brown, *West Indian Poetry* (London: Heinemann, 1984) 124; Robert D. Hamner, *Derek Walcott* (Boston: Twayne, 1981) 49; and Diana Lyn, "The Concept of the Mulatto in Some Works of Derek Walcott," *Caribbean Quarterly* 26.1&2 (March-June 1980): 61-62.
35. From a taped recording of the Walcott Celebration in May 1990, St. Lucia, provided by George Odlum.
36. Walcott, "The Muse of History," *Is Massa Day Dead?* ed. Orde Coombs (New York: Anchor) 5-6.
37. Walcott, *Sea Grapes* (New York: Farrar, 1970).
38. Rex Nettleford, introduction, *Dread: The Rastafarians of Jamaica,* by Joseph Owen (Jamaica: Sangster's, 1976) xiii.
39. Joseph Owens, *Dread: The Rastafarians of Jamaica* 3.
40. Owens 6.

41. Homi K. Bhabha, "Of Mimicry and Man: The Ambivalence of Colonial Discourse," *October* 28 (Spring 1984): 129.
42. Walcott, "The Caribbean: Culture or Mimicry," *Journal of Interamerican Studies and World Affairs* 16.1 (February 1974): 6.
43. Walcott, "The Wind in the Dooryard," *Sea Grapes* 58-60. Subsequent page references to this poem will appear in parentheses in the text.
44. Eric Roach, "I Am the Archipelago," *Voice Print,* ed. Stewart Brown et al (Essex: Longman, 1989) 196.
45. Orlando Patterson, *The Sociology of Slavery* (New Jersey: Fairleigh Dickinson UP, 1967) 182-195; and George Simpson, *Black Religions in the New World* (New York: Columbia UP, 1978) 117-121.
46. Edward Kamau Brathwaite, *Contradictory Omens* (Mona, Jamaica: Savacou, 1985) 64.
47. Edouard Glissant, Caribbean Discourse, trans. Michael Dash (Charlottesville: UP of Virginia, 1989) 66-67.
48. Walcott, "The Sea is History," *The Star-Apple Kingdom* (London: Cape, 1969) 25.
49. Robert Elliot Fox, "History as Dis-Ease," *Callaloo* 27: 9.2 (Spring 1986): 331.
50. D.S. Izevbaye, "The Exile and the Prodigal: Derek Walcott as West Indian Poet," *Caribbean Quarterly* 26 (March-June 1980): 75.
51. Lloyd Brown, *West Indian Poetry* (London: Heinemann, 1984) 140.
52. Walcott, "Caligula's Horse," *Kunapipi* xi.i (1989): 142.
53. Walcott, *Dream on Monkey Mountain and Other Plays* (New York: Noonday, 1970).
54. This text can be found in the collection of Walcott papers housed at the University of the West Indies, St. Augustine campus, Trinidad. As of 1990 these papers were not yet catalogued.
55. Patrick Taylor, *The Narrative of Liberation* (Ithaca: Cornell UP, 1989) 3.
56. Lloyd Brown, "The Revolutionary Dream of Walcott's Makak," *Critics on Caribbean Literature,* ed. Edward Baugh (New York: St. Martin, 1978) 59.
57. Jan Uhrbach, "A Note on Language and Naming in *Dream on Monkey Mountain,*" *Callaloo* 29: 9.4 (Fall 1986): 579.
58. Henry Louis Gates, *The Signifying Monkey* (New York: Oxford UP, 1988) 17.
59. Jahn 42-43.
60. Maya Deren, *Divine Horsemen: The Living Gods of Haiti* (New York: McPherson, 1991) 138.
61. Deren 145.
62. Jahn 45.

63. Alfred Métraux, *Voodoo in Haiti* (New York: Schocken, 1972) 110.

64. Milo Rigaud, *Secrets of Voodoo* (New York: Arco, 1969) 45.

65. Métraux 124-125.

66. Deren 30.

67. Harold Courlander, *The Drum and the Hoe* (Berkeley: U of California P, 1985) 20.

68. Edward Kamau Brathwaite, *History of the Voice* (London: New Beacon, 1984) 13.

69. Métraux 145.

70. Deren 113.

71. Walcott, *Dream on Monkey Mountain* 308.

72. Taylor 214.

73. Deren 144.

74. Robert D. Hamner, *Derek Walcott* (Boston: Twayne) 87.

75. George Lamming, *Season of Adventure* (London: Allison, 1979) 39-46.

76. Lamming, *The Pleasures of Exile* (London: Allison, 1984) 9-10.

77. Walcott, *Another Life* 69.

Chapter 3

Language as Salvation

I
must be given words to shape my name
to the syllables of trees
I must be given words to refashion futures
like a healer's hand.

—Brathwaite, "Negus," *The Arrivants*

Kamau Brathwaite and Derek Walcott share a passion and a commitment to change. Each poet sees his task as the remaking of Caribbean society. Through the transformative power of language, these poets attack the stereotypes and misreadings of history embedded in the society, a consequence of its confrontation with Europe. Rooted in a vernacular tradition, their concern with (re)membering the past determines the performance of this task. Their focus on the African elements of the Caribbean's history and culture includes a recognition of the diversity of the

Caribbean community and, as Wilson Harris puts it, a move-
ment towards a "visionary threshold of heterogeneous commu-
nity."[1] In this movement, language plays a crucial role in form-
ing community.

Brathwaite and Walcott appropriate the language of the col-
onizer and transform it by incorporating into the language the
manifestations of the African experience in the New World. They
share a revolutionary tendency to correct the distortions of his-
tory and in the process bring life to the new Caribbean self and
community they are engaged in reinventing. Kamau Brathwaite,
however, leaps ahead of Derek Walcott in bold experimentation;
in his latest works, he departs radically from earlier terrain.[2]
Utilizing what he describes as "video style," Brathwaite har-
nesses the technological possibilities of the computer and with
revolutionary force re-creates states of personal and societal
dread. "Video style" is his use of various computer fonts and sizes
of type that move beyond the conventional representation of
words on a page. In this current period, Brathwaite uses typog-
raphy in unique and dynamic ways to intensify and deepen the
poetic experience.

While each poet is engaged in repossessing the language, each
one views his relationship to his task differently. In an interview
with Charles Rowell, Derek Walcott was asked: "Do you think there
is an aesthetic reconciliation or synthesis of [your] British educa-
tion and [the] Caribbean landscape?" His reply was: "Are you say-
ing how do you relate Wordsworth's poetry to coconut trees?"[3]
Clearly, the implication here is that the Caribbean poet may attempt
to transform himself into something he is not by adopting the lan-
guage trappings of the colonizer to become, in other words, a
British poet in black face. But the Caribbean experience is a unique
one, and both Walcott and Brathwaite stretch and bend language
so that it reflects the history and reality of the Caribbean experi-

ence. This experience is the inhumanity and degradation of slav-
ery, the alienation of plantation existence, and the erasure of iden-
tity and selfhood. The experience is also the reality of the power
and memory of Africa. In addition, it is movement out of the pain
of self negation and dispossession into a new world of affirmation;
a visionary world. For Walcott, the first step in this movement
toward regeneration is the recognition of the humiliation of his peo-
ple. This is the "first act of recovery." Because of its colonial past,
the Caribbean world has been plagued by differences of race and
class, and its people have internalized the worthlessness of things
indigenous. According to Walcott, literature is a response to this
"doctrine of humiliation."[4] Literature becomes an act of subversion
in order to serve as the instrument of regeneration in the strug-
gle for the liberation of a people. Walcott consciously adopts the
mantle of the individual leader, assigning to himself the role of edu-
cator of the public consciousness.

On the other hand, Brathwaite submerges the individual self,
and his voice is always the voice of the community. Through his
voice the contemporary pains and possibilities of his community
are distilled and added to the archives of ancestral memory.
Brathwaite adopts the mask of the African griot. He is the seer
who is the repository of a people's wisdom, culture, and vision.
He is the memory and the consciousness of the race, and he
speaks in a language that draws its power from its African legacy
and its New World transformations. Brathwaite describes this lan-
guage as "Nation Language":

> [It is] the submerged area of that dialect which is much
> more closely allied to the African aspect of experience in the
> Caribbean. It may be in English: but often it is an English
> which is like a howl, or a shout or a machine-gun or the wind
> or a wave. It is also like the blues. And sometimes it is

English and African at the same time.[5]

Brathwaite's definition of "Nation Language" is easily applied to the language of his poetry. It is a gathering together of forces, African and Caribbean to sing of survival, to "howl" of pain, and to "shout" of liberation. Out of this clash of sounds emerges the freedom songs of self, community and nation. In the language of the visionary world of his poetry, Brathwaite moves beyond the retelling of past and present pain to create a world of possibility for Caribbean people and society. The creation of this world is Brathwaite's sacred mission. He is motivated by the force of his opposition to society's insistence on the worship of the present and the material and the erasure of the past from the collective memory.

Ever since their forced and torturous exodus from Africa, New World blacks have found themselves in a state of cultural and historical paralysis resulting in a crisis of identity. The creation of a literature of national identity is a necessary response to this crisis. Melvin Dixon, in discussing the Negritude movement, celebrates the resulting "birth" of literatures in the African diaspora:

> [These literatures] although established along lines of national language and culture, created an arena where blacks throughout the world could articulate their presence and condition. Each was a separate river remembering its source; each created a significant flow of theme and political passion ever circling the ancestral landscape, moving outward for independence and transformation of traditional oral forms of expression, and returning for renewal, regeneration, reunion with the past made present through language.[6]

As he returns to an African source for inspiration, "renewal," "regeneration," and "reunion with the past," Brathwaite's symbolic use of language is powerful and passionate. The process of this return is the essence of his power; he creates a Caribbean identity that is a merger of the intuitive African experience and the reality of the Caribbean existence. In the world of his poetry, he creates spiritual and physical landscapes offering solace and inspiration. These are landscapes peopled with presences, both human and spiritual, symbols of endurance and survival for the Caribbean community. Such conscious creations are the poet's antidotes to the pain of past and present history and sources of new life and identity.

In "New World A-Comin'," the lyrical and physical landscapes confront each other. The journey to slavery's plantations has left the poet's people crying for help:

O who now will help
us, help-
less, horse-
less, leader-
less, no
hope....[7]

Brathwaite places himself at the center of communal pain. The pain is immediate and present and is reinforced by the visual display of the poet's words on the page. The physical wrenching apart of words mirrors the trauma of a people's separation from their homeland. Brathwaite maintains this homeland in the memory of the New World inhabitants. But it is a homeland transformed by the New World experience. Paule Marshall, in discussing the language of Barbadian immigrants in America, shows how its power to transform and to be therapeutic becomes a coat-of-armor offering protection against the strangeness and the isolation of existence in a new country. She quotes Czeslaw Milosz, the emigré Polish writer who asserts that "Language is the only homeland."[8] Brathwaite is concerned with "language as homeland," a homeland that reflects both the African and the Caribbean experiences and symbolizes cultural preservation and identity. Brathwaite writes the African homeland into Caribbean history. He creates a place that fires the imagination of the dispossessed:

> This sacred lake
> is the soul
> of the world;
>
> winds whirl
> born in the soul
> of this dark water's world.   ["Chad," 105]

For the dispossessed, the recreation of a sacred mysterious place heightens the sense of longing and loss, but the poet insists that the place of Africa must be inscribed upon the collective memory. In "Timbuctu," he remembers the splendors of Africa: "[the] brilliance where our mosques / mock ignorance, mock pride, / burn in the crackled blaze of time,..." (106).

Africa is transformed into a multidimensional symbol in Brathwaite's poetry, but this symbol is always connected to the Caribbean experience and the poet prays that:

> ...[his] children's eyes
> will learn
>
> not green alone
> not Africa alone
> not dark alone

not fear
alone
but Cortez
and Drake
Magellan
and that Ferdinand
the sailor
who pierced the salt seas to this land.   ["Tom," 16]

Africa is the epitome of the glory and pain of the Old World expe-
rience. At the same time, the poet insists upon recognizing the
power of the New World experience. In this blend of the old and
the new worlds, Brathwaite insists upon hearing the voices of his
past. He recognizes their power to preserve a culture under
attack and their ability to heal the wounds in the psyche of the
colonized. These themes, poetic intentions, and the poet's pre-
scriptive use of language come together in a remarkable way in
the companion pieces, "Wake" and "Negus" (208 and 222).

By invoking the mourning rituals of a wake, Brathwaite's
"Wake" honors the African ancestors and their Caribbean descen-
dants. The poet prays for the power of "words" to initiate change.
The landscape of the Caribbean is arid; "the land is unbearably
dry / ...the hedges are dusty,...the tubes of the cane are dry / let
there be rain" (209). Current desolation is linked to the original
desolate journey, and the "ship / house on the water" is not only
the vehicle transporting the recent dead, it is also the slave
ship transporting Africans to the New World. The poet appeals
to the ancestors, and the "ninth night" ceremony of the dead is
used to intensify the appeal:

bless me with shadows
white calico of mutters;

> mother me with words,
>
> gems, spoken talismans of your broken tongue.   [210]

He asks for blessings from his "Ibo" ancestor whose "broken tongue" offers nurture and healing and moves the poet out of his dark world of pain and despair into a new world of creativity. The process is a searing one, mirroring the metaphysical need for creation out of destruction: "kill, destroy, restore me" (210). He will be restored by the miraculous power of the ancestral word. At this crucial moment on the threshold of his deliverance, he cries out to Attibon Legba: "Ouvri bayi pou' moi," open the gate for me (211). Brathwaite brings together the spiritual and the physical worlds, for Legba is the link between the supernatural and the real.

But the union he craves is not easily achieved, for the island world lacks substance; the gods are dormant. The word has been shattered into "syllables" and transformed from an agent of creation into an agent of destruction. The poet is "stoned with syllables" (212). At the end of "Wake," there is no rest. The struggle continues:

> We seek we seek
> but find no one to speak
>
> the words to save us;
> search
>
> there is no destination;
> our prayers reach
>
> no common sun.   [212-213]

"Negus" begins with the poet's statement concerning the impotence of the "Word" with which "Wake" ends. For the poet, words are the transmitters of memory; and, if they are not revived and brought into being, the connections to the past, to history and to culture, will be lost. This is the precise intention of the colonizer, to relegate the colonized to a state of cultural oblivion. Albert Memmi expresses it this way: "The colonized seems condemned to lose his memory."[9] Memory here is the collective memory of the race with its culture and institutions extending through time. The "word" that Brathwaite constantly invokes is the instrument of preservation and continuity.

Negus "was one of Haile Selassie's titles which Rastafarians freely employ as a substitute for Jesus."[10] Brathwaite recasts the Christian god to fit the Caribbean landscape. Ultimately, he rejects the Christian god and calls upon Legba, the link between African gods and humans. The poem is divided into two parts, the negation and the affirmation. Looking at the historical present, Brathwaite laments the loss of the "Word":

> it is not
> it is not
> it is not enough
> it is not enough to be free
> of the whips, principalities and powers
> where is your kingdom of the Word?   [222]

By "Word" the poet means a certain morality, a certain truth, a recreation, in present time, of a period when words were the sacred bond uniting individual and community and expressing the identity of both. In the first section of the poem there is a certain hesitation. The poet focuses on one word and repeats it; then, he adds words transforming the initial word into a phrase and repeating the phrase: "it / it / it / it is not / it is not / it is not enough" (222). The repetition of word is also the repetition of sound. Behind the words the African drums are beating resulting in a unity of creation and action. The poet names the wrongs and limitations of his society and invokes the power of the word to initiate change. Freedom is not enough if society undergoes no apocalyptic change. Brathwaite identifies the unacceptable: the worship of material possessions and the lack of fear of environmental and natural disasters. This leads to a disrespect of gods and customs and the freedom to "bulldoze god's squatters from their tunes, from their relics / from their tombs of drums" (223). The poet speaks out against the wanton separation of a people from their sources of identity. By returning to sources and by recalling ancestral customs, the Caribbean world will identify its values, discover its identity, and find its salvation.

Brathwaite's emphasis on values and the ethics and morality of freedom is critical to his purpose of identity formation. Ngugi wa Thiong'o makes a similar connection between values, language, and identity:

> Values are the basis of a people's identity, their sense of particularity as members of the human race. All this is carried by language. Language as culture is the collective memory bank of a people's experience in history.[11]

To Brathwaite, language is the symbol of a people's "sense of particularity." He uses language to maintain this "particularity" and to recognize and give validity to the national experience.

In the second movement of the poem, the poet as the messenger of culture and history invokes the power of the word: "I must be given words to shape my name / to the syllables of trees / I / must be given words to refashion futures / like a healer's hand" (223-224). The poet is healer, savior, and creator.

As creator, he remakes the world:

> I
> must be given words so that the bees
> in my blood's buzzing brain of memory...
> will make sky, will make heaven,
> the heaven open to the thunder-stone and the volcano
> and the un- / folding land.   [224]

Brathwaite brings into existence a new world. In order to do this, he must name the memories in his "buzzing brain," a brain teeming with relics of his Old World experiences. The instrument of creation is the "Word" that the poet associates with light and sound and matter. It is the opposite of silence and the void. At this point the poet becomes a supplicant of Legba. As he has already done in "Wake," he prays to Legba to open the gates connecting the gods and mortals:

> Att
> Att
> Attibon
>
> Attibon Legba
> Attibon Legba
> Ouvri bayi pou' moi
> Ouvri bayi pou' moi....   [224]

These words of intercession, the invocation at the beginning of a vodoun ceremony, rise from the depths of the soul and are appropriately rendered in vernacular speech, in Haitian creole. In this poem of renunciation and the affirmation of faith, it is fitting that Brathwaite invokes Legba at the moment of annihilation

and creation; for he is the god who is there in the beginning of
the world; he continues to be "at the threshold of every decision
and offers the options that decide our future."[12] In this New
World, the poet as the messenger of Legba will renounce the state
of being "semicolon" and "semicolony" and give voice to whole-
ness. Anne Walmsley objects to Brathwaite's use of the words
"semicolon" and "semicolony." She suggests that they are "an
annoying, not an illuminating, play on words."[13] But the poet's
words capture exactly the Caribbean's half and half condition,
half colonized and half free, half Caribbean and half European.
The poet will "raze" or eliminate the dualities, "blind" the God of
Europe and pray to Legba for wisdom and sight/insight:

> find me the rage
> and I will raze the colony
> fill me with words
> and I will blind your God.   [224]

His words are weapons initiating change. After the destruction
of colonial ways, the poet must necessarily rebuild his society;
he must rename it.

To Filoteo Samaniego, "naming becomes not only the initial
act but also the obligatory road of poetry."[14] The process of
"naming" is also a way of perceiving and of investing the object
with meaning. Brathwaite poses the question as well as supplies
the answer in "Naming": "What is a word / to the eye? / Meaning."
Named, the object is brought into existence and is given a life
of its own:

> The tree must be named.
> This gives it fruit
> issues its juices.   [217]

The poet returns to an Edenic place to carve out a new landscape that would offer promise and peace. The physical landscape comes alive; there is a sense of anticipation as the natural world awaits renewal:

> So the eye waits,
> the sun's gold weight
> lightens
>
> rain remakes trees
> leaves brighten the dolour
> the drying fish flies
>
> in the pool.   [218]

The "eye" of the poet benefits from this awakening in nature and his creative power, initially stifled, begins to soar, finding its inspiration in the "pool" of memory.

The preservation of memory, to the poet, is a sacred female task, and it is through the collective wisdom of the women that the culture will be preserved and the race saved. Brathwaite's women are survivors. They celebrate the ways and wisdom of the folk: "Eveie, chile? / You tek dat Miraculous Bush / fuh de trouble you tell me about?" ("The Dust," 62). In this world of personal and community deprivation, women form a circle of protection. They examine the physical and spiritual devastation around them and by giving voice to these realities hope to transcend them by finding solace, if not solution in the female collective. The women discuss "How Darrington Mule? / He still sicky-sicky" (63-64). Not only are the animals sick, but the vegetables "swibble up" (64). These are omens and symbols of the general sickness of the society and a manifestation of godly displeasure:

"Pastor / say las' night in the Chapel / that the Writin' Han' pun the Wall" (65). To further illustrate the possibility of imminent destruction, one of the women, Olive, retells a story from the past. This story, originally narrated by her grandmother, tells of a volcano's eruption in a neighboring island and the resulting disaster for the inhabitants of the region.

One woman's act of narration brings together past and present and expands to become a meditation on the cyclical nature of pain and a search for meaning:

> An' then suddenly so
> widdout rhyme
> widdout reason
>
> you crops start to die
> you cant' even see the sun in the sky....   [68]

But the instinct for survival is strong and "God sen' ev'ry month / a new moon" (68). Olive epitomizes female strength and power and the always present female voice which may go underground in times of disaster but always emerges stronger and more powerful:

> praise God that yuh body
> int turnin' to stone,
> an' that you bubbies still big;
> that you got a good
> voice that can shout
>
> for heaven to hear
> you....   [68]

Speaking for all women, Olive thanks God for life, sexuality, and the power of words to write the past into present history.

"Dust," the poem, becomes for Brathwaite a powerful symbol of continuity and the unity of community. The word "dust" in the poem is not only the volcanic ash of Olive's grandmother's story, but also the dust of Africa as it moves from the continent to the Caribbean. Brathwaite refuses to acknowledge any "separation between Africa and the Caribbean." He tells the story of living in St. Lucia, looking out on the morns in December, January, and February and seeing a haze in the sky. According to the poet, the haze enveloping the Caribbean "was really the harmattan dust from the Sahara blowing across the Atlantic." The poet describes this as "geo-psychic history":

> We must become aware that an ancestor such as Africa can
> be intimately with us through the centuries, influencing
> the climate, creating a situation of clarity in December,
> January and February when slave rebellions become possi-
> ble; because the time of the harmattan, the time when there
> is no rain, when your foot is not clogged by mud, when you
> can see your opponent clearly, this is the time when the
> slaves rebel.[15]

Brathwaite preserves this intuitive history, with its deep connections to Africa and the African experience, through the line of women. These women remember the past and in their stories preserve it. The recording of this history is made possible through the reality of the word. Its assimilation into the psychic consciousness of Caribbean people facilitates the process of personal and national recovery.

Language, for Brathwaite, is not only a symbol of the assimilation and preservation of the cultural past, it is also an instrument of rebellion and revolution. Brathwaite sings the song of rebellion and revolution in the speech of his people. The destruction of society and relationships is tearing apart the fabric of present Caribbean society. In his collection *Third World Poems*, "Manchile" is the story of relationships destroyed or perverted. Young girls are raped: "the girl raped comin' home from school / ...the girl raped in her home, in her own bed...."[16] The landscape of the poem is unremittingly desolate. An act of love becomes a mechanical exercise as the harshness of the public world intrudes upon the private world:

> ...she is locked still in her island
> your key will click, responsive to its prick
> of heat; the gear will shift, its metal tendons
> scraping, /
> wheels tearing the gravel as darkness explodes in the
> engine...
> an de long track a night tick tickin tick tickin
> machine pedal clatterin on
> and de clock stuck at 1.35 1.35 1.35 1.35   [33]

Surrounded by the metallic and the mechanical, the poet captures the woman's moment of frozen impotence. Time stops as she journeys back to a past no less brutal, with relationships just as degrading: an de man say mek i go wid im / and a can barely stan to look pan im...(34). The recognition of pain is cathartic, but there is no active call to revolution. The poem ends on the woman's plaintive cry: "...i sittin down here wid dis fine toot' comb / trying to scratch out de lies dat a tell" (34).

In "Manchile," Brathwaite's female persona gives voice to the pain in her personal life. "Springblade" expands to include the narration of communal pain and a call for change and action: "But there is goin' to be a revolution" (34). For Brathwaite, it is this naming that gives life and certainty to the concept of revolution. As he states, "the word (nommo or name) is held to contain secret, power."[17] The poet taps this power in order to present the stark reality of oppressive conditions in the Caribbean. In the world of the poem, the environment is harsh and unrelenting:

> the garbage knows it
> festering the silver sidewalks
> providing carrion for the crows and pigs
> the mountains have lost their green battle of innocence
> invaded by cut stone and crooks....   [34]

The poet is pained by the absence of heroes: Cuffy, Tacky, Bogle, and Garvey. Women become prostitutes in order to survive in this wasteland. But ultimately, the poet sings of endurance, perseverance, and hope in the form of the "hope of revolution." Brathwaite's voice as the vehicle of revolution is reminiscent of the Guyanese poet, Martin Carter, and his poem "Words." Words, for Carter, work in almost the same way as they work for Brathwaite. They bring revolution into being, and in this sense they are precious transmitters of a nation and a people's historical and contemporary reality:

> These poet words, nuggets no jeweller sells
> across the counter of the world's confusion
> but far and near, internal or external
> burning the agony of the earth's complaint.[18]

Carter, perhaps because of his experiences in the politically turbulent and riot-torn Guyana of the 1950s and the 1960s, and—particularly because of his imprisonment, is personally aware of the poet's role as a revolutionary who speaks out of the reality of his own harrowing experiences. It is this sense of urgency and commitment that both Carter and Brathwaite share: "Who will unlock must first himself be locked / who will be locked must first himself unlock" ("Words" 91). In a world of corruption, the poet is the visionary and the bearer of truth.

Brathwaite entitles the final section of *Third World Poems* "Irie." The poems in this section reflect the poet's conscious imposition of hope over despair. Ranging from the freneticism of "Guns" and "Fever" to the powerfully evocative world of "Shango" and the painful chronicle of the revolutionary blown to bits in "Poem for Walter Rodney," Brathwaite rewrites the past by writing his people and his region into history. By naming this section "Irie," the poet captures the ambivalence of life in the region. "Irie," a Rastafarian word meaning "an ultimate positive," suggests to a Rastafarian that all is well in his world; it is "tantamount to heaven or a strongly uplifting spiritual feeling."[19] The idyllic beauty of the islands and the ethereal vision of the Caribbean sea, however, provide a stark contrast to the simmering passion of the poverty and oppression of the region's masses.

"Guns" appeals to Ogun, the god of war and metal. This poem not only reflects the ambivalence of a Caribbean existence, but it also addresses the dual nature of the god Ogun to whom the poem appeals. The poet writes the god into his text and world: "and the cannibal eyes of the fiery mourners / are beautiful beautiful beautiful beautiful / o gun shot stigmata of song" (49). The gun shot, the mark of Ogun, is branded into the region's history. Robert Farris Thompson quotes the following praise-chant for Ogun in *Flash of the Spirit*:

Hoe is the child of Ogun
Axe is the child of Ogun
Gun is the child of Ogun

Ogun, salute of iron on stone
The blacksmith of all heaven.[20]

The hoe and axe are instruments of survival, and the gun
protects as well as destroys. Thus, Brathwaite invokes the cre-
ative protective powers of Ogun.

But after destruction comes hope, and the poet calls upon
Shango, the god of thunder and lightning: "There is new breath
here" ("Shango" 49). In the first movement of this poem a new
world is created. Initially, the poet utters sounds and intuitively
senses the beauty of this new world: "hah / there is a sound of
sparrows / ...ah / there is wind here" (50). Africa is written into
the world at the supreme moment of creation:

i take you love at last my love
my night my dream my Africa

softly of cheek now
sweat of pillow, thigh of thorn
tender to your fire

we make with salt this moisture
vision
we make from vision: black and bone and sound.   [50]

Creation, however, is incomplete without the gift of words,
words that identify and bring objects into existence:

listen
his vowels taste of wood

of cedar lignum vitae phalanx

those gutterals are his own.   [50-51]

With the gift of language comes the power to initiate change. Shango is the presiding deity and the ordering principle. According to Brathwaite, he is the "Pan African god of thunder, lightning, electricity and its energy, sound systems, the locomotive engine and its music."[21] Shango brings creation into being, and the experiences of the New World, honed in time, are ritualized and ordered into music:

> after so many twists
> after so many journeys
> after so many changes
>
> bop hard bop soul bop funk
> reggae new thing soul rock shank
> bunk johnson is ridden again.   [53]

Brathwaite utilizes repetition to establish sound. He believes that the power of the word is linked to the reality and substance the word achieves when it comes into being through the spoken word; its sound. The poet's concern with sound, the energy generated in its creation, and the naming of sound in music and words is directly linked to his search for origins and beginnings. Journeying to the heart of the ancestral experience, Brathwaite recaptures this experience while he grasps its very essence, bringing it into reality through the power of the word. This ability to name the unnameable is Kamau Brathwaite's special gift.

Brathwaite relentlessly pursues his appointed task of naming the African experience in the New World, offering to New World inhabitants both place and identity. He is musician, writer, and recorder of history:

> with this reed i make music
> with this pen i remember the word
> with these lips i can remember the beginning of the
> world   [53]

More than the keeper of the past, Brathwaite is the creator of a compassionate world: "...I suffer the little children / i remember the lilies of the field" (53). Brathwaite expands the poetic self to include powers of creation, to stamp his words upon the world and to generate fundamental changes in community and society. This task, however, is no easy one, for the environment is hostile and alien and the poet is "reduced / to a bundle of rags / a broken stick" (54). The poet's staff of knowledge is "broken"; his music silenced. Poetic intention and the pull of the past confront each other:

> your authority is these chains that strangle my wrists
> your authority is the red whip that circles my head
> your authority is the white eye of interrogator's
> terror....   [55]

Brathwaite struggles for freedom to reenter the past and transcend it. He cannot remain frozen in time. He must move beyond "the dreadness of the avalanches of unjudgement," and give voice to possibility and hope (55). Aware of the need for transcendence, the landscape of "Kingston in the kingdom of this world" becomes the battleground upon which the forces of destruction and the forces of creation struggle for supremacy (53-56). At the end of the poem no clear victory or defeat occurs. The poet, in a state of anticipation, awaits the return of his poetic voice. The community will be his vital source of rebirth and inspiration:

> awaiting the water of sunlight
> awaiting the lilies to spring up out of the iron
> awaiting your eyes o my little children   [56]

Out of the "iron" existence of Kingston, the reduction of the poetic self to a "driven rag" will come the renewal of soul in community. The stifling atmosphere of unyielding metal will eventually give way to hope as the poet regains his creative spirit, and writes his people and community into a present of possibility.

Brathwaite carefully prepares for this moment of reconnection. The sense of urgency increases in "Fever." The land anticipates rebirth; senses are alive: "Everywhere there were lips: bubble and bud .../ everywhere there were eyes..." (60). The community awaits the poet/savior. As the persona/poet descends from the visionary world to enter the real world of pain, Brathwaite creates a center that celebrates the sacred union of poet and community:

> everywhere there were eyes: dressing me in robes
> placing sandals under my feet: praising me
> everywhere there were hands: building the temple
>
> i was a door opening
> i was a window: looking onto a tree
> and there was a landslide of memories   [60]

At this sacred spot, the meeting place of poet and people, the past is recaptured in a "landslide of memories." As the poet journeys closer and closer to the present, he chronicles his people's journey through history. They had lost the drum and the dance. Some had died "crossing"; others had discovered other forms of escape: "rum" and "the long drag of the thighs of their women." In view of their present condition of hopelessness and the seeming failure of past freedom fighters, i.e., the *djukas* and the maroons, the poet moves to remedy the situation, to offer salvation. The *djukas* of Surinam, like the maroons, were fearless fighters and preservers of the African way of life. The ancestors of the *djukas* were slaves who fled the plantations of "coastal Surinam" in the seventeenth and eighteenth centuries. After prolonged fighting in the 1760s, they signed peace treaties with the Dutch government.[22] In moving towards salvation, Brathwaite recalls these freedom fighters of the past. Invoking them as symbols of struggle and possibility, he carves out his own path to salvation. He "move[s] down into the old watercourses," searching for the wisdom of the past and the vision of the ancestors. Brathwaite, however, always comes back to present realities, and, to reinforce the urgency of current time, he lists the daily concerns of ordinary people: bills must be paid; food is expensive; a roof destroyed in the last hurricane must be replaced. Finally, after listing these urgent and pressing matters, the poet, almost as an afterthought, and, in nation language, utters the poem's final statement: "an i mussn't forget that i ax the teacher to stop in and see / me tomorrow" (62). Such a deliberate use of nation language is Brathwaite's way of exerting control of place and space. As he moves between the spaces and places of the colonizer and the colonized, the poem is transformed into hallowed ground, where it is possible for his people to transcend physical and mental battering and to continue with the threads of their lives. The poet stores and preserves the memory of the race; he restores this memory through the medium of the language of the people. Thus, the poet is not only seer and visionary; he is also political activist. Language is the tool he employs to initiate political change.

Brathwaite's "Poem for Walter Rodney" is a fine example of the unity of politics and language. In this poem, Brathwaite celebrates the life and work of Walter Rodney, the Guyanese historian, socialist, revolutionary; even as he speaks out against the destructive political forces alive and flourishing in the region—forces responsible for Rodney's violent death. The manner of Rodney's death is a symbol of the region's social and political disintegration. Rodney was blown into fragments. His life and work are eternalized in Brathwaite's poem, but this is no simple personal tribute. The violence of the poet's language mirrors the violence of a desolate political landscape. He utters a desperate cry of rebellion: "POR CYAAAAN TEK NO MOORE" (64). At this moment of desperation and rebellion, the rebel leader is destroyed:

> the well
> of flame drilling aeeeeeeeeeeeeeeeeeeeee through your
>   flesh
> drrrrrrrraaatat drrrrrraaataaatat drrraaataaaatat tat
>   tat tat taaaaaaaat   [63]

The visual and auditory impact is striking. The cacophonous combination of consonant and vowel sounds mirrors the discord and violent disintegration present in the society at the time. The sounds of destruction and the inhuman, mechanical movement of the flame as it consumes the body describes the impersonal nature of organized violence. Rodney is eliminated physically, but the poet carves his memory into history. The heroism of his life and death becomes a motivational force empowering the region's dispossessed:

so that each man on his cramped restless island
on his backdam of land in forest clearing by the
   broeken river
where berbice struggles against slushy ground

takes up his bed and walks

in the power and the reggae of his soul/stice
from the crippled brambled pathways of his vision
to the certain limpen knowledge of his nam   [67]

Having endured the extremes of oppression, the people will sur-
vive. The poet plays on the words "solstice" (i.e., "soul/stice").
When pushed to the extreme limits of endurance, strength comes
from the power of the spirit of the people. His vision, once "crip-
pled," will expand in the awareness of his "nam," the essence of
his existence; as Brathwaite puts it, "the core of [his] culture."[23]

In this poem of darkness, violence, and the elimination of
a life, the poet ultimately transforms death into new life: "he was
cut down plantation cane because he dared to / grow and grow-
ing/green...because his bridge from man to men meant doom to /
prisons of a world we never made" (68). Rodney's mission was
to educate his people and to eliminate the "prisons" of oppres-
sion and poverty. His death remains a reminder of the absolute
power of oppressive governments to create, physically, the polit-
ical climate they desire and want to maintain. In this drive for
control, citizens are dispensable and human lives worthless.
Brathwaite, even as he narrates the dire situation, carves Rodney's
message into the public consciousness. In his death there is
renewal, for the "dreadren" will disseminate his message: "but
there are stars that burn that murders do not know / soft dia-
monds behind the blown to bits" (68). Rodney's memory is pre-

cious, and the poet imbues it with the fragile yet durable creations of the natural world.

In the imaginary landscapes of his poetic world, Brathwaite memorializes the Caribbean's history and its heroes. Aware of the rapid advance of technology in a highly materialistic contemporary world, Brathwaite is convinced that cultural rootedness is redemptive. It offers freedom from the pain of the past. To move beyond the past, however, is no simple task. Gordon Rohlehr suggests that "it involves...erecting spirit on a foundation of encrusted materialism, rediscovering or recreating the lost idea of the holy."[24] Brathwaite has set himself this holy task. Brathwaite can accomplish this task because of his poetry's power to live its own truth and to embrace new worlds as well. He technologizes the text by utilizing what he has described as video style. Video style is Brathwaite's use of computer fonts to create varying sizes of type and symbols allowing him to harness the power of language to represent emotional landscapes in the poetic text. Video style is an example of Brathwaite's daring exploration of language. In explaining his artistic intent, Brathwaite writes: "What I am trying to do is create word sculpture on the page, word sculpture in the ear."[25] Extremely conscious of existing in a world of contradictory forces, where the lyrical is often subsumed by the crass, the poet's visual/video language mirrors these contradictions. Brathwaite's style is spare without softness or luxury. It is intense and packed with feeling. Underneath the destruction he narrates, is his own anger at the fragmentation of Caribbean society. Yet, Brathwaite is convinced that the humanity he reveals must be honored, loved, and valued. In a world of contradictions, the poet realizes that people become agents of destruction, anger, and despoliation which corrupt both self and space. But even as he confronts demonic forces and discordant powers in the increasingly discordant allegorical landscapes he creates, Brathwaite's internal poetic world has a vitality and an acceptance of living moments which suggest that change and regeneration are possible.

The Zea Mexican Diary, where Brathwaite chronicles his response to his wife's illness and death, is a fine example of his growing experimentation with video style.[26] In this autobiographical work, the poet occupies a very lonely space, and there is a constant collision between the straining for self-disclosure or revelation and the certainty of imminent death and emptiness, between the self inviolate and the self vulnerable. Brathwaite attempts to explode the barriers enclosing the self, to grasp the unknown, and to recapture (however briefly) the security and wholeness that his relationship with his wife provided. This attempt becomes increasingly impossible: "...we who love look on w/out [sufficient] faith & understanding & so the hope gets less / the dream gets tarnished & heaven weaker weaker weaker (61). In the text the print becomes smaller as hope diminishes. This visual ingenuity mirrors Brathwaite's private world of despair.

While Brathwaite's journey is purgatorial, it is at the same time destructive of both the artistic and the social self. Faced with the physical manifestations of his wife's illness, the normal, painful daily rituals of communication and survival, Brathwaite formalizes his private pain, his suffering, and his uncertainty of self; but the public stance does not move him out of his private hell, nor does it offer him comfort. His language becomes sparse and intense, creating an effective barrier between the poet and his world:

> ...I came to reach far out far
> out in space and into the very wound & darkness of
> our/selves out there/ far out/ deep down in/side...
> out there...And it seemed as if I might win...

was winning...if only I cd find the strength...
the certitude...that power of the miracle...
ice cold heat...lava of icicle...pure freedom
of my very breath/ our breathing origines....   [43]

The arbitrary splitting of words, the use of oxymoron and of
ellipses create a duality of emotional meaning. On one level,
Brathwaite is hurling downwards into an emotional abyss from
which there seems to be no escape. On the other hand, he clings
tenaciously to a slim thread of hope that the rootedness of rela-
tionship will overcome the degeneration of the flesh.

With the destruction of the poet's social self comes an over-
whelming isolation that is the literary equivalent of a religious
retreat. The poet withdraws into an intensely private world in
which he is trapped in the lonely human space between two
unknowns; the eternal darkness of physical death into which his
wife will enter and the void that will be created by her absence.
Again, the poet blames himself and holds himself responsible for
his wife's illness:

                                                        ...the tales
she must have heard the agonies of doubt/selfdoubt her
love might well have tried to justify xplain/xplain away
forgive & must have caused her generosity to hide &
harbour like a pearl inside her heart/her hurt until it
built itself into this tumour and how I feel Olorun/God
has now withdrawn from me because I did not preciate
its gifts of àshe: the always possibility: creative cross-
roads: open doors: Mawu Ogou the Eshu/Legba: Loas   [78]

Even the world of his gods offers no comfort, for the poet has
failed to appreciate the significance of communications, the

lessons of the crossroads. Olorun, instead of providing a new body, new breath, new life, has withdrawn from the physical world, thus evoking Brathwaite's *cri de coeur*.

"If she should die - go from me now - **why why why why** -I know i will not only lose my life my love my love -

my very very very friend -and there are o too few of these - **I**

may forever lose the light the light - the open doors."   [78]

The typescript imitates the volume, depth, and magnitude of his lament and captures intensely, the nuances of feeling.

Brathwaite's song of painful lamentation functions as the prelude for the diary's Sunday 7, September 1986 entry, the day of his wife's death. The section is entitled "**Middle Passages.**" According to Gordon Rohlehr, "Middle Passage [is] a metaphor of [Brathwaite's] private journey as straitened subject."[27] The poet finds salvation on his journey by moving beyond the body to the spiritual spaces where feelings lie, carrying "the pain that troughs within [him] as [he] walk[s] towards the silence" (94). The enactment of ritual offers protection and the possibility of healing in two ways. First, on a physical level, the poet involves himself in tasks that force him to continue functioning; for example, he covers his wife's body with "the adinkra cloth," and finds some comfort in words of prayer: "...the words didn't much matter...**but the weight of their meaning was heavy - li - / ke stones**...coming out of me unrolled away from deep deep / down & dungeon" (98). Broken words and syllables fall like weighted stone. Second, the poem itself becomes ceremony, a formal enactment of the ritual of pain, and, as a result, a certain splendor emanates from the poem. By achieving a ceremonial stance, pain becomes imaginative, creative and openly expressive. Brathwaite's video style permits entrance into his internal emotional world, transforming personal pain into a mythic public experience.

At the heart of *The Zea Mexican Diary* is a self consumed by pain, but ultimately, the poet finds solace in the rituals of community. A tree planting ceremony, together with the enactment of Christian and Yoruba rituals, returns the poet to the circle of community: "I put some of the ashes on my tongue & swallowed her" (199).[28] Before the ashes are "poured into the planting of her tulip tree," the poet "touched the ashes w/ [his] middle-finger tip & placed what was stuck there upon the forehead...of the four [participants in the burial ceremony], embracing each one" (199). The poet is priest, his wife divine; he is transformed. Now moving beyond human need, he can minister to the community. In the freedom of his imagination, the poet is at one with his wife; he has consumed her and achieves a new level of consciousness. Existing at ease at the crossroads between spirit and world, the poet now spans worlds of pain and despair as well as worlds of exhilaration and self-discovery. The planted stalk of the tulip tree "vibrated there in the sunlight like music like the string of life it had become" (206). Having experienced the moment of ultimate transformation, the poet undergoes an epiphany. His mastery of video style contributes to Brathwaite's intense awareness of the sacred power of the word. It allows him to pursue his task of reenvisioning a world in which Caribbean people have a definite awareness of the sanctity of self and historical rootedness.

Walcott, too, attempts to re-create a similar Caribbean world in which its citizens have a definite sense of self and place. But unlike Brathwaite, whose imaginative ingenuity lures the reader into a direct involvement in the ensuing exploration of emotion and situation, Walcott creates a certain distance from which he evaluates the ways of his region and people as he writes them into history. Brathwaite, by repeatedly conjuring up landscapes of psychic and physical pain, forces these realities upon the reader's consciousness. Walcott, however, does not delve into the heart of the community and become enveloped in its pain in quite the same way. While Brathwaite's world is dominated by community, Walcott's world is dominated by self. Walcott constantly attempts to separate the individual from the communal. As a result, very often the poet and the personae he creates exist in spaces of alienation on the fringes of community. In spite of his attempts to anesthetize pain, the region's awful history always brings him back to reality. Walcott reorders Caribbean history and constructs a past that functions as a foil to the inherited evils of the region.

Out of the region's landscape emerges the figure of the "castaway," the persona of one of Walcott's earlier poems. Castaway and poet exist apart from society in a world of apparent nothingness: "A net inches across nothing. / Nothing: the rage with which the sandfly's head is filled."[29] The poet meditates upon the inevitability of death and the miracle of rebirth, and is led to a consideration of his role as creator, maker, and remaker of worlds: "I make thunder split" (9). He is suffused with the power of Shango, the African god of thunder and creation. As he becomes fully aware of his creative powers, he resolves to "abandon dead metaphors," symbols of the absence of a vibrant creative life. He dedicates his own life to correcting the "gospel" (10). The "gospel" is the colonizer's negative message of the region's lack of creativity and promise. The future is stifled by past history: "That green wine bottle's gospel choked with sand, / Labelled, a wrecked ship, / Clenched seawood nailed and white as a man's hand" (10).

As poet/creator, and speaking in his public voice, Walcott is willing to be sacrificed for the benefit of the public sensibility; this clearly links him to divinity. But his private voice is not as strident, and the internal voice of the poet speaks of hesitations and divisions. He is "schizophrenic, wrenched by two styles."[30] This ambiguity of language is the result of the conflict between the language of authority and nation language or the language of rebellion. While claiming that he is never repressed by language, Walcott is very much aware of the relationship between language and the circumscribed world in which he lives. He is also familiar with the ways in which living in this peculiar world informs the language of his daily existence: "To change your language you must change your life" (61). But in "Codicil," there is a strain of despair permeating Walcott's poetic world. He is disillusioned: "I cannot right old wrongs" (61). Disillusionment comes not only from the inequities of the past, but also from the servile curryfavoring of the present:

> Once I thought love of country was enough,
> now, even I chose, there's no room at the trough.
>
> I watch the best minds root like dogs
> for scraps of favour.   [61]

Walcott remains on the periphery; yet, he is deeply aware of the scramble for connections, power, and the literal and spiritual deaths surrounding him. He imposes on this bleak landscape some semblance of life and renewal.

The poet is always the source of this renewal and vibrancy. He views the poetic self as the universe in miniature, and, in spite of his moments of desolation, he firmly believes that this self is in tune with the timbre of the universe. The poetic act and the creative act are one: "Resisting poetry I am becoming a poem."[31] In the process of "becoming" and transformation, he gains in wisdom and sanctity and moves towards language:

> Slowly my body grows a single sound,
> slowly I become
> a bell,
> an oval, disembodied vowel,
> I grow, an owl,
> an aureole, white fire.   [12]

But the journey toward language is not smooth and the poet is "gripped by demons of inaction" (12).

These "demons" are slain in the struggles to discover "...truth, the style past metaphor / that finds its parallels...in simple, shining lines, in pages stretched / plain as a bleaching bedsheet...."[32] He destroys the inaccuracies and misrepresentations of history and creates new "pages," where he gathers together the lush richness of the Caribbean islands, their folk and folklore while ever-present in the background is the history-laden Caribbean sea.

"Tales of the Islands," the sonnet sequence appearing in *In a Green Night,* illustrates the very detailed way in which the poet makes the landscape come alive. Ranging from the beauty of the Doree River, the stone cathedral at Choiseul to Cosimo de Chretien's boarding house, a relic from an earlier time, to the eccentric Miss Rossignol who "sang to her one dead child," Walcott places the islands in time and history. He captures both the nostalgia and the pretense of Miss Rossignol's time: Miss Rossignol, who "had white skin / And underneath it, fine, old-fashioned bones," and "flew to vespers every twilight"; yet, "tipsy as a bottle when she stalked / On stilted legs to fetch the morning milk."[33] The economy of language, the precision of words, and the power of the images capture the mixture of forced gentility, repression, and the awareness of color and class that are all part of the legacy of the region.

However, not all of the characters in "Tales of the Islands" are in Miss Rossignol's category. In "Chapter VI" of the sonnet sequence, the persona describes a "fete," a Caribbean party. Walcott utilizes the language of the islands, the peculiar mixture of standard English and its Caribbean transformation as a part of his attempt at the preservation of the national culture:

> Poopa, da' was a fete! I mean it had
> Free rum free whisky and some fellars bating
> Pan from one of them band in Trinidad
> And everywhere you turn was people eating
> And drinking and don't name me but I think
> They catch his wife with two tests up the beach
> While he drunk quoting Shelley....   [28]

The use of nation language brings into being the lyrical speech of the islands. In this vignette, islanders enjoy the music of the steelband. Yet, the description has touches of unrest. There is the hint of marital infidelity, and past corruption of African religious practices in the narrative of the child sacrificed by "practitioners of native art." But the poet distances himself from any form of evil that threatens the serenity of the island vision he is presenting. What is important to Walcott's persona is the "jump and jive" (28). However, it is not possible to erase the memory of the past from the consciousness of the present, for the practice of African religions lives on in the Caribbean.

While Kamau Brathwaite publicly integrates the religions of Africa into the life of the Caribbean, Walcott's involvement with

African religions and folklore is not as open or public. They do, however, inform his poetic world. Generally, his connection to the African experience is negated by critics who focus exclusively on his classical and European influences; but, as Michel Fabre puts it, he presents "the authentic tone of Caribbean folk sensibility."[34] It is not possible for Walcott to achieve this authenticity without recognizing the Caribbean's rootedness in African custom and ritual. An air of mystery and exoticism and a sense of delving into the unknown surface whenever Walcott hints at the existence of an African ritual world in the Caribbean: "They lead sheep to the rivulet with a drum, / Dancing with absolute natural grace / Remembered from the dark past whence we come" (28). Walcott satirizes the attitude of Europeans to African religious practices. The community organizes a "fete" for a visiting anthropologist who views it as "great stuff." The choice of language is a camouflage protecting the sanctity of the religion. By adopting the mask and language of a public performance, the true meaning of the ritual is protected from alien eyes. Alien eyes often desecrate, encouraged by those willing to peddle the customs of the ancestors. Walcott is against this view of customs and rituals as commodities: "...our art objects are not sacred vessels placed on altars but goods placed on shelves for the tourist. The romantic darkness which they celebrate is thus another treachery, this time perpetuated by the intellectual."[35]

The preservation of island culture is Walcott's personal mission. He molds the customs and rituals of the island, bringing them to life and preserving them in the language of the Caribbean. "Pocomania," for example, is a poem that celebrates the Afro-Caribbean religious experience of Pocomania, a religion of possession and a mixture of African/Caribbean and Christian religious beliefs. It brings together "the Christian Trinity, the Angels and Saints, the Prophets and the Apostles, combining

these...with the spirits including the Ancestral dead."[36] Walcott
captures the vitality of movement as the participants strive
toward possession. Edward Seaga, in his discussion of Pocomania,
mentions that "at the moment of possession [possessed] indi-
viduals are all considered to be located as a group in the spirit
world" (8). As the possessed journey through the spirit world,
obstacles are met and overcome suggesting that salvation is
only possible in community. "Pocomania" is an example of the
possibilities of the Caribbean cauldron. Religious symbols are
transformed into their uniquely Caribbean forms by the merger
of African and Christian symbols; for example, "the lamb bleeds
on the Coptic cross" (35), and the sacrament of the eucharist
meets the feasting table of Pocomania. The rhythm of the verse
moves towards a joyous crescendo, a release of pain and the
achievement of freedom of the spirit in spite of the recognition
of earthly turmoil, deprivation, and physical degeneration:

> Lower the wick, and fold the eye!
> Anoint the shrivelled limb with oil!
> The waters of the moon are dry,
> Derision of the body, toil.   [35]

Walcott, aware of the imperfections existing in Caribbean
society both past and present, is driven to animate the world of
his present reality. But, Walcott's confrontation with the imper-
fections of Caribbean society is different from Brathwaite's, who
descends into the alleys and yards of the region's poverty-
stricken, gathering together their songs of pain. Walcott's songs
lack the immediacy and raw terror of Brathwaite's narration of
life in the region's Trench Towns and Tiger Bays. Walcott, too,
seeks to alleviate pain, but because of the space he creates
between himself as distant artist and the region's poor and

oppressed, the pain is romanticized. He wants, however, to bring to life the Caribbean experience; therefore, the process of naming, so central to poetry becomes for him a process of animation and intellection.

Appropriating the power of naming, Walcott commands the world and changes it. "Origins" is his *cri de coeur.*[37] The persona enters the world "nameless" and without memory. But this position is not tenable, for without memory "a gap in history closes" (12). Presently, he remembers the rivers of the African continent. During the African period, "an infant Moses" is born who grows to adulthood. His function in this phase is to "rechristen...trees." What he actually does is to rename the flora and fauna of the New World and to mythologize the act of memory:

> Now the sibyl I honour, mother of memory,
> Bears in her black hand a white frangipani, with berries
> of blood,
> She gibbers with the cries
> Of the Guinean odyssey.   [12]

The black sibyl carrying "berries of blood" is an eternal reminder of the Africans' journey to the New World. In the third section of the poem, Walcott apostrophizes the Troumassee river in his native island, St. Lucia. The river, a "brown tongue," embodies in its depths, the different stages of the region's history. As a symbol of eternity and timelessness, it constantly preserves the story of the region's tortured past and longsuffering present as it journeys through poverty-stricken villages to the sea.

The sea is a powerful symbol in this poem about beginnings in the New World. The poet searches the "shallows" of the coast to find his "name" and identity, for the transplanted people have learnt the colonizer's "alphabet of alkali and aloe," alkali and aloe symbolizing the bitter, painful process of the acquisition of an alien language. At the same time, the poet writes the memory of the Guinean ancestors into history in the language of the colonized:

> We praise those whose back on hillsides buckles on
> the wind
> To sow the grain of Guinea in the mouths of the dead,
> Who, hurling their bone-needle nets over the cave
> mouth,
> Harvest ancestral voices from its surf....   [15-16]

Walcott's legitimate obsession with origins permeates the world of his poetry. His poem "Names," dedicated to Kamau Brathwaite, mythologizes the origin of language in the Caribbean:

> My race began as the sea began,
> with no nouns, and with no horizon,
> with pebbles under my tongue,
> with a different fix on the stars.[38]

Walcott acknowledges the infinite origins of his people, the expansiveness of the New World, and the ability of its people to absorb and transform the world around them. At the same time, he also acknowledges, through the metaphor of "pebbles," both the presumed "imperfection" of Caribbean speech and the sense of a new and powerful language waiting to explode. Walcott reiterates Brathwaite's forceful statement in "Pebbles": "You cannot crack a pebble, / it excludes / death."[39] Both poets shatter the myth of the limitations of Caribbean language. Pamela Mordecai, augmenting Brathwaite's central symbols of missile and capsule to represent the essential European and African worldviews, sees the pebble as a "powerful missile which 'will slay / giants'."[40] The pebble here is Brathwaite's symbolic "capsule" that with missilic force shatters misconceptions about Caribbean speech and language. Walcott's "pebbles" have the same transformative force. In this new space, the possibilities for language are vast; and the poet creates a persona, the new Caribbean person who will fill this space, enter history, and name the disparate elements of the past:

> Have we melted into a mirror,
> leaving our souls behind?
> The goldsmith from Benares,
> the stone-cutter from Canton,
> the bronzesmith from Benin.   [32]

Naming becomes a necessity for the poet who "began with no memory, / ...began with no future" (32). Yet, this is not quite accurate; Walcott himself is always conscious of the layers of memory hidden in the unconscious area of the mind. In this poem, he is both creator and created:

> and my race began like the osprey
> with that cry,
> that terrible vowel,
> that I!   [33]

The "terrible vowel," "I" is fraught with the awe and wonder of creation, the power to animate and to make new. There is a certain feeling of expansiveness as the poet filters through his imagination, the immensity of the New World, the intense beauty of its landscape, and the strength of the ancestors who survived the crossing. Walcott's inscription of landscape, together with the connectedness of people and place, inform his construction of Caribbean identity. As Robert Elliot Fox suggests, "Identity really begins with a recognition of the spirit of place, and the network of one's relationships with those actually present as well as those who still survive in living memory" (338).[41]

The problematics of identity in the Caribbean has been particularly traumatic. Colonizer and colonized have battled as Caribbean people fought against the reduction of self and world that European colonizers sought to perpetuate. In this battle, the process of naming plays an important part, for naming can function in a number of ways. To the colonizer, it is an act of power and control over an alien world that has been conquered. By naming the elements in this world, the colonizer exerts control over the lives and actions of the colonized and demands their total allegiance. Joyce Jonas describes the process in this way: "A colonized world, people, psyche—even landscape—is a function of the controlling Word: hegemony finds its ultimate strength in language."[42] But the relationship between colonized and colonizer is not without its ambiguities and paradoxes. When faced with the colonizer's insistence upon the right of everything to be a noun, "the African acquiesced, / repeated and changed them" ("Names" 34). The African inhabitants of the New World adopt the persona of the trickster figure, Anancy, and while appearing to conform to the colonizer's use of language and meaning, develop strategies to protect their cultural heritage. New World inhabitants, by the act of naming, impose their own order upon the universe they are forced to inhabit:

> Listen, my children, say:
> moubain: the hogplum,
> cerise: the wild cherry,
> baie-la: the bay,

with the fresh green voices
they were once themselves
in the way the wind bends

our natural inflections.   [34]

Walcott's "pebbles under [the] tongue" have preserved and pro-
tected his people's "natural inflections." While the poet stresses
the vibrancy and the music of the language of his people, the
voice here is one of command: "listen" and "say." In other words,
the poet is the leader of this movement to reclaim language. By
commanding his community to rename the "nouns," the poet
envisions a pre-slavery, pre-plantation world where it is possi-
ble to be in control of the environment and of one's existence.
Such an idealized poetic creation becomes the source of the
renewal of self and world that the poet undertakes. The vision-
ary landscape is prepared for the reception of the word and its
magical, transformative powers.

Upon this landscape, Walcott superimposes the beauty of his
own land, St. Lucia. He celebrates the villages and the people who
endure and survive there. He presents a litany of place names
eternalizing the "sun-bleached villages," "Laborie, Choiseul,
Vieuxfort, Dennery."[43] All this is a part of the poet's intent to write
the region into history. After listing the native fruit of the island,
he invokes language: "Come back to me / my language" (36).
Walcott is not only praying to be granted the power of words to
describe the elements of his homeland, he is also praying for
inspiration, vision, and the ability to absorb himself totally in the
New World landscape. Out of his complete absorption comes the
ability to view this world with new eyes. The landscape is the
poet's text from which bursts forth the songs/poems coming into
being through the power of his voice. The songs celebrate and

preserve the experience of New World peoples. Walcott captures the essence of the land and the beauty and the fluidity of movement of his people. A young woman walks down steps "as spring water eases over shelves of rock...her smile like the whole country, / her smell, earth, / red-brown earth" (39).

In "Sainte Lucie," Walcott achieves a unity of people and place. He captures the rhythms of his people and their intimate relationship with the land upon which they exist and endure, a relationship bred out of reverence. Because of his abiding reverence for the land, the poet finds words that shatter the view of the Caribbean as "other." Through language, Walcott brings into existence a place blessed by his vision. He bestows a special identity upon the people of the region that is completely at variance with the negative identity bestowed by its colonizers. Walcott reclaims his St. Lucian identity in the creole of his island: "moi c'est gens Ste. Lucie. / C'est la moi sorti; is there that I born" (39).

The identity that Walcott is so carefully crafting is no where more clearly visible than in Section V of "Sainte Lucie," subtitled "For the Altarpiece of the Roseau Valley Church, Saint Lucia." At the heart of this poem is a mural painted by Walcott's childhood friend, Dunstan St. Omer. St. Omer, in the mural, and Walcott, in the poem, celebrate the intrinsic beauty of the St. Lucian folk:

> and the massive altarpiece
> like a dull mirror, life
> repeated there,
> the common life outside
> and the other life it holds;
> a good man made it.   [46]

In this hallowed spot "the common life" is sanctified and memorialized. What is interesting is the manner in which the poet balances the beauty and terror of human life. He juxtaposes the fecundity of the valley and its destitution. In this valley, "fat with things," exist "broken mules," "swollen children," "dried women," and "their gap-toothed men." Walcott, like his friend St. Omer, captures the St. Lucian peasants' blind perseverance in the face of suffering and, in his text, etherealizes them for all time. These are the faces of St. Lucia, "the real faces of angels" portrayed with love and compassion. When Walcott portrays the folk of the Caribbean and the region's haunting beauty, his poetry is most powerful. He captures the essential qualities of his people and his region and eternalizes them in his visionary world. At these moments, his poetry achieves a tone of humility far removed from the imperial stance he sometimes adopts.

As he looks back on earlier poetic stances, Walcott, however, is not always content. In *Midsummer,* a more mature Walcott, burdened by the weight of years, looks back with dissatisfaction at the almost imperial stance of his earlier work:

When I was greener, I strained with a branch
to utter every tongue, language, and life at once.
More skillful now, I'm more dissatisfied.
They never align, nature and your
own nature. Too rapid the lightning's shorthand,
too patient the sea repeatedly tearing up paper,
too frantic the wind unravelling the same knot,
too slow the stones crawling toward language every night.[44]

With age has come the tempering of the poet's craft. His "pebble" image, earlier vibrant and mobile, in his later years is transformed into weighty and almost immobile "stones." The movement toward language has become ponderous and hesitant. Walcott equates history with time and is therefore ever conscious of its transient nature. The changes he has envisioned are achieved very slowly. Natural creation and human nature are in conflict. Walcott embraces the world of nature in order to preserve it. He wants it to be a vital part of his visionary landscape and a suitable and sympathetic background upon which to inscribe the story of his people's existence. The task he has set himself is so vast that it is almost overwhelming. He realizes that if language is to be the agent of transformation in the rewriting of Caribbean history, the elemental memory of Africa must inspirit language. In other words, the pain of the Middle Passage and the dehumanization of colonization has to be written into this history. He recognizes the unique interaction between the old and new worlds and the way in which this interaction informs Caribbean identity. Walcott, in his essay "The Muse of History," describes the experience this way: "Exiled from your own Edens you have placed me in the wonder of another and that was my inheritance and your gift."[45] It is this inheritance that he attempts to preserve.

Walcott comes to realize that preservation implies the recognition of the value of this inheritance; this means acknowledging the reality of race, for as Walcott himself affirms: "A raceless critic is a primate's dream."[46] What Walcott means by raceless is not only the acknowledgment of all his New World ancestors, but particularly the recognition of the African ancestors who are generally absent from the region's official history. Embarking upon a restless penitential journey towards a discovery of his place in the world, he discovers the beauty of his New World homeland and his place in it. He has to write this world into existence, for "the earth drinks / language as precious, depending upon the race" (71). In his newly created world, Walcott eliminates political barriers and rises above the deadening arena of politics. He will "on dank ground, using a twig for a pen, / write Genesis and watch the Word begin. / Elephants will mill at their water hole to trumpet a / new style" (71). Concerned with the concept of the poet as the maker and the bearer of language, Walcott officiates at the sacred moment when the "word" is given the power of life. The poet as wordmaker and as interpreter has the ability to bring his visionary world into being as well as to interpret it for the uninitiated. In the process of interpreting the world of his creation and focussing on the nature of Caribbean identity, Walcott explores the nature of the artist and his relationship to his craft. Very often this relationship is analogous to that of God and creation:

> If my craft is blest;
> if this hand is as
> accurate, as honest
> as their carpenter's
>
> every frame, intent
> on its angles, would
> echo this settlement
> of unpainted wood
>
> as consonants scroll
> off my shaving plane
> in the fragrant Creole
> of their native grain;
>
> from a trestle bench
> they'd curl at my foot,
> C's, R's, with a French
> or West African root.[47]

The artist as carpenter shapes the language and brings new words and new worlds into being. Walcott's "fragrant Creole" is intended to capture the beauty and delicacy of a new language that is informed by the poet's sensitivity to the physical environment of the New World. The letters achieve their own peculiar grace and a life of their own as they "curl" at the "foot" of the poet/carpenter.

"Cul de Sac Valley" is a poem central to the understanding of the mind and work of Walcott. It is a blend of the poet's extreme sensitivity to the beauty of the natural world around him, his regard for the creole of his island and his determination to establish a Caribbean identity. According to Walcott, "a panel of sunrise / on a hillside shop / gave these stanzas / their stilted shape" (9). Inspired by this effect of nature, he meditates on the unique language of the Caribbean. The words might be English, but an English that reflects the particular realities of existence in the Caribbean: "What you wish / from us will never be, / your words is English, / is a different tree" (10). To maintain its distinct Caribbeanness, the landscape that Walcott describes becomes a closed text to the outside world, a world in which language is often used to control and to imprison.

Within this circumscribed landscape, people go about the business of surviving: a young woman "sits to a supper / of bread and fry-fish," "shack windows flare"; and in the warmth of the tropical night, an "odour of saltfish" permeates the air (14-15). Walcott creates an atmosphere of normalcy. He eternalizes the spirit of his people in a language that symbolizes their rootedness in African and New World experiences. The language of the Caribbean possesses this special quality: "...although the language employed is English, the experience recorded is not, and...the new experience may profoundly alter the language and the form employed."[48]

This union of English and the creole of the Trinidadian calypso is clearly seen in "The Spoiler's Return."[49] Walcott utilizes both the rhythm and the conventional rhyme scheme of the calypso:

> I sit high on this bridge in Laventille,
> watching that city where I left no will
> but my own conscience and rum-eaten wit,
> and limers passing see me where I sit....   [53]

By utilizing end-rhymes, the free-flowing movement of the rhyme scheme suggests a certain aimlessness and a concern with the frivolities of life. The scene is set for Spoiler's return from hell to critique the society in which he had lived. While Stewart Brown insists that Walcott's Spoiler "is only marginally based on the figure of Spoiler the real calypsonian," the connections are in fact much deeper.[50] Walcott, like the calypsonian, is aware of his responsibility as the conscience of the nation. The audience of the calypsonian, while caught up in the jazzy rhythms of the music and the ambiguities of the language, is always very much aware of the calypsonian's sense of public responsibility and his need to sing about societal needs and inadequacies. He sings of society's limitations in the language of the people. Thus the link between poet and calypsonian is obvious. Keith Warner puts it this way: "The calypsonian as folk poet and repository of the oral tradition shows a keen sense of language pattern and rhythm."[51]

The calypsonian's facility of language, quick wit, and his ability to extemporize, gives him a false sense of power over his world and the people in it. Spoiler the calypsonian, like Walcott the poet, is very much aware of the limitations of this power. Ultimately, power and the real ability to change the lives of the people remain the purview of the region's politicians. Gordon Rohlehr remarks on this contradiction of which calypsonians have always been conscious:

If on one level calypsonians seemed to be overcompensat-
ing, through grandiose rhetoric, for their real social and
political impotence, it should always be remembered that
within their own group they were the most grounded persons
who, because of their role as spokesmen, commentators
and men-of-words, had developed a subtle consciousness of
language.[52]

In "The Spoiler's Return," Walcott experiences deeply this sense
of "social and political impotence," and his choice of persona is
no accident. As Warner suggests, "in calypso after calypso,
Spoiler presented himself as the victim of an absurdity over
which he had little control."[53]

On the other hand, Walcott through Spoiler, his persona,
attempts to reassert this control, using the power of the
Trinidadian creole to raise the issue of Caribbean identity so cen-
tral to the region:

> . . . . he send me
> back up, not as no bedbug or no flea,
> but in this limeskin hat and floccy suit,
> to sing what I did always sing: the truth,
> Tell Desperadoes when you reach the hill,
> I decompose, but I composing still.   [53]

On one level, this is a reference to Spoiler's calypso "Bed Bug" in
which he states that after death a human being returns to earth
as "an insect or animal." Spoiler chooses to live his second life
as a bed bug.[54] Walcott actually quotes from the calypso: "I'm
going to bite them young ladies, partner, / like a hotdog or a ham-
burger" (53). On another level, it is a reference to poetic integrity,
commitment, and the desire to uphold the "truth." These are dif-

ficult tasks and, when faced with the gnawing advance of cor-
ruption, it is no wonder Spoiler shouts: "I see these islands and
I feel to bawl / 'area of darkness' with V.S. Nightfall" (54). This
reference is a not-so-subtle one to Naipaul's statement con-
cerning the Caribbean's permanent condition of darkness and
ignorance as he sees it.[55] Utilizing the invective of the calyp-
sonian, Walcott's Spoiler attacks the politicians:

> Is crab climbing crab-back, in a crab-quarrel,
> and going round and round in the same barrel,
> is sharks with shirt-jacs, sharks with well-pressed fins,
> ripping we small fry off with razor grins....   [54]

Walcott uses the language of the calypso to launch a scathing
attack on the politicians of the region. The image of politicians
like crabs trying to get to the top of the same barrel heightens
the poet's distaste for the selfish, useless activities of many
Caribbean politicians. According to Stewart Brown, even Dr. Eric
Williams does not escape[56]:

> the slime crab's carapace is waterproof
> and those with hearing aids turn off the truth,
> and their dark glasses let you criticize
> your own presumptuous image in their eyes.
> Behind dark glasses is just hollow skull,
> and black still poor, though black is beautiful.   [55]

Walcott attacks politicians whose rhetoric lures the masses into
an artificial sense of well-being by pushing self-pride, determi-
nation, and sacrifice for country. However, the poor continue to
exist in poverty, and radicals are eliminated: "All those who
promise free and just debate, / then blow up radicals to save the

state" (55). Walcott is referring here to the assassination of the Caribbean historian and revolutionary, Walter Rodney.

Spoiler speaks with authority about the "hell" of Trinidad having just returned from hell. The entire poem is an attack on the evils of the historical past and its manifestations in current time. In each era, it is left up to men of vision to fight the battles of the dispossessed while all around them people and islands suffer immensely because of the corruption and greed of those in power. Walcott suggests, as he has done before, that the region has merely exchanged the original colonizers for a new breed in shirt-jacs. After his intense attack on the region's politicians, Spoiler ends his song without fanfare and in the language of the people: "All you excuse me, Spoiler was in town; / you pass him straight, so now he gone back down" (60). Walcott effectively utilizes the calypsonian's language of vicious and strident attack to address the greed and corruption existing in the Caribbean. The poet channels his language towards the initiation of change, and while he is often despairing, he is never hopeless. Language is a vessel of dissemination possessing transformative powers. The poet's words are a testament to the New World experience of endurance and survival and a written record of his journey from elemental memory to an identity grounded in history.

His urge to record experience for preservation and change is Walcott's particular mission, and it is no where more clearly seen than in his description of the land and the people of St. Lucia. "Roseau Valley" moves between an almost romanticized past; even the suffering of the island people is romanticized, and a present dominated by government and unions. The poet captures the societal changes experienced by the inhabitants of Roseau Valley: the change of production from sugar to bananas, the unrest of the workers and the desperate conditions of the island's poor. The poet's voice is almost despairing, for he can write his land and people into history, but he is uncertain of the power of his art to effect permanent change. For example, the chapel at Jacmel "stays old as the valley," while the workers remain "gently chained" in poverty. Roseau remains "connect[ed] to heaven," but "breath went out of the mill."[57]

In spite of the poet's momentary despair, the symbol of "breath" as a life-giving force is a metaphor for the task that Walcott has set himself. His poetry breathes life into the land and the lives of his people and sings of triumph and possibility: "From this village, soaked like a grey rag in salt water, / a language came."[58] It is a language that uniquely captures the sights and sounds of the Caribbean. Walcott quickly points out that the language gains its power from its ability to absorb and preserve the customs of the Caribbean:

> There are different candles and customs here, the dead are
> different. Different shells guard their graves. There are dis-
> tinctions beyond the paradise of our horizon. This is not the
> grape-purple Aegean. There is no wine here, no cheese, the
> almonds are green, the sea grapes bitter, the language is that
> of slaves.   [35]

Walcott's insistence upon difference emphasizes the particular-ity of the Caribbean experience; it is precisely because of the ele-ment of bitterness attributable to the reality of slavery, that Walcott's people have grown in strength. In the idyllic setting of the Caribbean, the remembrance of slavery continues to haunt the literary imagination.

Remembrance of the past is an integral part of the folklore of the Caribbean, and Walcott's poetic world is peopled by well-known folk characters. In a poem ironically entitled "White Magic," Walcott celebrates the folklore of the region. The names of folk characters may change from island to island, but their abilities generally remain the same. Walcott introduces the "gensgagee" or old higue who has the ability to slip out of her "wrinkled skin," suck the blood of sleeping children, and turn herself into a ball of fire. Other creatures of the night are the "half-man wolf" and the fairmaid, "a pale woman" who flies to her "forked branch," and Papa Bois, ruler of the woods.

Walcott makes the point that these creatures and their tales, figments of the Caribbean imagination, are dismissed as the superstitions of a simple people or merely the characters of European mythology transported to the Caribbean:

> Dryads and hamadryads were engrained
> in the wood's bark, in papyrus, and this paper;
> but when our dry leaves crackle to the deer-
> footed, hobbling hunter, Papa Bois,
> he's just Pan's clone, one more translated satyr.   [38]

The inclusion of characters from the world of Caribbean folklore into Walcott's poetic world is the poet's attempt to preserve the culture of his people, a culture always under attack both within and outside of the society. Harold Simmons' comment, in 1963, on the decline of the folk arts in St. Lucia is still very relevant today, not only for St. Lucia, but also for the entire Caribbean as well:

> Increased literacy, the coming of newspapers and radio
> have combined with better transport to lessen the author-
> ity of the "older heads" in their homes,the torch bearers of
> tradition....one might say that economic and social changes
> have undermined the function of successive parts of the folk
> tradition, and that their place has been taken by the prac-

tices of the larger society, or the sophistication motivated by magazines and movies.[59]

The current tendency of Caribbean society to mimic the societies of North America and Europe mitigates against the preservation of the traditional cultural forms of the region. This mimicry is a modern reworking of the need of eighteenth and nineteenth century Caribbeans to pattern themselves after the colonials of the time. Walcott attacks the growing tendency to denigrate the traditions of the folk. But such attempts have always existed. Caribbean folk traditions have been attacked over the years, i.e., by established churches, governments and people who view themselves as the "upper-crust" of Caribbean society. By including vital folk figures in the world of his poetry, Walcott aims, not only at preserving a dying culture, but at giving Caribbean cultural forms the respectability they deserve. In doing so, he fights against the stereotypical perceptions of both Caribbeans and Europeans: "these fables of the backward and the poor / marbled by moonlight, will grow white and richer. / Our myths are ignorance, theirs are literature" (39). Walcott has long been involved in a movement of preservation. For him, the folklore of the Caribbean is a living, breathing entity that enriches the life and literature of the region. The language of the region is the vehicle of preservation as well as its deliverance. It honors and protects the culture of the ancestors and its transformations in contemporary society:

> What would deliver the [New World person] from servitude was the forging of a language that went beyond mimicry, a dialect which had the force of revelation as it invented names for things, one which finally settled on its own mode of inflection, and which began to create an oral culture of

chants, jokes, folk-songs and fables; this, not merely the debt
of history was his proper claim to the New World.[60]

In their own way, New World poets are the guardians of history.
They protect the past by inventing new names for the elements
of the New World and their own experiences in it. In this way, they
ensure the survival of the folklore and its informing presence in
the life and literature of the region.

In the process of ensuring the survival of the folklore,
Walcott idealizes and anesthetizes immediate pain and suffering.
For example, the epigraph to "The Light of the World" comes from
a song by Bob Marley: "Kaya now, got to have kaya now, / Got to
have kaya now, / For the rain is falling" (48). "Kaya" is marijuana,
and its invocation sets the tone of the piece. The voice of the
poem is the poet's voice, and he is on a "sixteen-seater transport"
plying people and their belongings between Gros-Islet and the
Market in St. Lucia. Marley's song of the epigraph is blasting forth
on the transport's stereo, but for the poet the journey is con-
templative and nostalgic. While the poet's eyes are busily occu-
pied with two women, one he admires who was "like a black
Delacroix's Liberty Leading the People," and the other "in a yel-
low bodice / and yellow shorts, with a flower in her hair" whom
he lusts after, his mind goes back in time to his childhood expe-
riences. There was the same traffic, the same busyness, the
same enduring quality of labor. In the present, an old woman
"hobbled" toward the transport with a basket, leaving behind a
heavier basket that she was unable to carry:

> She said to the driver: *"Pas quittez moi à terre,"*
> which is in her patois: "Don't leave me stranded,"
> which is, in her history and that of her people:
> "Don't leave me on earth," or, by a shift of stress:

"Don't leave me the earth" [for an inheritance].   [50]

The suffering of the peasants, of the simple folk, is frozen in time. The poor are always "stranded"; the era is irrelevant, and the poet is consumed by his own sense of inadequacy: "I had left them on earth, I had left them to sing Marley's songs of a sadness as real as the smell of rain on dry earth, or the smell of damp sand (51). Walcott is aware that as much as he would like to embrace the folk and change their lives, he is separated from them by his position as poet/outsider, and while he might want to change their situation, this is not possible. As he himself puts it: "There are things that my craft cannot / wield, and one is power."[61] The poet's power lies in his insight and awareness. All he can do is to utilize the power of his New World language to bring the reality of his people's existence to public consciousness. "Kaya," the poet's symbol for the public amnesia provides no solution; it merely maintains the status quo. Derek Walcott's poetry ranges from joyful, lyrical celebrations of his people and his region to harsh attacks on the destructive nature of Caribbean politics and politicians, to meditations on the past and the history of slavery. But, whatever his subject, like Kamau Brathwaite, he is constantly exploring the language and rhythms of the Caribbean, always returning to the Caribbean's ancestral roots. Both poets utilize the shaping power of language to forge and to preserve a distinct Caribbean identity.

Notes

1. Wilson Harris, "A Talk on the Subjective Imagination,"
   Explorations (Denmark: Dangaroo, 1981) 65.
2. See Kamau Brathwaite's use of "video style" in *The Zea Mexican
   Diary* (Madison: U of Wisconsin, 1993); *Barabajan Poems*
   (Kingston and New York: Savacou North, 1994); and *DreamStories*
   Essex: Longman, 1994).
3. See Derek Walcott's interview with Charles Rowell in *Callaloo* 34:
   11.1 (Winter 1988): 83.
4. Walcott address, Medgar Evers College (CUNY), Black Writers
   Conference, New York, March 26, 1988.
5. Kamau Brathwaite, *History of the Voice* (London: New Beacon,
   1984) 13.
6. Melvin Dixon, "Rivers Remembering Their Source," *Afro-American
   Literature,* eds. Dexter Fisher and Robert B. Stepto (New York:
   MLA, 1979) 26.
7. Brathwaite, "New World A-Comin," *The Arrivants: A New World
   Trilogy* (London: Oxford UP, 1973) 10. Subsequent poems from
   this collection are identified in parentheses in the text.
8. Paule Marshall, "The Making of a Writer: From the Poets in the
   Kitchen," *Reena and Other Stories* (New York: Feminist Press,
   1983) 7.
9. Albert Memmi, *The Colonizer and the Colonized* (Boston: Beacon,
   1967) 103.
10. Gordon Rohlehr, *Pathfinder: Black Awakening in The Arrivants of
    Edward Kamau Brathwaite* (Trinidad: Rohlehr, 1981) 262.
11. Ngugi wa Thiong'o, *Decolonizing the Mind* (New Hampshire:
    Heinemann, 1988) 15.
12. Gary Edwards and John Mason, *Black Gods: Orisa Studies in the
    New World* (New York: Yoruba Theological Archministry,1985) 8.
13. Anne Walmsley, "Dimensions of Song," *Bim* 13 (July-Dec.1970):
    163.
14. Filoteo Samaniego, "Naming Things in a New World," *Diogenes*
    (Summer 1979): 97.
15. Brathwaite, "History, the Caribbean Writer and X/Self," *Crisis and
    Creativity in the New Literatures in English,* eds. Geoffrey V. Davis
    and Hena Maes-Jelinek (Amsterdam: Rodopi, 1990) 30.
16. Brathwaite, "Manchile," *Third World Poems* (Essex: Longman) 32.
17. Brathwaite, "The African Presence in Caribbean Literature," *Roots*
    (Havana: Casa de las Américas, 1986) 236.
18. Martin Carter, *Selected Poems* (Georgetown: U of Guyana P, 1989)
    91.

19. Tracy Nicholas, *Rastafari* (New York: Anchor, 1979) 39.

20. Robert Farris Thompson, *Flash of the Spirit* (New York: Vintage, 1983) 53.

21. See Brathwaite, *Notes to X/Self* (Oxford: Oxford UP, 1987) 130.

22. Richard Price, *Maroon Societies* (Baltimore: Johns Hopkins UP, 1979) 293.

23. Brathwaite, "Gods of the Middle Passage: A Tennament," *Caribbean Review* 11:4 (1982): 18+.

24. Gordon Rohlehr, "Song of the Skeleton: Flowers of the Harmattan," unpublished paper presented at the Interdepartmental Conference in English, University of the West Indies, St. Thomas W.I. (1985): 27.

25. Quoted from Brathwaite, back cover of *DreamStories.*

26. Brathwaite, *The Zea Mexican Diary* (Madison: U of Wisconsin P, 1993).

27. Gordon Rohlehr, "Dream Journeys," *World Literature Today* (Autumn 1994): 766.

28. See E.B. Idowu, *Olódùmarè: God in Yoruba Belief* (New York: African Islamic Mission, 1988) 142. Idowu discusses a special cult of Olódómarè where devotees worship within a circle of ashes. The circle symbolizes the eternal. In the circle the worshipper with outstretched hands offers a split kola-nut to the God. Brathwaite clearly brings together the Christian sacrament of communion and the ritualistic worship of the Yoruba God.

29. Derek Walcott, "The Castaway," *The Castaway* (London: Cape, 1969) 9.

30. Walcott, "Codicil," *The Castaway* 61.

31. Walcott, "Moon," *The Gulf* (New York: Farrar, 1970) 12.

32. Walcott, "Nearing Forty," *The Gulf* 67.

33. Walcott, "Tales of the Islands," *In a Green Night* (London: Cape, 1969) 27.

34. Michel Fabre, "Adam's Task of Giving Things Their Name," *New Letters* 41 (Fall 1974): 93.

35. Walcott, "What the Twilight Says: An Overture," *Dream on Monkey Mountain and Other Plays* (New York: Noonday, 1970) 8.

36. Edward Seaga, "Revival Cults in Jamaica," *Jamaica Journal,* reprint vol. 3.2 (June 1969): 4.

37. Walcott,"Origins," *Collected Poems* (New York: Farrar, 1986) 12-16.

38. Walcott, "Names," *Sea Grapes* (New York: Farrar, 1976) 32.

39. Brathwaite, *The Arrivants* 196.

40. Pamela Mordecai,"The Image of the Pebble in Brathwaite's Arrivants," *The Caribbean Poem, Carib* 5, (Kingston, Jamaica, WIACLALS (1989): 63.

41. Robert Elliot Fox, "Derek Walcott: History as Dis-Ease," *Callaloo* 27:9.2 (Spring 1986): 338.
42. Joyce Jonas, *Anancy in the Great House* (New York: Greenwood, 1990) 130.
43. Walcott, "Sainte Lucie," *Sea Grapes* 35.
44. Walcott, "IX," *Midsummer* (London: Faber, 1984) 19.
45. Walcott, "The Muse of History" 27.
46. Walcott, "LI," *Midsummer* 71.
47. Derek Walcott, "Cul de Sac Valley," *The Arkansas Testament* (New York: Farrar, 1987) 9.
48. Gareth Griffiths, *A Double Exile: African and West Indian Writing Between Two Cultures* (London: Boyars, 1978) 141.
49. Derek Walcott, *The Fortunate Traveller* (New York: Farrar, 1980) 53.
50. Stewart Brown, "Spoiler, Walcott's People's Patriot," *Wasafiri* 9 (Winter 1988/1989): 14.
51. Keith Warner, *Kaiso! The Trinidad Calypso* (Washington: Three Continents, 1985) 43.
52. Gordon Rohlehr, *Calypso & Society in Pre-Independence Trinidad* (Trinidad: Rohlehr, 1990) 65.
53. Warner 113.
54. Warner 112.
55. V.S. Naipaul, *Middle Passage* (Middlesex: Penguin, 1982) 29.
56. Brown 13.
57. Walcott, "Roseau Valley," *The Arkansas Testament* 17.
58. Walcott, "Gros-Ilet," *The Arkansas Testament* 34.
59. Harold Simmons, "Notes on Folklore in St. Lucia," *Iouanaloa,* ed. Kamau Brathwaite (St. Lucia: n.p., 1963): 41.
60. Walcott, "What the Twilight Says: An Overture," *Dream on Monkey Mountain and Other Plays* (New York: Noonday, 1970) 17.
61. Walcott, "The Arkansas Testament," *The Arkansas Testament* 116.

Chapter 4

Epic Rhythms
in the Caribbean

                    making
                    with their
                rhythms some-
                    thing torn
                    and new

                    —Brathwaite, *The Arrivants*

But they crossed, they survived. There is the epical splendour

                    —Walcott, *Omeros*

The development of an epic voice in the Caribbean has been the direct result of the region's historical marginality. Writers and poets of the region, intensely aware of the negativity of the region's official history, create an epic space that celebrates the region's progress and achievements. Franco Moretti, in his study *Modern Epic: The World System from Goethe to García Márquez*, shows how the epic form itself comes "close…to the ideology of progress."[1] For Caribbean writers of the epic, the "ideology of progress" depends on the integral concept of creolization.

Creolization is the process by which the various and distinct cultural groups in the Caribbean interact with each other, resulting in the emergence of a language and a culture that is distinctly Caribbean. Creolization becomes a metaphor for Caribbean unity and possibility. At the center of the experience of creolization is the African experience in the New World. Anyone of perception who has studied the history, culture, and literature of the Caribbean recognizes that the African experience dominates the creolization process; yet, Kamau Brathwaite continues to be attacked for this assertion. Bruce King in *Caribbean Conundrum* takes Edward Chamberlin to task for "defining…the West Indian poetic tradition as "black." He goes on to state that Chamberlain accepts "Brathwaite's view of creolization as essentially Afro-Caribbean."[2] King's response shows his own bias and his inability to accept creolization with its focus on the African elements of Caribbean culture as a transformative force in the region. Neither Brathwaite nor Chamberlain, however, suggests a theory of African superiority or the exclusion of other cultures.[3] Brathwaite's position is perfectly clear: Creolization "result[s] in subtle and multiform orientations from or towards ancestral originals." "Caribbean culture," Brathwaite maintains, "can be seen in terms of a dialectic of development taking place within a seamless guise or continuum of space and time; a model which allows for blood flow, fluctuations, the half-look, the look both/several ways; which allows for and contains the ambiguous, and rounds the sharp edges off the dichotomy."[4]

One of the effects of creolization is the politicization of the Caribbean. Any process that attempts to bring together the disparate elements of Caribbean society is a threat to the existing regional and neocolonial power structures. In addition, creolization has both a political and a visionary thrust inspiring the possibility of being a real force for change. Rex Nettleford best captures the spirit of the process:

> The Caribbean is to be seen more as a cultural unit, the product of the process of creolization which goes beyond biological mixing to the *creation* of a unique and distinctive sensibility capable of coping with *difference* without resort to intolerance or deterioration into psychic despair.[5]

As a force for unification, creolization has historically been viewed as a revolutionary concept by those interested in maintaining the status quo in the Caribbean. In their separate existences as English, French, and Spanish islands and the Guianas, Caribbean territories will never achieve political or economic self-sufficiency.[6] The poets of the region are ahead of the politicians in recognizing the transformative and unifying powers of the creolization process. Edouard Glissant suggests that creolization is not an isolationist concept, for today "infinite varieties of creolization are open to human conception."[7] Creolization opens endless possibilities for interrelationships. The form of the epic provides an infinity of space in which the writers of the region can confront a painful past while exploring the possibilities of interrelationships. In this space, history is rewritten, the silenced come into voice and the Caribbean confronts its relationship to the past and to history.

Wilson Harris, in "History, Fable and Myth in the Caribbean and the Guianas," makes the following assertion:

...the apparent void of history which haunts the black man
may never be compensated until an act of imagination opens
gateways between civilizations, between technological and
spiritual apprehensions, between racial possessions and
dispossessions in the way the *Aeneid* may stand symbolically
as one of the first epics of migration and resettlement
beyond the pale of an ancient world.[8]

Harris recognizes the problematics of history. He is also con-
scious of the civilizing possibilities of Caribbean culture and of
creolization as bridges between the technologies of the modern
world and the wisdom of traditional folk culture. By inventing
an epic imaginary space, Kamau Brathwaite and Derek Walcott
transcend their own time. They explore the isolated fragments
of Caribbean history searching for meaning and a way to end
colonial and neocolonial domination. They return to origins to
create an epic world in which the imagination is supreme.

The beginnings of a Caribbean epic voice are a part of the
literary history of the region. A.J. Seymour's "The Legend of
Kaieteur," which was put to music by Philip Pilgrim and produced
as a "choral fantasy" in 1944, contributes to the epic genre. In
"The Legend," Seymour immortalizes the myths and legends of
Guyana's indigenous people. He sings of the ancestral spirit
Kaie, who sacrificed himself for his people, and of the great spirit
Makonaima, the father of the Akawaio Indians. He celebrates the
beauty and majesty of the towering Kaieteur Falls on the Potaro
River in Guyana's interior. As the narrative begins, Seymour cap-
tures the grandeur and the mystery of the falls and the power
of the spirit, Makonaima:

Now Makonaima, the Great Spirit dwelt
In the huge mountain rock that throbbed and felt

The swift black waters of Potaro's race
Pause on the lip, commit themselves to space
And dive the half mile to the rocks beneath.
Black were the rocks with sharp and angry teeth
And on those rocks the eager waters died,
Lost their black body, and up the mountain side,
Above the gorge that seethed and foamed and hissed
Rose resurrected into lovely mist.[9]

While Seymour's "Legend" is firmly rooted in the Amerindian ethos, Wilson Harris in *Eternity to Season* returns to a Greek classical world.[10] Unlike Derek Walcott, whose characters in *Omeros* are essentially Caribbean,[11] Harris superimposes Homeric figures from the *Iliad* and the *Odyssey* onto the Guyanese landscape. As Seymour himself puts it in *The Making of Guyanese Literature*: "For [Harris] in these poems, the central figure is Ulysses, mastering time and space and bridging the world from eternity to season."[12] In Harris's work, Greek names are juxtaposed with Guyanese names. One poem in the collection is entitled "Troy," while another is called "Canje." Ulysses surfaces in Cumberland, a village on the Courantyne coast in Guyana. Harris attempts to relocate history's victims to a psychic territory of strength. The problem in the Caribbean has always been the position of black people in society, for slavery's shadow continues to cast its pall over the present. Inevitably, poets and artists of the region consciously or unconsciously affirm its role in the shaping of Caribbean identity.

Harris realizes that this task requires "an act of imagination." In his work, the Caribbean situation is analogous to that of ancient Greece and Rome. In their wanderings in search of rootedness and stability, Odysseus and Aeneas never lose their connections to history and community, and history is never separated from the process of migration in the imagination of Homer and Virgil. Perhaps this is what attracts Derek Walcott to the Greek experience, although he insists that in *Omeros* he is not writing a Caribbean epic.[13] Clearly, he is attracted to the Homeric wanderings and the pull of the sea and sees in the Caribbean experience the same mixture of tragedy and triumph, the survival of the human spirit, and the inevitability of the force of history.

Kamau Brathwaite, in *The Arrivants,* more solidly aligns himself to the tradition of the African oral epic described by Isidore Okpewho as:

> a tale about the fantastic deeds of a man or men endowed with something more than human might and operating in something larger than the normal human context and...[a tale] of significance in portraying some stage of the cultural or political development of a people.[14]

Derek Walcott also recognizes the Caribbean epic's origins in the African oral tradition: "Epic was compressed in the folk legend. The act of imagination was the creative effort of the tribe."[15] *The Arrivants* is Brathwaite's Caribbean epic. He brings together past and present time in a powerful portrayal of his people's existence in the old world, their exodus, and their survival in the New World. As these experiences are filtered through his imagination, he invokes the gods of Africa and their new forms in the Caribbean, calling upon them to offer guidance, inspiration, and hope.

Both Brathwaite and Walcott utilize elements of the epic genre to suit their individual purposes and to create a distinctly Caribbean form. In discussing courtly epic, Erich Auerbach notes that "only members of the chivalric-courtly society are worthy of adventure, hence they alone can undergo serious and significant experiences."[16] Walter Ker observes: "Whatever Epic may mean, it implies some weight and solidity."[17] Although the inhabitants of the epic worlds of Brathwaite and Walcott are very far removed from "chivalric courtly society," classical Greek or Roman society, the Teutonic world of *Beowulf* or the divine world of the Miltonic epic, the spirit of epic permeates their worlds. Brathwaite and Walcott write of the exodus and the massacre of a people, of thousands of dead Africans interred in the depths of the Caribbean sea; they eternalize their people's songs of endurance and survival on the literal and symbolic plantations of the Caribbean; they celebrate the life of the simple worker and peasant and sing of the ethereal beauty of the landscape and the mystery of the sea. Out of this revisioning of place and history comes the creation of Caribbean identity.

Brathwaite and Walcott approach this tenuous process of identity formation quite differently. Bakhtin, in discussing the epic genre, insists on the importance of selecting what "should be preserved" from the past:

> One may, and in fact one must, memorialize with artistic language only that which is worthy of being remembered, that which should be preserved in the memory of descendents; an image is created for descendents and this image is projected on to their sublime and distant horizon.[18]

Both poets are imbued with a strong sense of history; they must preserve the glories as well as the psychic scars of the tribe. Brathwaite wants to re-create the glory of African kingdoms, the power of the African gods, the trauma of the Middle Passage, and the Africans' existence on the slave plantations of the Caribbean. Walcott, in *Omeros*, comes closest to this vision of Brathwaite's. Both poets are keenly aware of the connections between the imagined world of literature and the real world of society, and the role of the imagination in the creation of identity.

Brathwaite's approach to identity creation is rooted in the communal. In his work, he represses individuality and the self. On the other hand, Walcott is more self-consciously aware of his role as individual creator and world shaper. By subsuming the role of the individual, Walcott objectifies the communal, and his poetic act of regeneration appears less successful than Brathwaite's. Emphasis on community is crucial. Given the region's fragmented history, it is only by acknowledging the communal voice that the process of healing and regeneration can begin. Glissant, very much aware of the need for a communal voice, suggests that: "A new epic voice is needed [in the Caribbean], not one of individual identity, but of common, human identity."[19] That voice of "common, human identity" is Brathwaite's. Ranging through historical time, he reconstructs the history of his people, their achievements, and inherent possibilities.

Brathwaite has created the word "nam" for this cyclical concept of reinvention and re-creation and the belief in the limitless possibility of the human soul. The notion of nam is at the very center of Brathwaite's visionary world, and, symbolically, it epitomizes the poet's determination to create a Caribbean identity that reflects the history of the region and the experiences of its people. To achieve this formidable task, Brathwaite adopts the epic voice. Joan Dayan's comment on *X/Self* can aptly be applied to *The Arrivants*: "Brathwaite's epic tells the story of the colonizing of minds, the costuming of souls."[20] Beyond his story of colonization and mimicry, Brathwaite's first trilogy shows how a return to ancestral sources decolonizes minds, and how Caribbean peoples must rediscover their nam. Brathwaite has defined his concept of nam in several places, but nowhere more powerfully than in his discussion of history and *X/Self*.

"name,"...is another form of "nam": the name that you once
had has lost its "e," that fragile part of itself, eaten by
Prospero, eaten by the conquistadores, but preserving its
essentialness, its alpha, its "a"protected by those two intran-
sigent consonants, "n" and "m." The vibrations "nmnmnm"
are what you get before the beginning of the world. And that
"nam" can return to "name" and the god "Nyame."[21]

The word "nam" expands to embrace the glory of past history, the
immensity of origins, and the power of the ancient gods. It also
contracts to ward off the sterility of the periods of colonization
and slavery, and between these two poles it is the fragile
Caribbean self that the poet preserves and celebrates. This self
can only exist and survive in community.

The Arrivants is Brathwaite's story of Caribbean community
and the rebirth of identity.[22] He focuses on the essential elements
of community: a people's history, customs and rituals, the hero-
ism of their daily struggle for survival and their relationship to
divinity. Brathwaite, as is so clearly indicated in his poetry, ignores
the concept of chronological time. He leaps through history enter-
ing the time of early African kingdoms, journeying to the begin-
nings of slavery, the Africans' transportation to the New World, and
finally plunging into the New World experiences of colonization
and neocolonization. As Christine Pagnoulle puts it:

...time is a labyrinth in which there is no fixed centre; time
is a mesh of overlapping lanes, avenues and blind alleys that
have to be explored without any preconceived idea and
connected in new, visionary ways if the world (and the
word) is to make sense.[23]

Brathwaite's blurring of time allows him space to correct the misreading of history that has relegated his people to virtual obscurity. Like the epic poets of old, he brings to public consciousness not only his people's glory, but also their degradation in all its ugliness. Brathwaite's emphasis on the seamy aspects of European colonization and neocolonization is a conscious descent into a world of evil and graphic brutality from which he reconstructs a new world of possibility and hope.

"New World A-Comin'" fuses time and space, glory and pain. Hawkins and Cortez are memorialized along with the "imprisoned" Prempeh, the Asante king and his sister, Asantewa.[24] Into this collection of personages, illustrious and infamous, the poet also adds Geronimo, the Maroon, Tackie and Montezuma. Such a range across continents points to the common tragedy of the dispossessed. In the second section of the poem, Brathwaite describes the enforced exodus of the African. He contrasts the warmth, the lushness, the fertility of the old land with the coldness, the aridity and the barrenness of the Middle Passage journey. The old world is remembered and out of the clash between old and new, a new form emerges:

> . . . . this ship floats
> to new worlds, new waters, new
> harbours, the pride of our ancestors mixed
>
> with the wind and the water
> the flesh and the flies, the whips and the fixed
> fear of pain in this chained and welcoming port.   [11]

The paradox of "chained and welcoming" strikingly emphasizes the contradictions within the New World experience.

Brathwaite's tendency to weave in and out of various historical periods highlights the incapability of the Africans' untenable position regardless of place or time. The character Tom who keeps reappearing in "Rites of Passage," a section of *The Arrivants,* illustrates this reality. Tom conjures up in the reader's imagination a figure subservient and servile, a figure without a true understanding of existence as the "other" or the outsider in society. But such a reading is not Brathwaite's intention. He transforms Tom into an archetypal figure representing the memory of the tribe. Tom's mind moves from the "screams" and the "lashed sore" to earlier times and heroic men:

> . . . . . . Atumpan talking and the harvest branch-
>
> es, all the tribes of Ashanti dreaming and the dream of Tutu,
> Anokye and the Golden Stool, built
> in Heaven for our nation by the work
> of lightning and the brilliant adze....[25]

Even as the poet recalls heroic moments, by a linguistic twist, he carves his people's fragmented past into memory. The literal splitting of "branch- /es" symbolizes the divisions of the African tribes and their separation from traditional history and culture. While Tom formally "sing[s] / nothing / now," "remember[s] / nothing / now," "suffer[s] / nothing /now," his amnesia is merely a protective ploy: "and hold my hat / in hand / to hide / my heart" (15). The poet utilizes the epic technique of combining both the heroic past and mundane present. Tom appears again in "All God's Chillun" (17-21). On the plantations of America's South, he is mocked and hated by both blacks and whites. To whites, he appears as a measure of their degradation; to blacks he becomes a constant symbol of their powerlessness and servility. But Tom remembers a glorious past. Brathwaite presents simultaneously a vista of past glory and present dehumanization. Tom is presented with a narrative of heroism and achievement generally consigned to a dead past. Brathwaite deliberately revitalizes past glories in order to promote revolutionary action, change, and creativity. Brathwaite's Tom is also a wanderer, and as he roams through London, once more he becomes the symbol of mass degradation and despair: "I died alone, without the benefit of fire" (22). The poet is here referring to the epic fire of knowledge as well as of comfort. As so often happens in his poetic world, after Brathwaite has piled up image upon image of utter hopelessness, there is a lyrical moment of calm where, by reentering the past, mind and body are regenerated and re-armed for the struggles ahead:

> Bring me now where the warm wind
> blows, where the grasses
> sigh, where the sweet
> tongue'd blossom flowers
>
> where the showers
> fan soft like a fisherman's
> net thrown through the sweet-
> ened air   [23]

In a moment of rejuvenation, Tom is transposed, in time, to a time in which he can find hope and peace in the beauty of natural creation far removed from "the fire trail / of fear" (25).

But the "fire trail" is always present, and when Brathwaite specifically addresses the Caribbean situation, the blaze becomes an inferno. "Calypso" captures the violence of the Caribbean's introduction to the plantation system: "The islands roared into green plantations" (48). This "roar" into existence means profits for the European colonizers and poverty for the people: "It becomes an island dance / Some people doing well / while oth-

ers are catchin' hell" (49). At the end of "Calypso," Brathwaite has
his people "nigratin' overseas..." (50), in this way, they continue
their epic wandering. They have become the world's "niggers";
homeless, selfless, and endangered. They are found at the ports
of the world "with their cardboard grips, / felt hats, rain- /
cloaks."[26] In a tremendous leap of time, Brathwaite moves back
to the advent of Columbus and the birth of destruction: "hot
splintered courage, bones / cracked with bullet shot, / tipped
black boot in my belly, the / whip's uncurled desire?" (53).
Brathwaite focuses relentlessly on the tragic history of his peo-
ple. Journeying through time and place, he discovers the truth
of Caribbean people's existence from their days in the Old World
to their existence in the New.

Wherever his people embark on worldly wanderings, ques-
tions concerning identity arise:

Have you no language of your own
no way of doing things
did you spend all those holidays
at England's apron strings?   [55]

Even the drum, the instrument of identity and connectedness
loses its power: "Our colour beats a restless drum / but only the
bitter come" (56). Brathwaite moves his wandering tragic people
from Africa to the Caribbean back to the European capitals of the
world, then to the United States. But their fate remains the same.
They exist in "Castries' Conway and Brixton in London, / Port of
Spain's jungle / and Kingston's dry Dungle / Chicago Smethwick
and Tiger Bay" (40). Migration does not bring relief; it intensifies
hopelessness:

Never seen

```
a man
travel more
seen more
lands
that this poor
path-
less harbour-
less spade.                                    [40]
```

However, Brathwaite finds a path and a harbor for his people. "Wings of a Dove" moves from acceptance and desperation to hope and renewal. The poet attacks the rising tide of materialism sweeping over the region. Jamaica as Babylon can be any island in the Caribbean. The wandering Tom is transformed into "Brother Man the Rasta / man" (42), but in spite of his religion and the "pipe of his ganja," he can find no peace. He is consumed by desperation. Poverty locates him outside the circle of success. The poet places his wanderer at the center of a very surrealistic experience. His mind, clouded by ganja, transforms his surroundings:

```
. . . . . . . . the mice
eyes, hot pumice
pieces, glowed into his room
like ruby, like rhinestone
and suddenly startled like diamond.            [42]
```

In the sudden brilliance, he is transfigured. Adopting the mantle of prophet and guardian, his voice rising from the depths of his soul in lamentation, he sings the sorrow songs of his people. He catalogues the agents of destruction as well as the agents of hope. Finally, lifting his voice in a rising crescendo, he appeals to his god. His god is an African god celebrated by drumming: "So beat dem drums / dem, spread / dem wings dem, / watch dem fly / dem, soar dem / high dem, / clear in the glory of the Lord" (45). The scene is set; the Rasta Man has resorted to the safe harbor of ritual to find comfort and salvation. He is convinced that the destruction of the material world is imminent, and that the new world is at hand:

> So beat dem burn
> dem, learn
>
> dem that dem
> got dem nothin'
>
> but dem
> bright bright baubles
>
> that will burst dem
> when the flame dem
>
> from on high dem
> raze an' roar dem
>
> an' de poor dem
> rise an' rage dem
>
> in de glory of the Lord.   [45]

In this passage, the poet's use of sound symbolism is an integral part of the meaning of his words. The repetition of "dem" captures the insistent roar as the sound of the drums rises unremittingly to a frenzy.

In this frenzy of sound, Brathwaite creates the setting for
his apocalyptic vision of the uprising of society's poor and
downtrodden. His words increase in power and force as he
moves his people through various stages of rebellion: "burst,"
"raze an' roar" and "rise an' rage." The "baubles" are ephemeral
and will be consumed by "rage" which suggests both the violence
of God and the violence of the dispossessed. The poet implies
that there is going to be a sudden spontaneous uprising, the cul-
mination of a history of various forms of mental and physical vio-
lence against the poor. While the poet's prophetic vision is one
of ultimate doom, he suggests ways of avoiding the apocalypse.
Repeatedly, he insists that salvation lies in the acceptance and
performance of customs and rituals, and while the drums here
summon the poor to revolution, in Brathwaite's visionary world,
drums also transmit messages between the gods and their peo-
ple and are essential instruments in the ritual of healing.

The drum in African culture goes beyond revolutionary
and religious functions. It symbolizes origins, and, as Maureen
Warner-Lewis suggests, it "come[s] to symbolize Africa itself":

> ...the drum is closely linked in learned African philosophy
> with the Word, in the sense in which St. John the Apostle
> used it at the start of his Gospel—the original utterance
> which created life out of nothingness and chaos, and then
> established order in that creation. The drum is therefore a
> divine tool of the Supreme Being, a womb or beginning of
> created life.[27]

It is not surprising that drums play a major role in *The Arrivants*.
Brathwaite merges the ritual and symbolic functions of the drum
in this work dedicated to the African narrative of origins and jour-
neys, Old World history, and New World reality.

"The Making of the Drum" details the mechanical motions of the ritual, but underlying the mechanical is the deeply spiritual yearning for connections to the African deities:

> we have killed
> you to make a thin
> voice that will reach
>
> further than hope
> further than heaven, that will
> reach deep down to our gods where the thin
> light cannot leak, where our stretched
>
> hearts cannot leap.   [94]

The poet calls for a descent into the self that reaches beyond hope and religion. Brathwaite is suggesting a move beyond the imposed religions of the colonial legacy. A journey into the self reveals the presence of the African gods who offer anchor and identity to "stretched hearts."

Brathwaite's drum poems are ceremonial performances. There is a formality and precision of vocabulary resulting in a grandeur of tone that is entirely in keeping with the epic world the poet creates. The drum encloses, to borrow Wilson Harris' famous phrase, "a womb of space" from which silence and identity will emerge out of darkness and the void[28]:

> Here in this silence
> we hear wounds
> of the forest;
> we hear the sounds
> of the rivers;

vowels of reed-
lips, pebbles
of consonants,
underground dark
of the continent.   [95]

The act of giving voice is a creative one and leads the poet back
to God: "God is dumb / until the drum / speaks."[29] Once more the
poet returns to origins and the ancestral memory. He returns to
the original place, the ancestral home. New World Africans

walk...through the humble
dead to meet
the dumb
blind drum
where Odomankoma speaks   [97]

In "Atumpan," Odomankoma, the sky god, creator, speaks.
According to Brathwaite's notes, he begins the poem by imitat-
ing the sound of the drum: "Kon kon kon kon / kun kun kun kun"
(98). This merger of sound and symbol takes the poet back to the
past and to beginnings and awakenings. He allows the past to
speak, to divulge its secrets: listen / let us succeed / listen / may
we succeed... (99). Brathwaite addresses the profound human
importance of the Caribbean's struggle for identity in a world
largely alien to blacks. He celebrates blackness and, as Marina
Maxwell suggests, "his crystallization of the interior dialogue of
the black [person] today is the emergence of a confidence of exis-
tence and of potential wholeness."[30]

The journey towards "wholeness" is not an easy one for a
people relegated to the periphery of New World society.
Brathwaite's people wander throughout the world and find no

peace. Even their journey to Africa is fraught with ambivalence. In "The New Ships," after an exodus of three hundred years, the narrator returns to Ghana:

> I travelled to a distant town
> I could not find my mother
> I could not find my father
> I could not hear the drum
>
> whose ancestor am I?   [125]

The poet's rhetorical question merely points to his solution to the problem of identity and ancestry. Separated for so long from the ancestral home, Caribbean people are not simply transplanted Africans. The culture of Africa is firmly rooted in their consciousness; therefore, the identity being forged cannot be complete without the recognition of its African antecedents.

Brathwaite paints a dire picture of the consequences of the loss of connections to Africa. The Caribbean becomes a wasteland of divided people alienated from their ancestors: "the / eyes / of our elders / are dead" (130). The silence of ignorance envelops the landscape. The picture is one of death and disintegration. But, underneath the mask of silence and ignorance lies a yearning for life and new beginnings: "hearts / rustle their secrets, / blood shiver like leaves" (131). The persona cries for guidance: "Will / your wood lips speak / so we see?" (131). But the path to sight/insight is a violent one, and in "The Golden Stool," the clash between the reverence for history and tradition and the mercenary nature of society erupts. The poet castigates the African slavers for their part in the destruction of a people. For such transgression there is no forgiveness: "no elder to lead you / again through the branch- / es. through the path- / ways of prayer, / to Onyame's now / leafless air" (145). The "pathways" to knowledge have been destroyed. Such a sin results in the wrath of Onyame, the creator, and the only way to salvation is further destruction. Onyame destroys in order to renew:

> And when the cycle is ripe
> I, giver of life to my people,
> crack open the skull, skill
>
> of shell, care-
> fully carved craft
> of bones, and I kill.   [146]

What is being destroyed is the New World vision of history that negates the African experience and reinforces the view that black Caribbean identity is worthless. In response, the poet carefully rebuilds the structure of self and society through the new aware-ness of the past and the wisdom of the reclaimed ancestors. In the unfolding of the trilogy, the poet has been gradually moving towards this process of rebuilding. In the final section of *The Arrivants,* "Islands," Brathwaite focuses on Caribbean transfor-mations, showing how new gods and rituals inform identity and offer strategies for rebirth and revitalization. In Brathwaite's recreated Caribbean, God is Jah, the name used by the region's Rastafarians. "Islands" begins with the poem, "Jah," which sets the tone of rejection, for Rastafarians "reject Western 'Babylonian' cul-ture."[31] The poet, like God, reorders the New World:

> God is glass with his type-
> writer teeth, gospel
> jumps and pings off the white
> paper, higher and higher   [162]

The aim of the new gospel is to recall the memory of the past: "For the land has lost the memory of the most secret places" (164). Ancestral sacred places have been desecrated. In this barren landscape, where there are no sacred places and the "gods have been forgotten or hidden," the poet speaks out against empty rituals: "A prayer poured on the ground with water, / with rum, will not bid them come back" (164). Anancy, the spider/spirit, is at work however. Brathwaite focuses on Anancy's godlike powers before he fell from grace. He adopts the persona of the spider-god and, in his role as trickster, "spin[s] webs in the trees" (164), waiting for the right moment to put his creative powers to work.

As a New World figure, Anancy brings with him the protective talent of subterfuge. He is able to remove himself from dangerous situations. Brathwaite's Anancy "prefers to spin webs in the trees." Joyce Jonas's interpretation of the image of the spider spinning its web is a particularly striking one that makes excellent sense in the understanding of Brathwaite's purpose:

> Like Anancy, the artist escapes the disastrous prospect of nonbeing by weaving a (fictive/narrative) thread and climbing it to freedom. He takes the strand of linearity (oppressive history or plot) and complicates it by making a patterned web of connections and interrelationships—a woven "text" that turns history/his story into oracular myth, an infinite play of signifiers.[32]

The artist as spider/creator is a particularly relevant symbol for the New World. He weaves the disparate strands of the region's myths and history into a holistic text that is the source of new perceptions and therefore of new strengths. The text invites a new reading of the past and history and inscribes upon the imaginary landscape the poet's epic vision of the Caribbean's struggle for visibility and identity. Through *The Arrivants*, Brathwaite brings this struggle into existence. In "Ananse," he is the keeper of the language and therefore of the collective memory. He is also the keeper of sound: "he spins drum- / beats, / silver skin / webs of sound / through the villages" (165). Anancy's sounds bridge the gap between worlds. The drums call to African chiefs as well as New World heroes. Anancy is also an integral part of the present society and maintains his function as "world-maker, word-breaker, creator..." (167). Brathwaite utilizes the duality of the Anancy figure. In the New World, Anancy—wearing the disguise of the trickster—plays with language and works to conceal meaning. He creates a sacred space to lodge New World history.

Discussing the artist's dual role as bringer of truth and trickster, Wilson Harris notes:

> [The artist] stands therefore at the heart of the lie of community and the truth of community. And it is here, I believe, in this trickster gateway—this gamble of the soul—that there emerges the hope for a profoundly compassionate society committed to freedom within a creative scale.[33]

Harris believes that the Caribbean's limbo dance "reflects a certain kind of gateway or threshold to a new world" (6). Limbo originated on the slave ships of the Middle Passage. As Harris tells the story, space was so limited that the slaves were forced to twist themselves into shapes as flexible as spiders. The limbo dancer moves under a stick, which in the course of the dance, narrows the space between the stick and the floor. The objective is for the dancer to spread his limbs as close to the floor as possible in order to dance under the stick without knocking it over. Both Harris and Brathwaite see Anancy, the spider, in the dancer's flexibility of limb and ability to enter exiguous space. Limbo becomes the symbol of the space, or the "gateway" connecting Africa and the Caribbean.[34]

Appropriately, the second section of "Islands" is entitled "Limbo." In this tenuous space, the connections to Africa are submerged. The inhabitants of the islands are isolated from custom and tradition, finding themselves in the precarious position of reaching back to Africa and at the same time trying desperately to give their lives substance and meaning in the New World. For the poet, the state of limbo is a crucial part of the journey towards wholeness. Caonoba, in "The Cracked Mother," represents the "other," a victim of the vagaries of history.[35] She stands in fear at the threshold of a New World existence, unable to cast away the terrors of the colonial experience. But Brathwaite also moves his people away from the terror of the past, and, in "Shepherd" (185), there is a growing awareness of new beginnings and hope. The poet takes his people through various stages of recovery, and in "Caliban," they come to realize the saving grace of history (194). The shattered psyche of the New World person cannot be made whole until it is possessed by the reality of the New World existence. The longing to return to an idyllic Africa has to be transformed into a recognition of the Africa within.

"The Cracked Mother" addresses the fragmented and tormented psyche of the Caribbean person subjected to the culture and religious beliefs of the colonizing powers. Caonoba's mother sees Columbus as a powerful force, and he becomes for her a symbol of achievement. Brathwaite's comments on "The Cracked Mother" in his notes to the recording of "Islands":

> We now hear the sea-saw effect of the imposition of an alien god on an integrated personality. Caonoba, the Carib daughter of this section, trapped in a convent garden, surrounded

by black-robed nuns, experiences the collapse and frag-
mentation of her world through a series of water-images end-
ing in hurricane and emotional blindness.[36]

The perception of Caonoba's mother is "cracked." Unable to see
clearly, she believes her daughter's salvation, and that of her peo-
ple, will only be realized if they adhere to the new customs and
religion. Caonoba is more perceptive. The Christianity of the col-
onizer only divides the indigenous population: "Christ on the
Cross / your cruel laws teach / only to divide us / and we are lost"
(182). The natural violence in the form of a hurricane with which
the poem ends mirrors Caonoba's personal mental turmoil. Out
of this violence comes a new awareness. Old ways of domination
will be destroyed; "new maps" will be "drafted" and there will be
a new "dawn." The questions that end the poem are rhetorical,
for the poet slowly moves towards the creation of a landscape
of hope: "...How will new maps be drafted? / Who will suggest a
new tentative frontier? / How will the sky dawn now? (184).

"Shepherd" moves the Caribbean people closer to possession
and trembling toward speech. Initially, the voice of the narrator
is silenced: "Dumb / dumb / dumb / there is no face / no / lip /
no moon" (185). The messenger—the woman in "white calico"—
prepares the way for the entrance of the African gods. Libations
are poured, and, in the silence, "the drum speaks," bringing into
existence the voice of the gods. The poet creates in the New
World symbols of the old gods: "The orange on the table, the
grapefruit, the cashew / nut: these are our votive offerings"
(189). The gods are, thus, liberated. They do not remain consigned
to the depths of the sea with the casualties of the Middle Passage:
"they...walk up out of the sea / into our houses" (190). They
need to be recognized and their voices heard.

Movement towards recognition comes in "Caliban." Here, the

poet/narrator sings of the sorrows of his people: their dire poverty, their mindless slaughter over the years, the worldwide, barren cityscapes created by men. Brathwaite embarks on a backward excursion into time and history:

It was December second, nineteen fifty-six.
It was the first of August eighteen thirty-eight.
It was the twelfth of October fourteen ninety-two.
How many bangs how many revolutions?   [192]

Moving from the date of Fidel Castro's initial steps towards revolution to the date of Emancipation and finally to the date of Columbus's violent and disruptive entrance into the Caribbean, Brathwaite suggests that what remains constant is Caliban's position as "other," enslaved both mentally and physically. However, in the poem's second and third section, the poet moves toward regeneration and healing. Caliban dances the limbo towards a new consciousness. He goes through the process of dancing the limbo without any awareness of its significance, but in time he is transformed, and the limbo "stick is the whip / and the dark deck is slavery." Caliban descends into the darkness of the unconscious and, as he emerges, undergoes an epiphany:

out of the dark
and the dumb gods are raising me

up
up
up

and the music is saving me

hot

slow

step

on the burning ground.   [195]

For Caliban, history has come home. The past is seared into his conscious memory becoming the foundation upon which his New World identity will be built.

"Jou'vert" signals the beginning of this new day in the Caribbean. Jouvay, originating from the French *jour overt,* meaning "opening day," is an integral part of Trinidad's carnival ritual. In the hours before dawn, people find their bands and begin the journey to Independence Square. Members of the Jouvay bands cover themselves in mud, oil, dirt and paint or dress themselves in old clothes. The ritual of Jouvay commemorates the past and the days when "slaves lit the night with their torches." Libations are poured honoring the ancestors. The spirit of Jouvay goes back to the original rejoicing of the slaves at the end of the cane season. After the cane was burned, the slave masters would permit the slaves to celebrate. The occasion marked "freedom, emancipation, no more work." Jouvay provides the passage into Carnival and into an existence removed from harsh realities. Revellers coat their skins with mud and oil to facilitate entrance into the ritual space of carnival.[37]

Brathwaite, in "Jou'vert," brings together Old and New World experiences, and out of this amalgam comes the distinctive Caribbean identity he has been intent upon creating. The drum remains the central symbol, not only connecting mortals to the gods, but also binding together the New World community. It also links the deities from both worlds: "Christ will pray / to Odomankoma / Nyame God / and Nyankopon" (267). In the pow-

erful force of this merger, "sorrows / burn to ashes." Images of
new life and renewal abound in the newly created landscape;
"flowers / bloom along the way." Images in "Jou'vert" embody the
merger of the two worlds:

> flowers bloom
> their tom tom sun
>
> heads raising
> little steel pan
>
> petals to the music's
> doom   [269]

There is a certain inevitability to this Caribbean awakening. The
poet uses "doom" here in the sense of destiny, for in spite of the
region's dark history, the intensity of its encounter with the
devastation of slavery and colonization, there is movement
beyond the "black and bitter / ashes." As Michael Dash aptly puts
it, ["Jou'vert"] represents the dawn of the risen god/word and the
poetic vision retrieved with all its positive and healing reso-
nances."[38] "Jou'vert" celebrates survival beyond immeasurable
odds, and a tone of jubilation pervades the poetic landscape.
Pamela Mordecai, too, acknowledges the ebullience of the verse:
"...the verse is sweet with the sweetness of flesh that is close to
the bone."[39] Brathwaite filters his people's history through his
poetic imagination. In placing their experiences and history in
an epic landscape, he preserves the vision of wholeness and iden-
tity that he has so carefully crafted.

At the end of *The Arrivants,* the poet brings into being a new
Caribbean world inhabited by people who have explored the
torturous past and have come to an awareness of the meaning

of history and their place in their New World homeland. They are

> making
> with their
>
> rhythms some-
> thing torn
>
> and new   [270]

In *Omeros,* his epic work, Derek Walcott is also engaged in creating "some- thing / torn / and new" out of the various "rhythms" of the Caribbean. Although he adopts Homeric names for his characters, Omeros is Walcott's Caribbean epic. In a conversation with Lewis Lapham, Walcott suggests that Omeros is not merely a "layover of Homer, pretentious or pompous," for people are often named, but have no real awareness of what their names mean.[40] Walcott focuses not on the Homeric analogies, but on the act of naming. He molds the epic form into a font containing the meaning of human existence and history in the Caribbean. The Caribbean's epic wandering is the African exodus, and its epic war is the battle against slavery in its various historical and contemporary manifestations. This war is at the heart of *Omeros.* By bringing these fragmentary experiences to life, Walcott, as epic poet/narrator, transforms them into a narrative of totality.

This act of transformation is not a simple task, for under the poet's pen, the work of art becomes the medium that reshapes the world and reveals a new order. Consumed by his belief in the messianic role of the poet, Walcott assumes control, provides direction and brings together the fragments of history and experience. His adaptation of the epic form provides the vast framework he needs, for, if the work is to have life and meaning, it must become public and shared. As the poet himself explains, the error of his narrator, is to "dignify people through literature," and Major Plunkett's error is to "dignify people through history." It is necessary to move beyond literature and history to "a simplicity which sees people without adornment."[41] Walcott moves beyond the colonized spaces of literature and history to disclose both historical wounding and contemporary rehabilitation.

Omeros, a long narrative poem in seven books, is Walcott's celebration of the life and history of the people of St. Lucia in particular and the people of the Caribbean, in general. The protagonist Achille, a simple fisherman, is engaged in the elemental struggle for survival in the face of a not always benevolent Nature and a present world corrupted by history. He is surrounded by simple people: Helen who loves him, but abandons him to live with Hector; Hector who follows the road to modernization and surrenders his fishing boat for a jitney; his friend, Philoctete whose leg has an incurable sore; and Ma Kilman who operates the "No Pain Cafe" and protects and cultivates the memory and the wisdom of the African ancestors. In addition, interacting with the native population are Major and Maud Plunkett representing the colonial presence on the island and in the region. Major Plunkett, who had fought with Montgomery in North Africa, spends much of his time engaged in historical research. Weaving in and out of the narrative is the figure of Omeros. He is blind Seven Seas, the African griot; he is also the derelict who is refused sanctuary in St. Martin-in-the-Fields' church in London. Throughout the text, Omeros remains a constant symbol, for black Caribbeans, of a quest for revelation and survival.

Walcott, as epic poet, adopts the persona of prophet, and returns Caribbean people to an African Golden Age through Achille's journey from the Caribbean to Africa. He creates for the modern reader a myth of Africa complete with legendary heroes. Walcott's myth informs the establishment of the Caribbean home-land. This Caribbean homeland gains a special visibility when the poet enters the poem in a real way. In the middle of the world of Achille and his friends, Walcott inserts a moving tribute to his mother:

> She floated so lightly! One hand, frail as a swift,
> gripping the verandah. The cotton halo fanned
> from her shrunken crown, and I felt that I could lift
>
> that fledgling, my mother, in the cup of my hand
> and settle her somewhere else....   [XXXII 165]

Walcott in fact settles her "somewhere else"; in his imagi-nation, the amnesia that accompanies his mother's advancing years is linked to the amnesia of his people—people who "had forgotten a continent in the narrow streets." He transposes him-self to another time and wills the spirits to speak:

> Now, in the night's unsettling noises, what I heard
> enclosed my skin with an older darkness. I stood
> in a village whose fires flickered in my head
>
> with tongues of a speech I no longer understood,
> but where my flesh did not need to be translated;
> then I heard patois again, as my ears unclogged.   [XXXII.I. 167]

Whenever the poet or his wandering alter ego, Omeros, enters the work, a moment of revelation or truth is experienced. The poet is covered with the mantle of an "older darkness" that is Africa, and his body understands intuitively the nature of the experience even though the language is alien to him as a man of the present time. This moment of voiceless recognition forces Walcott to an appreciation of the beauty of his native patois and its African connections.

The entrance of the poet's dead father into the work presents another such moment of revelation. This encounter occurs on a beach, a "mud-marked seafront" where "people took evening walks." In this setting, the poet's father appears. During their conversation, the poet discloses his longing to belong, to be a part of a great tradition, a tradition that would offer a sense of identity and public pride, and would "carry [him] over the bridge of self-contempt...when [he] felt diminished" (XXVI.III. 187). The father also offers advice to his son and all other Caribbean wanderers and exiles: "Once you have seen everything and gone everywhere, / cherish our island for its green simplicities, / enthrone yourself," and above all, do not forget that "in its travelling all that the sea-swift does / it does in a circular pattern" (XXXVI.III. 187-188). Born in the Caribbean and assaulted by the forces of history, it is impossible for Walcott to deny a Caribbean identity completely. The distinct awareness of place, history, and the region's "green simplicities" are sources of the poet's empowerment. Achilles discovers that the quest for identity might lead to other harbors, but inevitably these harbors prove to be alien and provide no peace. The quest, therefore, becomes mythic, and the journey becomes a mythic journey of reconciliation to an African homeland. In an epic sweep of time and space, Walcott returns Achille to his ancestral homeland, Africa. In a variation of the classic descent into the underworld, Walcott places Achille in a trance-like situation where the landscape of Africa appears to him "like the African movies / he had yelped at in childhood" (XXV.I. 133). The experience profoundly disturbs him, and in one second he experiences a vision of his place in time, both its origin and its culmination. He is also overwhelmed by feelings of pain and shame. But this is the first step towards the attainment of self-respect and recovery. The awareness of his own inadequacies forces him to find strength in a mythical Africa that has always existed in his imagination.

Walcott very carefully constructs the interaction between reality and myth. He brings together Achille and his father Afolabe, and out of this meeting of past and present, Achille's sense of loss is heightened. He feels alienated from a culture and a tradition. His interaction with his ancestors causes him to recognize his lack of an historical base, and he yearns to achieve his father's sense of self and grounding in history. During this period, he is exposed to the customs and rituals of his people and hears the griots sing of their exploits, their sorrows and their joys:

> . . . . but he learned to chew
> in the ritual of the kola nut, drain gourds of palm wine,
> to listen to the moan of the tribe's triumphal sorrow
>
> in a white-eyed storyteller to a balaphon's whine,
> who perished in what battle, who was swift with the arrow,
> who mated with a crocodile, who entered a river-horse
>
> and lived in its belly, who was the thunder's favorite....
>
> [XXVI.I. 139]

A transcendent moment for Walcott's protagonist and a searing emotional experience, the return to an African homeland involves more than an individual search for identity and a personal affiliation with an original home. Achille's experience guarantees continuity as he confronts the historical past and realizes the extent of his deprivation.

This sequel in *Omeros* is reminiscent of "The New Ships" in Brathwaite's *The Arrivants* (124-129). Brathwaite's narrator, like Achille, is returned to the past to experience the history and wisdom of his people. In both instances the result is a new awareness and knowledge. Again, while both poets focus on the past and on history, each one leads his protagonist back to the present, each poet now endowed with the wisdom of the past. It becomes their sacred mission to use their new knowledge to shape the identity of their comrades in the New World.

In creating this myth of rediscovery, Walcott uses Achille to bridge the gap between humans and the gods:

> and he climbed a track of huge yams, to find that heaven
> of soaring trees, that sacred circle of clear ground
> where the gods assembled. He stood in the clearing
>
> and recited the gods' names.   [XXVI.I. 140]

At this sacred spot, Achille, deprived of tradition and culture in present time, can give voice to the names of his gods. Walcott skillfully manipulates time in this section of the work. Afolabe and his people speak of a future already experienced by Achille: "the future reversed itself in him. / He was his own memory..." (141). The confrontation between past and future brings him no peace: "Make me happier, / make me forget the future" (XXVI.II. 141). Forgetting, however, is no solution, and Walcott's purpose is not only to make Achille remember, but also to discover the meaning of what he remembers. While he discovers meaning, it brings him no peace. Transported to Africa, Achille is entrapped between the past and the future and becomes fully conscious of the horror and the terror of his people's experience in the present. The juxtaposition of past and present shocks Achille into an awareness of the connections between his African heritage and his New World existence. His people dance the dances of the African warriors. He discovers the sameness of things:

> the same chac-chac and ra-ra, the drumming the same,
> and the chant of the seed-eyed prophet to the same
> response from the blurring ankles. The same, the same.
>
> [XXVI.III. 143]

Walcott also returns Achille to the past to experience the actuality of his people's early history. He experiences a slave raid that "yielded fifteen slaves / to the slavers waiting up the coast." In the aftermath of the raid, "Achille walked the dusty street / of the barren village. The doors were like open graves" (145). But the griot sings his song of a future time and a "sorrow that would be the past" (148). He sings the songs of the ancestors from Benin and Guinea who endured the crossing and survived. Walcott creates the incredible sense of loss and separation resulting from this forced exodus. The simplicity of language as the poet lists everyday articles missed by the displaced Africans increases the pathos. The hunter cried for his lance, the fisherman for his river, the weaver for his straw fishpot. In addition, "They cried for the little thing after the big thing. / They cried for a broken gourd" (XXVIII.III. 151). The "broken gourd" symbolizes the displacement of a people as well as their attempt to protect their cultural heritage in the painful, forced journey to the New World.

The fact that Walcott is a dramatist is evident. He returns to a central concern of his drama, the regenerative power of ancestral ritual. In *Omeros*, Walcott's focus on ritual, and the griot's role in re(membering) the ancestral past, place Achille, the wanderer, in an imagined universe of possibility. First,

however, Achille must come to terms with the original dis-
placement and alienation of his people. Second, he must make
sense of his return to the African homeland. In the space
between the actual exodus from Africa and Achille's mythic
return, Walcott suggests that his protagonist can achieve psy-
chic healing only through his new reading of history. As Lillian
Feder notes, "the vitality of myth" lies in its power "of express-
ing a variety of contemporary approaches to the inherited past,
to time, history, and the yearning for order and meaning in a
skeptical age."[42]

An "inherited past" envelops both the symbolic and real
worlds of *Omeros* and gives coherence and meaning to the
Caribbean world Walcott is defining. Belonging and identity come
through an understanding of the "inherited past," and the African
gods who inspirit it.[43] When a hurricane descends upon Achille's
island, all that the people of the village can do is "listen to the gods
in session" (52). Walcott consciously invokes the African gods. The
drums of Shango, the god of thunder and lightning, are heard
throughout the land. Walcott presents both the old gods and
their New World counterparts in a grand merger of the two worlds.
At this demonstration of supernatural force, Shango is joined by
Erzulie, the New World goddess of love. The music of her ra-ra
joins the grand symphony of the gods. Ogun and Damballa also
take part in the ceremonial show of power and force:

> Fete start! Erzulie
> rattling her ra-ra; Ogun, the blacksmith, feeling
> No Pain; Damballa winding like a zandoli
>
> lizard, as their huge feet thudded on the ceiling,
> as the sea-god, drunk, lurched from wall to wall, saying:
> "Mama, this music so loud, I going in seine".... [IX.III. 52]

Bringing together the music of both worlds, Walcott integrates the African and the Caribbean elements of New World identity. Ogun, the god of war and iron, is the "patron of hunters and warriors."[44] It is interesting that here Walcott places Ogun in the company of Damballa, the Haitian god associated with the rainbow, "which in ancient Dahomean lore was thought to be the great serpent come out from the underworld to drink after a rain."[45] Walcott includes Damballa at this point as a symbol of hope and the promise of integration. Achille, "in his shack," experiences this spectacle of the power of the gods. Valleys are destroyed as well as the "year's banana crop." The gods consciously imprint the memory of their power on the minds of their subjects in an attempt to keep the past always at the forefront of consciousness for "Too much had been forgotten" (IX.III. 54).

Ma Kilman, the owner of the "No Pain Cafe," embodies the memory of the past and the connection between Africa and the New World. Philoctete's physical wound (he has a festering sore on his ankle) is an obvious manifestation of slavery's bondage and historic wounding of the Caribbean's psyche:

> He believed the swelling came from the chained ankles
> of his grandfathers. Or else why was there no cure?
> That the cross he carried was not only the anchor's
>
> but that of his race, for a village black and poor
> as the pigs that rooted in its burning garbage,
> then were hooked on the anchors of the abattoir.   [III.III. 19]

Philoctete and his people are trapped animals forever anchored in a world where the impoverished black masses remain powerless and their only certainty is the inevitability of death. In this situation of powerlessness and pain, Ma Kilman is a source of restoration and healing. She represents the submerged wisdom of the African elders. In order to heal Philoctete, Ma Kilman must rediscover ancestral wisdom and knowledge. Because of the nature of Ma Kilman's mission, she remains at a distance from society. The villagers sense her untapped powers. To function in her role as healer, she must reach deep down into ancestral memory from which healing powers emanate. She finds herself in a "dark grove...in which the bearded / arms of a cedar held council" (XLVII.II. 237).

In Yoruba belief, groves are "sacred and secret." They are found in forests where the trees grow tall and the leaves are so thick that the sun is often blocked out. Some trees are viewed as the homes of spirits and very often ceremonies of worship take place at the "foot" of these trees. According to Omosade Awolalu, "because of the singular air of strangeness and quietness about them, they instil a sort of awe even in the minds of the worshippers."[46] In discussing the symbolic nature of the sacred place and its function as the link between the world of the real and the world of the supernatural, Awolalu quotes Mircea Eliade:

> [The sacred place] constitutes a break in the homogeneity of space; this break is symbolized by an opening by which passage from one cosmic region to another is made possible (from heaven to earth and *vice versa*; from earth to the underworld.[47]

Walcott utilizes the mythology of the sacred grove. He creates a space that will link Ma Kilman to two worlds, the real world of her existence in St. Lucia and the mythic world of ancestral Africa.

In this space, Ma Kilman discovers a flower "whose odours diverted the bee from its pollen"; this flower possesses healing properties (237). A swift carried the seed in its stomach from Africa to the New World: "She aimed to carry the cure / that precedes every wound" (XLVII.III. 239). While the journey to the New World was fraught with horrors, the Africans carried within them the seeds of their own deliverance. Ma Kilman comes to the realization that the ancestral memory is not dead, but simply waiting to resurface. As Walcott puts it, Ma Kilman "glimpsed gods in leaves, but their features [were] obscured" (242). He captures the feeling of Ma Kilman's growing awareness as she waits for the moment of recognition when the gods will grant her knowledge:

...... the deities swarmed in the thicket

of the grove, waiting to be known by name; but she
had never learnt them, though their sounds were within her,
subdued in the rivers of her blood. Erzulie,

Shango, and Ogun; their outlines fading, thinner
as belief in them thinned....   [XLVII.I. 242]

Here Walcott uses myth to explain the dying power of the gods in the New World. As belief in the gods declines, their power is concentrated in the evil smelling flower Ma Kilman discovers. In discovering the flower and its potent powers, Ma Kilman once more calls into existence the latent power of the gods. Walcott, shrouded in the mantle of the artist and engaged in the act of re-creation, fully realizes that a world cannot be remade with flawed systems. Ma Kilman, in discovering a cure for Philotete's physical illness, facilitates his psychic recovery. As Philotete emerges from the healing bath in which Ma Kilman has immersed him, the "tears trickled down his face": "So she threw Adam a towel. / And the yard was Eden. And its light the first day" (XLIX.II. 248).

The Eden of the Caribbean, its new day, like the Golden Age of Africa, is a part of the grand myth that Walcott creates. Caribbean identity is inextricably linked to separation from Africa, the Middle Passage, slavery, and colonization. Walcott invents another place and time, an African Golden Age and a Caribbean new day. He presents a mythical, glorified past that informs Caribbean identity. Deliberately blurring in his epic scheme the lines between myth and history, he invents an amorphous space at the center of which the collective memory of the Caribbean endures. For Walcott, the invention of myth in the Caribbean is closely associated with memory. It is also a cultural and political act intended to influence the present and the future. For Walcott, the creation and preservation of myths and their transmission from generation to generation in a people's collective memory is liberating. Conscious of the interconnectedness of memory and epic, Walter Benjamin defines memory as "the epic faculty *par excellence*." He further suggests that "only by virtue of a comprehensive memory can epic writing absorb the course of events on the one hand and, with the passing of these, make its peace with the power of death on the other."[48] In the liberating epic space of *Omeros,* Walcott not only achieves historical absorption and reconciliation with the past, but the past also lives in the present and survives it.

An example of such a moment of integration is Walcott's description of a childhood memory. He recalls women, virtually enslaved, carrying baskets of coal on their heads, worming their way up the hills of St. Lucia. Walcott transforms this moment from a narrative of pain and hardship into a moving account of female strength and endurance, a celebration of the female spirit and an act of liberation. He connects the women of St. Lucia to the circle of ancestral survivors:

> Kneel to your load, then balance your staggering feet
> and walk up that coal ladder as they do in time,
> one bare foot after another in ancestral rhyme.   [XIII.II. 73]

The image of ascent suggests the possibility of freedom and escape as in the Negro spiritual "We Are Climbing Jacob's Ladder." While the St. Lucian women escape metaphorically into the company of the ancestors, the reality of their pain is infernal:

> Hell was built on those hills. In that country of coal
> without fire, that inferno the same colour
> as their skins and shadows, every labouring soul
>
> climbed with her hundredweight basket, every load for
> one copper penny, balanced erect on their necks
> that were tight as the liner's hawsers from the weight.
>
> The carriers were women, not the fair, gentler sex.
> Instead, they were darker and stronger, and their gait
> was made beautiful by balance....   [XIII.II. 74]

The strength, purity, and beauty of the women's movements are all part of Walcott's general purpose to move beyond the terror and the pain to a celebration of endurance and survival: "But they crossed, they survived. There is the epical splendour" (XXVIII.I. 149).

In order to give voice to the epic splendor of the Caribbean, the poet becomes an archaeologist and attempts to unearth remnants of the past. He soon realizes that only the spiritual ruins tell an epic tale, for the physical ruins attest solely to violence and destruction. Acknowledging the evocative power of ruins in "The Muse of History," Walcott writes:

> The epic-minded poet looks around these islands and finds
> no ruins, and because all epic is based on the visible pres-
> ence of ruins, wind-bitten or sea-bitten, the poet celebrates
> what little there is, the rusted slave wheel of the sugar fac-
> tory, cannon, chains, the crusted amphora of cut-throats, all
> the paraphernalia of degradation and cruelty which we
> exhibit as history, not as masochism....[49]

It is not the physical ruins that concern the poet; rather it is his-
tory's less obvious statements. Although Walcott refers to the
Caribbean's visual historical relics, for example, the ruins of
Vigie and the Morne in St. Lucia, he is also interested in intan-
gible ruins, remnants of the psychology of slavery and colo-
nization so firmly etched in the Caribbean psyche.

It is, however, possible to find more than a "little" to cele-
brate, and Walcott later notes in the same essay: "The epic poem
is not a literary project. It is already written; it was written in the
mouths of the tribe, a tribe which had courageously yielded its
history."[50] Walcott gives voice to the history of the tribe. Ma
Kilman represents the timelessness of tribal history. In the
circle of her existence, past, present and future time meet and
confront each other. The lives of the powerful and the powerless
converge. The Plunketts and ordinary villagers are brought
together, and each group tries to tap into her powers for its own
good. The Plunketts represent colonial domination in the
Caribbean. On an intellectual level, Major Plunkett, who had
fought in North Africa with Montgomery and is married to an Irish
woman, is well aware of the devastating effects of colonial pol-
icy and arrogance:

> We helped ourselves
> to these green islands like olives from a saucer,

munched on the pith, then spat their sucked stones on a plate,
like a melon's black seeds.   [V.I. 24]

Attracted to the beautiful black Helen, once the Plunkett's maid,
and now a waitress, "he felt a duty / towards her hopelessness,
something to redress / (he punned relentlessly) that desolate
beauty / so like her island's" (V.III. 30). Without fully under-
standing the nature of Helen's pain, Plunkett sees himself in the
role of benevolent, well-meaning patriarch. Ironically, he wants
to write her into history, but a history viewed through male,
white, colonizing eyes: "Helen needed a history, / that was the
pity that Plunkett felt towards her. / Not his, but her story"
(V.III. 31). Helen having been written out of history by the
Plunketts of the world, is now to reenter history shaped by
Major Plunkett's patronizing perception—a perception typical of
colonial arrogance. Walcott's narrator, distant from the movement
of the unfolding narrative, sees "the rage of [Helen's] measuring
eyes" and suggests the suppressed violence ready to erupt (36).

Relationships between the Plunketts and the people of the
island have been colored by the inevitability of the facts of his-
tory. Ranging from Africa's involvement with Europeans and the
slave trade, the European presence in the Caribbean to the dec-
imation of American Indians, Walcott sets the stage and amasses
the evidence for continuing antagonisms between the colonizer
and the colonized. Plunkett relentlessly pursues his historical
research on the European presence in St. Lucia, not too pleased
by the realization he comes to that *History* "will be rewritten /
by black pamphleteers, History will be revised, / and we'll be its
villains, fading from the map..." (92). Walcott reveals that history
must be revised if a national identity is to be forged in the
Caribbean. According to George Lamming, only "when there is a
liberated regional Caribbean of one people, [will] an environment

[be] created in which we may be able to say: 'here man truly is man, and the world he lives in is a human place.'" [51]

Helen's relationship with the Plunketts mirrors the uneasy relationship between Caribbean islands and colonial powers. It also points to the problematics inherent in the colonial relationship that mitigate against the creation of a communal "human place." Historically, Europeans, secure in their belief in Christian right and might, nevertheless, are attracted by what they view as the exoticism of the islands. Plunkett associates Helen with exoticism and "otherness" and is obsessed by the beauty of "this Judith from a different people" (97). He masks his lust with benevolence: "My thoughts are pure. / They're meant to help her people, ignorant and poor" (XVIII.II. 97). Maud Plunkett, too, has learned the lessons of empire well. She believes that Helen, in the servant class, should be subservient and suitably awed in the presence of her mistress. Both women are consumed by suppressed rage and forced to mask their true feelings. Helen, who is pregnant, is forced to ask Maud for money to have an abortion. Her poverty chains her to dependency. The relationship between native and colonizer remains one of patronage.

Imprisoned by history and circumstance, Major Plunkett views himself as a representative of the British Empire whose responsibility is the custodial care of the natives. He has moments when he becomes uncomfortable in this role, but if he relinquishes this power, he will be diminished in the eyes of society. Maud Plunkett is also imprisoned. She is living in an alien country, and while she feels herself superior to the natives with whom she comes in contact, she lives a life of isolation. She is isolated from the islanders and from the inner life of Major Plunkett. Her life is one of passive female existence: "She preferred gardens to empires" (254). But she really has no choice, for in her culture men amass "empires" while women cultivate "gardens." Her reaction to Helen is also laced with envy. She is aware of Helen's power over men, including Major Plunkett. But both Plunketts clothe with politeness their basic reactions to the people and to the society in which they find themselves. Sometimes, however, the true reaction emerges and the veneer of civility is eroded. For example, when he narrowly escapes being forced into a ditch by Hector's jitney and is cursed at by a passenger, Major Plunkett responds: "I am not a honky. / A donkey perhaps, a jackass, but I haven't spent / damned near twenty years on this godforsaken rock / to be cursed like a tourist" (LI.I. 256).

Plunkett's wife dies, as she must, for Walcott allows no room for personal growth in the environment in which she finds herself. At her death, the poet/narrator forcibly enters the narrative:

> I was both there and not there. I was attending
> the funeral of a character I'd created;
> the fiction of her life needed a good ending   [LIII.II. 266]

In the re-created world, where the poet is shattering old fictions of inequality and supremacy, Maud Plunkett must be eliminated. She represents the old colonial order. Although in her personal world she is powerless, in the Caribbean, she remains a symbol of the unattainable.

Walcott's vision is also one of hope. In his rewriting of history, he reshapes the colonizing mind. He leads Major Plunkett to Ma Kilman and the "No Pain Cafe" in search of solace and a reconnection with his dead wife. Plunkett wants the opportunity to ask forgiveness for the pain he had caused her in life. She, too, had been a colonial subject, for Major Plunkett was always in control. Now deeply affected by her death, he wants to assure himself that she is in "heaven." Ma Kilman gives him this assurance, and he is "bound...for good to another race" (307). Before leaving the cafe, Maud's apparition appears to him. Major Plunkett's contact with Ma Kilman and her mysterious African powers affect him profoundly. He is transformed: "He discovers the small joys / that lay in a life..." and "he began to speak to the workmen / not as boys who worked with him, till every name / somehow sounded different" (LXI.III. 309). Walcott suggests that colonizer and colonized need to meet in a space beyond the ordinary realm of everyday living. In this space, faith in human possibility is supreme and the tempering presence of ancestral memory can assert its civilizing influence.

Clearly conscious of the impossibility of achieving such a unity of consciousness in the real world, Walcott fills the void of alienation in the world of the imagination. In the world of the contemporary Caribbean, slavery and the dread of plantation society may appear to be relegated to the past, with independence and achievement the mood of the times; however, the reality is quite different. In the beautiful and lush landscape of *Omeros,* poverty is endemic, and the historical attitudes and antagonisms between colonizer and colonized still flourish. But over and over again, Walcott sings of the simple lives of his people and their continued survival in the face of evil, both human and natural. He captures the drama of their passions, their pettiness, and their daily attempts to assert selfhood and claim a Caribbean identity that recognizes its African connections.

This drama is played out in the other world of *Omeros,* the world of the local folk. Here, Achille and Hector are rivals for the love of Helen. But the two worlds of *Omeros* are not distinct and separate. The lives of their inhabitants are inextricably interwoven. Achille works on the Plunkett's pig farm during the hurricane season. Helen, at one time was the Plunkett's maid, and her beauty entices the men of both worlds. It destroys the friendship between Achille and Hector. While these relationships unravel, the life of the island continues. Helen adds her troubling presence to the unfolding histories of the people with whom she comes in contact. Walcott creates in Helen a figure who embodies all of the island's ambiguities. She is a survivor who adapts to the changing life of the island and at the same time attempts to maintain a sense of selfhood. Achille resents any adaptations on her part. He also resents the growing capitalist influence on the island, the "Soul Brothers" singing, but also "losing their soul," and "the smell of fresh bread drawn from its Creole oven, / its flour turned into cocaine, its daughters to whores..." (XXI.I. 12).

Achille's resentment, while it is focused on Helen, is not the traditional European battle of superiority between the sexes, between the male perception of a self-effacing passive female and the dominant aggressive male. Helen is trapped between the old simple ways of the island and new alien patterns of behavior that are in conflict with the values of traditional Caribbean society. Therefore, what is at work here is Achille's distaste for the changes sweeping over his island. With a growing capitalist influence, the evils of industrialized society encroach upon the lives of the island people. Islanders are discarding traditional occupations and becoming involved, usually in menial tasks, in new capitalist enterprises. Helen is a waitress; Hector abandons fishing to become owner and driver of a jitney transporting the island's people between the city market and their homes in the countryside.

These changes in the society affect the narrow vision of the woman in society, lessening the distance between the ideal and the real. In the life and poetry of the region, the woman has traditionally been presented as a person of great strength and endurance, the epitome of survival and the preserver of the region's culture. In Brathwaite's *Mother Poem,* for example, the woman represents Barbados, survival, the connections to Africa, and the continuation of the race.[52] She epitomizes survival and is superhuman and distant, the embodiment of steel and strength. Her capacity for love and passion is hidden underneath the magnitude of her struggle to exist.

In Walcott's poetic world, black women are associated with violence, revolution, and the darker side of passion; while their sisters of a lighter color are linked to love's lyrical moments. Walcott transforms the black woman into a mechanical force, totally lacking in human feeling, but driven by the passion of revolution. Walcott's black woman is "shawled like a buzzard"; she "was as beautiful as a stone in the sunrise, / her voice had the gutturals of machine guns,...her sex was the slit throat of an Indian."[53] In "The Light of the World," Walcott's persona sits on a bus admiring a black woman as he fantasizes about making love to her: "I wanted her to change / into a smooth white nightie that would pour like water / over the black rocks of her breasts."[54] Even here, at a projected moment of ultimate tenderness, Walcott compares the woman's breasts to rocks with the connotations of indestructibility, unyielding strength and petrification. On the other hand, Anna, Walcott's fair representation of love and beauty has "mellowing breasts."[55] Both portrayals of the black woman, Brathwaite's superwoman and Walcott's metallic revolutionary, are responses to the stereotypical presentations of the black woman by early European and Caribbean writers. Walcott, in *Omeros,* creates a New World Helen, symbol of the black Caribbean woman who is the epitome of beauty, passion, and desirability.

Walcott's creation of Helen as revolutionary and passionate is an interesting contrast to Joan Dayan's portrayal of the Caribbean woman as passionate but frail. In "Caribbean Cannibals and Whores," Dayan suggests the adoption of Erzulie, the Haitian goddess of love, as an appropriate symbol of the Caribbean female's response to the numbing effects of colonization. This adoption would then initiate the creation of "a new ethics of voice."[56] But the duality of Erzulie is just as problematic as the exclusive images of woman as rabid revolutionary or divine superwoman. Erzulie, both in her role as " mother of man's myth of life",[57] and as the epitome of sensuality and sexuality, reinforces both past and current limited visions of the Caribbean woman. Images that focus on superhuman strength or an all-consuming and stifling sexuality are also misrepresentations. In fact, Dayan establishes a polarity between the woman of strength and the woman of fragility:

> Female strength is fundamental to Caribbean society. And although an "official" image-making culture, increasingly supported by the mass media, projects the mystique of an ideal woman—pale, diffident, refined, and at home—the daily lives of women in urban ghetto or countryside defy such stereotypes of femininity.[58]

The image of the "pale" and "refined" lady of leisure prevalent in advertisements in the Caribbean is evidence of the new wave of postindependence colonization that has its roots in the movement to Americanize the Caribbean. The Caribbean has become the dumping ground for America's outdated images of white women. The intent of the new image builders, generally politicians indebted to American business and politics, is again to destroy the Caribbean's links to Africa and to substitute American dependency for European dependency. Walcott's positive characterization of Helen is his response to the contemporary stereotyping of Caribbean women. Grace Nichols, in "Caribbean Woman's Prayer," beseeches God to give politicians courage to:

> mek dem see dat de people

must be

at the root of dih heart

dat dis

place ain't Uncle Sam backyard[59]

Dayan suggests that the strength and endurance epitomized in the lives of the region's vast numbers of poverty-stricken citizens negate the stereotypical images of weakness. However, while this is so, the tragedy is that the new waves of the Caribbean's elite brown middle and upper classes are being seduced by their perceptions of the glitter and materialism of the United States. They refashion the old stereotypes in order to foster difference and to maintain a false sense of superiority and power.

In this sense, Walcott's portrayal of Helen in *Omeros* attempts to address both past dualities and current misconceptions. He presents the reality of the black woman's existence in Caribbean society and captures the heroism of her simple but epic struggle for survival. When Helen makes her first appearance in *Omeros,* Walcott writes: "I felt like standing in homage to a beauty / that left, like a ship, widening eyes in its wake" (24-25). At this point Helen appears to be the traditional beauty who launched a thousand ships, set on a pedestal by adoring male eyes; very soon, however, it becomes obvious that Helen is a fighter and a survivor, a woman who wants to assert her independence: "she dint take no shit / from white people and some of them tourist—the men only out to touch local girls" (33). In a confrontation with Helen, Achille realizes that "he had startled a panther" (39). This reenvisioning of the black woman and acknowledgement of her beauty is in direct contrast to her traditional portrayal as servant and prostitute. Major Plunkett lusts after Helen, but in his colonial mind, when he is not being patronizing and feeling regret for the errors of history, she remains his wife's servant and a whore. In his reimagining of the Caribbean woman, Walcott pays tribute not only to female beauty and sexuality, but also to the black woman's right to independence. Dayan, in looking at the images of women in the Caribbean suggests that they appear "in varying texts as a sign of a lost ideal or a pressing reality."[60] Walcott, in his portrayal of Helen, addresses both the ideal and the real. Such an attempt is certainly new for poets of his generation. Helen is not only Helen, lover of Achille and Hector, servant of the Plunketts, and the object of Major Plunkett's lustful gaze; she is also a woman fighting for the survival of self and identity in a world in which black women are generally discarded and debased. In addition, she is St. Lucia, the "Helen of the West." In his epic world, Walcott reenvisions both his island and the Caribbean as empowering territories that allow for the freedom of the female spirit in spite of struggle and survival. In *Omeros,* he captures and immortalizes this battle.

As the intensity of passions develop in *Omeros,* Achille, Hector, and Helen become more than characters in the unfolding drama. Each begins to symbolize warring forces at work in Caribbean society. Achille, the simple fisherman, represents the old ways and a return to simple values and ancestral wisdom. Hector is impatient with the past, and the present is not moving as rapidly as he would like into a future over which he has control. The sale of his canoe and the purchase of the "Comet, a sixteen-seater passenger van," solidifies his movement away from the old ways. Yet, the new ways bring him no peace, and he dies violently driving the Comet along the winding roads of his island. Helen survives, and her pregnancy signifies continuity in time.

Through the interconnections of these characters as they move beyond common tragedy, the poet celebrates the spirit of continuity, survival, and rebirth. "Through the year, pain came

and went. Then came Christmas" (LV.I. 272). Walcott focuses on
the celebrations that occur in the Caribbean the day after
Christmas—Boxing Day. On this day of masquerades, Achille
transforms himself:

> Today he was not the usual king-fish fighter
> but a muscular woman, a scarf round his head.
> Today was the day of fifes, the prattling skin
>
> of the goat-drums, the day of dry gourds, of brass bells
> round his ankles, not chains from the Bight of Benin
> but those fastened by himself. He was someone else
>
> today, a warrior-woman, fierce and benign.
> Today he was African, his own epitaph,
> his own resurrection....   [LV.I. 273]

Again, the poet focuses on transformation not only for survival,
but also as a vehicle in the search for and possession of an
identity. Unlike the celebration in Britain, Boxing Day celebrations
in the Caribbean are not part of the religious celebrations of
Christmas. These celebrations have their origins in the time of
slavery. Then, the day after Christmas was one of four holidays
slaves were given annually. On this day, the slaves' dress, man-
ner, and relationship with their masters were transformed. As
Orlando Patterson puts it: "Their relationship with their mas-
ters...assumed the character of a kind of ritual license."

In addition, as part of the "temporary metamorphosis,"
they even adopted what were called "gala day names" that were
the names of local whites of standing and substance.[61] This
renaming forms part of a ritual of transformation and a passage
of escape from the pain and monotony of their daily existence

as slaves. Their musical instruments, calabash rattles and drums, reveals the link to Africa, but their existence is firmly rooted in the Caribbean. In Achille's transformation, Walcott stresses the presence of Africa in the Caribbean. He is Mother Africa, a "warrior-woman, fierce and benign. / Today he was African, his own epitaph, / his own resurrection" (LV.I. 273). This moment is a sacred one in Walcott's text, and it is full of the transformative power of ritual. The preparation for, and the enactment of the ritual of masquerade move Achille out of the everyday world of struggle and survival into a world of spirit that offers him and his people comfort and hope. Achille becomes teacher and leader. Initially, Helen does not take the ritual seriously, but he explains its importance and its connection to Africa, and she "did not laugh anymore, but she helped him lift / the bamboo frame with its ribbons and spread them out / from the frame, and everything she did was serious" (LV.II. 275).

Identifying Achille's rebirth as Mother Africa with the resurrection myth removes Achille from the world of reality and includes him in the company of mythic figures. The poet, at the moment of Achille's transformation, offers Africa as the source of healing for colonial wrongs. In order to assume an identity and to claim selfhood, Walcott locates the dispossessed in their own mythic world, peopled by figures familiar to the communal unconscious. In his masquerade costume, Achille is "resinous and frightening. He smelt like trees / on a ridge at sunrise, like unswaying cedars" (LV.II. 276). Achille is linked to a mythic and elemental memory. The dance he will participate in with Philoctete will return them to the Caribbean's heart of darkness, the initiation into slavery and the Middle Passage; it also moves them out of this darkness:

All the pain

re-entered Philoctete, of the hacked yams, the hold
closing over their heads, the bolt-closing iron,
over eyes that never saw the light of this world,
their memory still there although all the pain was gone.

[LV.III. 277]

This dance is one of remembrance and expiation. Walcott
employs the ritual of the dance and the myths of re-creation and
rebirth to fill the spiritual void left by the colonial erasure of self.
In this way, he brings Caribbean people back to a sense of root-
edness in the past.

Omeros celebrates the simple life of Caribbean people and
their history of endurance and survival despite almost insur-
mountable obstacles both metaphorical and real. The life of
Walcott's protagonist, Achille epitomizes this psychic struggle.
But Achille learns his lesson:

Measure the days you have left. Do just that labour
which marries your heart to your right hand: simplify
your life to one emblem, a sail leaving harbour

and a sail coming in ...   [XIII.II. 72]

Walcott's epic is an epic of spirit. Achille looks out towards
the horizon and his vision expands to embrace his ancestors,
those who survived in Africa as well as those—the casualties of
the crossing—whose bones are buried in the depths of the sea.
It is this expansion of horizon, the recognition and inclusion of
an African past, that gives grounding to Caribbean identity. With
the creation of identity, Walcott moves Caribbean people from
their marginalized position and places them firmly at the cen-
ter of human consciousness. This struggle "to control the bur-

den of...history and incorporate it into our collective sense of the future," George Lamming sees as "the most urgent task and the greatest intellectual challenge."[62] In going back to the sources, the history, and the mythology of the African people, both Derek Walcott and Kamau Brathwaite accept the "challenge" to provide a spiritual and intellectual home for the Caribbean people. In the visionary world of their poetry, folk traditions are preserved. These traditions form an integral and humanizing force in the Caribbean identity each poet is re-creating:

> The drums beat from the blood, the people danced and spoke their un-English English until our artists, seeking at last to paint themselves, to speak themselves, to sing themselves, returned...to the roots, to the soil, to the sources.[63]

Notes

1. Franco Moretti, *Modern Epic: The World System from Goethe to García Márquez* (London: Verso, 1996) 54.
2. Bruce King, "Caribbean Conundrum," *Transition* 62 (1993): 151.
3. See J. Edward Chamberlin's discussion of early Caribbean history and the development of a Caribbean poetic tradition in *Come Back to Me My Language: Poetry and the West Indies* (Urbana: U of Illinois P, 1993) 1-29.
4. Kamau Brathwaite, "Caribbean Man in Space and Time," *Carifesta Forum,* ed. John Hearne (Jamaica: The Institute of Jamaica & Jamaica Journal, 1976) 204.
5. Rex Nettleford, *Inward Stretch Outward Reach: A Voice from the Caribbean* (New York, Caribbean Diaspora Press, 1995) ix-x.
6. For a well-documented overview of historical creolization and the failure of federation in the Caribbean see William A. Green, "The Creolization of Caribbean History: The Emancipation Era and a Critique of Dialectical Analysis" 28-40; and Elizabeth Wallace, "The "Break-Up of the British West Indies Federation," in *Caribbean Freedom: Economy and Society from Emancipation to the Present* 455-475, eds. Hilary Beckles and Verene Shepherd (London & Jamaica: Currey & Randle, 1993).

7. Edouard Glissant, *Caribbean Discourse* 250.
8. Wilson Harris, "History, Fable and Myth in the Caribbean and the Guyanas," *Caribbean Quarterly* 16.2 (June 1970): 17.
9. A.J. Seymour, "The Legend of Kaieteur," *The Guiana Book* (British Guiana: Argosy, 1948) 8.
10. Harris, *Eternity to Season* (Guyana, n.p., 1954).
11. Derek Walcott, *Omeros* (New York: Farrar, 1990). Subsequent poems from this edition are identified in parentheses in the text.
12. Seymour, *The Making of Guyanese Literature* (Guyana: n.p., 1978) 45.
13. From a private transcript of "A Conversation Between Derek Walcott and Edouard Glissant" (New York: Poets' House, 11 April 1991).
14. Isidore Okpewho, *The Epic in Africa* (New York: Columbia UP, 1979) 34.
15. Walcott, "The Muse of History," *Is Massa Day Dead?* ed. Orde Coombs (New York: Anchor, 1974) 13.
16. Erich Auerbach, *Mimesis* (New York: Anchor, 1976) 139.
17 Walter Ker, *Epic and Romance* (New York: Dover, 1957) 4.
18. M.M. Bakhtin, *The Dialogic Imagination,* trans. Caryl Emerson and Michael Holquist (Austin: U of Texas P, 1981) 18-19.
19. From a private transcript of "A Conversation Between Derek Walcott and Edouard Glissant (New York: Poets' House, 11 April, 1991).
20. Joan Dayan, "The Beat and the Bawdy," review of Edward Kamau Brathwaite's *X/Self, The Nation* (9 April 1988): 507.
21. Brathwaite, "History, the Caribbean Writer and X/Self," *Crisis and Creativity in the New Literatures in English,* eds. Geoffrey V. Davis and Hena Maes-Jelinek (Amsterdam: Rodopi, 1990) 34.
22. Brathwaite, *The Arrivants: A New World Trilogy* (London: Oxford UP, 1973). All quotations from *The Arrivants* are identified by page number in parentheses in the text.
23. Christine Pagnoulle, "Labyrinth of Past/Present/Future in Some of Kamau Brathwaite's recent Poems," *Crisis and Creativity in the New Literatures in English,* eds. Geoffrey V. Davis and Hena Maes-Jelinek (Amsterdam: Rodopi, 1990) 449-450.
24. Brathwaite, "New World A-Comin'," *The Arrivants* 9-11.
25. Brathwaite, "Tom," *The Arrivants* 13.
26. Brathwaite, "The Emigrants," *The Arrivants* 51.
27. Maureen Warner Lewis, *Notes to Masks* (Benin: Ethiope, 1977) 16.
28. Harris, *The Womb of Space* (Westport, Connecticut: Greenwood, 1983).
29. Brathwaite, "The Gong-Gong," *The Arrivants* 97.

30. Marina Maxwell, "The Awakening of the Drum," *New World* 5.4. (1971): 44.
31. Brathwaite, Notes to *The Arrivants* 273.
32. Joyce Jonas, *Anancy in the Great House* (New York: Greenwood, 1990) 2.
33. Harris, "History, Fable and Myth in the Caribbean and the Guianas," *Caribbean Quarterly* 16.2 (June 1970): 16
34. Wilson Harris, "History" 6.
35. Brathwaite, "The Cracked Mother," *The Arrivants* 180-184.
36. Gordon Rohlehr, quotes Brathwaite's comments in *Pathfinder: Black Awakening in the Arrivants of Edward Kamau Brathwaite* (Trinidad: Rohlehr, 1981) 207.
37. John W. Nuley and Judith Bettelheim, *Caribbean Festival Arts* (Seattle: U of Washington P, 1988) 87-88.
38. Michael Dash, "Edward Brathwaite," *West Indian Literature*, ed. Bruce King (Connecticut: Archon, 1979) 223.
39. Pamela Mordecai, "The Image of the Pebble," *The Caribbean Poem,* Carib 5, Jamaica, WIACLALS (1989): 77.
40. Walcott, in Conversation with Lewis Lapman, *Thirteen Live*, New York PBS, 14 February 1991.
41. Walcott, in Conversation with Lewis Lapman.
42. Lillian Feder, *Ancient Myth in Modern Poetry* (Princeton: Princeton UP, 1971) 4.
43. John Figueroa, *"Omeros"* in *The Art of Derek Walcott*, ed. Stewart Brown (Wales: Seren, 1991) 211. Figueroa states categorically that *Omeros* "is not an epic, and it hardly touches on the gods." Figueroa negates Walcott's reconceptualization of epic form and his acknowledgment of African gods.
44. William Bascom, *The Yoruba of Southwestern Nigeria* (Prospect Heights, Illinois: Waveland, 1969) 82.
45. Harold Courlander, *The Drum and the Hoe* (Berkeley: U of California P, 1985) 20.
46. Omosade J. Awolalu, *Yoruba Beliefs and Sacrificial Rites* (Essex: Longman, 1979) 116.
47. Awolalu 117.
48. Walter Benjamin, "The Storyteller," *Illuminations: Essays and Reflections* (New York: Harcourt, 1968) 97.
49. Walcott, "The Muse of History" 8-9.
50. Walcott, "The Muse of History" 9.
51. George Lamming, *Conversations: George Lamming: Essays, Addresses and Interviews*, eds. Richard Drayton and Andaiye (London: Karia, 1992) 300.
52. Brathwaite, *Mother Poem* (Oxford: Oxford UP, 1977).

53. Walcott, *The Star-Apple Kingdom* (London: Cape, 1980) 50-51.
54. Derek Walcott, "The Light of the World," *The Arkansas Testament* (New York, Farrar, 1987) 50.
55. Walcott, *Another Life* (Washington, D.C.: Three Continents, 1982) 92.
56. Dayan, "Caribbean Cannibals and Whores," *Raritan* IX:2 (Fall 1989): 46.
57. Maya Deren, *Divine Horsemen: The Living Gods of Haiti* (New York: McPherson, 1991) 138.
58. Dayan, "Caribbean Cannibals and Whores" 56.
59. Grace Nichols, "Caribbean Woman's Prayer," *Caribbean Women Writers,* ed. Selwyn R. Cudjoe (Wellesley: Calaloux, 1990) 2.
60. Dayan, "Caribbean Cannibals and Whores" 50.
61. Orlando Patterson, *The Sociology of Slavery* (New Jersey: Fairleigh Dickinson UP) 236.
62. Lamming, *Comming Comming Home: Conversations II: Western Education and the Caribbean Intellectual* (St. Martin: Nehesi, 1995) 25.
63. Brathwaite, *Folk Culture of the Slaves in Jamaica* (London: New Beacon, 1971) 34.

Conclusion

here is the chant of light
the new source of singing
this is the ending
this is the beginning

—Goodison, "Ceremony for the Banishment of the King of Swords"

Historically, literary and cultural critics have positioned Kamau Brathwaite and Derek Walcott as contending forces located at opposing poles of Caribbean discourse. Kamau Brathwaite has been viewed as exclusively Afrocentric in orientation, while Derek Walcott has been celebrated as the Caribbean's most prominent English poet, well-versed in the classical tradition.[1] Such a polarity denies the similarity of the poets' vision and encourages a critical discourse that imprisons each poet in a world narrowly defined by critics who engage the poetry in isolation from the historical and cultural realities from which it emerges. In perpetuating this polarity, the literature, like the region, is once again colonized.

Kamau Brathwaite clearly intends his poetry to speak to members of the Caribbean's black population, so that they may recognize their position in society, become cognizant of their identity, and discover their connectedness to a creolized Caribbean culture. However, his intention is not isolationist. With recognition of their own place in the society, and an acknowledgment of this place by the rest of the population, the entire society moves towards integration and the identification of a common Caribbean identity that moves beyond race. While Derek Walcott might deny it vehemently, his poetry, too, is rooted in the African experience. The ambivalence that surfaces so often in his work is a result of his attempts to give both African and English ancestors equal voice, but in the Caribbean's diverse world, the African experience is the dominant one. In the world of both poets, the civilizing rituals and customs of the African ancestors add a deep appreciation for the grandeur and vibrancy of the physical world, at the same time they provide a way of integrating the national landscape into the Caribbean psyche.

In the territories of their imagination, Kamau Brathwaite and Derek Walcott engage in rewriting the fictions of official colonial history in order to create a Caribbean narrative of possibility. The intent of such a narrative is to fill the deliberately cultivated historical and cultural void and to provide a New World identity as a response to the annihilation of self inculcated in Caribbean people by both European and Caribbean colonials and their modernist counterparts. The poets' task is one of inordinate struggle against both reactionary politicians and an often naive population, while they simultaneously remain keenly aware of their own responsibilities and the transformative power of literature. Literature's role in "rebuilding a national cultural heritage" is an essential part of the political struggle to achieve independence and freedom from colonial rule, as Edward Said recognizes:

> For in the decades-long struggle to achieve decolonization and independence from European control, literature has played a crucial role in the re-establishment of a national cultural heritage, in the re-instatement of native idioms, in the re-imagining and re-figuring of local histories, geographies, communities.[2]

The reclamation of cultural forms—its linkage to an African past and its role in identity creation—becomes an integral marker of a refashioned Caribbean national territory as well as the particular legacy of Kamau Brathwaite and Derek Walcott. This legacy reechoes with new life and vitality in the imaginative landscapes of the region's contemporary poets. Younger poets (for example, Lorna Goodison, Jean Binta Breeze, Grace Nichols, Cynthia James, Fred D'Aguiar, Kendel Hippolyte, and Mutabaruka) locate their texts in an already repossessed Caribbean territory. Kamau Brathwaite's mythic quest for connections to an African homeland is an integral part of these aesthetics of time and place. Both poets' honing of the writer's craft, their experimentation with language (particularly Brathwaite's bold experimentation with nation language and his "video style"), allow the younger poets to explore new imaginary landscapes and cast new stylistic inventions. With supreme mastery of craft, they leap beyond fragmentation to a spiritual universe where individual and communal experiences become part of the limitless possibilities of the human spirit. Existing in a postmodern world and having leaped beyond historical chaos and the loss of identity, contemporary poets can now explore the unfolding daily drama of imagination, spirit, and relationship, for as Wilson Harris suggests, "a post-modernism that is bereft of depth or of an appreciation of the life of the intuitive imagination is but a game for a dictatorship of technologies aligned to sophistry and nihilism."[3] As the Caribbean world continues to flounder in its dependency on the United States and the rest of the Western world, Caribbean people become more entrapped in the relentless technologizing of the West. Much in evidence is a movement away from a life of the spirit and a growing celebration of the technologies of the material world.

In response to the confusions and shifting, tenuous landscapes of the postmodern world, contemporary poets create imaginary sites of empowerment where existence has meaning and values and beliefs are worthwhile. In opposition to this state of moral permanence is the increasing growth of a worldwide descent into violence and spiritual chaos. To ensure survival in the face of chaos, the female poets, in particular, invent spaces, personae, and images sacred to their experience as women and directly connected to an African ancestral past.

As an example, many of the female poets invoke Nanny, the Maroon warrior, as their source of both inspiration and resistance.[4] This is a major departure from the tendency of the past, for Nanny, while she is the bridge between Africa and the New World, is firmly located in a distinct Caribbean ethos. As a figure of resistance, Nanny inspirits the imaginary landscapes created by the female poets, transforming ordinary moments of existence into moments of rebellion, meditation, reconciliation, and ultimately a renewal of strength. Lorna Goodison's Nanny is a transcendent figure in ways Walcott's Ma Kilman is not. An examination of Goodison's "Nanny" poem clearly illustrates this reality.[5] Goodison's Nanny is imbued with superhuman qualities, for it is her mission to retrieve the collective past. She travels through time and space and her journeys explore the past and history. In addition, her journey from Africa is a subversive act. Trained in Africa in the ways of resistance, Nanny is deliberately sold into slavery to spearhead the resistance movement in the New World:

> And when my training was over
> they circled my waist with pumpkin seeds
> and dried okra, a traveller's jigida
> and sold me to the traders
> all my weapons within me.
> I was sent, tell that to history.   [45]

While Nanny's consciousness is a collective one, Goodison uses this wandering figure to explore the complexity of the female self, a self unexplored in the work of earlier male poets. Nanny carries within her the seeds of resistance as well as the seeds of healing. The ultimate warrior, she is a woman for whom physical motherhood is not a necessary option. Instead, she chooses racial motherhood. In a "state of perpetual siege," her "womb was sealed with molten wax of killer bees" (44). With this image, Goodison acknowledges the fearsome power of sexuality. The deliberate suppression of Nanny's sexuality allows Goodison to create a figure who represents the epitome of resistance, a figure capable of destruction, not merely procreation. The history of Nanny's African experience and the experience of her journey to the New World is inscribed on her body. Well aware of the African powers of survival and healing, as well as New World rebellion and strategies of resistance, Nanny inhabits the lonely space of self-knowledge; she "became most knowing / and forever alone" (70).

Like Lorna Goodison, Jean Binta Breeze and Grace Nichols use the Nanny figure to symbolize female resistance and the inherent ancestral strength of women. Binta Breeze's Nanny is a warrior who "puffin pon a red clay pipe," sits and plans ways of bringing her people to freedom:

> an ebery smoke fram er pipe
> is a signal fi de fight
> an de people dem a sing
> mek de cockpit ring
> an de chant jus a rise, jus a rise
> to de skies
> wid de fervour of freedom[6]

Grace Nichol's Nanny is "Ashanti Priestess" and "Maroonic woman" who, "mouthing a new beginning song," conjures up strategies of resistance and survival. Resistance in women's poetry is female-centered, and the poets gather together sources and origins to write out of a complex and exhilarating integration of self and place. The Caribbean is thus both home and homeland, and the poets, in acknowledging ancestral roots and imagined presences, pay tribute to the region's wild spirits. Like the earlier poets, contemporary poets are equally bound to an ancestral past and the concept of Africa as woman, healer, nurturer, and keeper of a people's cultural heritage.

The female poets, just as their male counterparts, are intensely aware of the woman's body as territory and battleground. But instead of merely acknowledging this as metaphor, they reclaim the female body as a site of public and personal empowerment. Cynthia James in her invocation to "On Moaning Ground-Dream One" cries out:

> Mother
> seal me

point me the way
wash my mouth
that my tongue

not betray
wash my feet
that when I mark
time be light
wash my hands
that all I write
serve world
serve deed
serve light[7]

James's appeal "Mother / seal me" is reminiscent of Goodison's Nanny whose "womb was sealed / with molten wax / of killer bees" (69). Both poets create an archetypal figure in whose person sexuality is deliberately forfeited for public service. The image of a sealed womb also symbolizes a protected space suggesting fragility and vulnerability as well as vibrancy and creativity. Female poets transform this space into a sacred female one:

Mother of origins, guardian
    of passages;

generator of new life in the flood
    waters, orgasm,
birth waters, baptism.[8]

Here in the process of transformation, Olive Senior's water imagery echoes the powerful symbolism seen earlier in the works of Kamau Brathwaite and Derek Walcott. The female poets like their male counterparts, focus on the sea as repository of history, a reminder of the Africans dark days of journey and resettlement. But they stretch the image much further. Out of the cataclysmic union of old world and new emerges the new life of the Caribbean. The myths have already been created and history reclaimed; therefore, contemporary poets can now move on to pay tribute to the ancestral experience and acknowledge its relevance to the diversity of the Caribbean experience.

Brathwaite and Walcott have contributed immensely to the validation of the Caribbean experience. Brathwaite, particularly—by celebrating all aspects of the folk experience and foregrounding nation language, the language of the folk—has stretched the boundaries of language. Both men have made it possible for contemporary poets to capture the experiences of the Caribbean in the language of the Caribbean. Fred D'Aguiar's persona Mama Dot, who is rooted in African cosmology, comments on the frustrations of existence in a postindependent Guyana:

> Every meal is salt-fish these days; we even
> Curry it. Send a box soon. Pack the basics:
> Flour, for some roti; powdered milk;
> And any news of what's going on here.
> No luxuries please, people only talk, shoes
> Can wait till things improve (dey bound
> Fe improve cause dem cawn get no worse!)[9]

Like Fred D'Aguiar, Jean Binta Breeze, in "Riddym Ravings (The Mad Woman's Poem)," captures, in the vernacular of the region, the poverty, joylessness, and the sense of a country under siege:

> fah wen hungry mek King St. pavement

bubble an dally in front a mi yeye
an mi foot start wanda falla fly
to de garbage pan eena de chinaman backlat
dem nearly chap aff mi han eena de butcha shap
fi de piece a ratten poke
ah de same time de mawga gal in front a mi
drap de laas piece a ripe banana
an mi—ben dung—pick i up—an nyam i[10]

Breeze and D'Aguiar are clearly direct descendants of Kamau Brathwaite in their development of the use of nation language to explore all aspects of the Caribbean experience. They do more than capture what Lloyd Brown describes as the "multifaceted reality that is the West Indian experience."[11] In addition, they maintain the live aspect of the poetry so that poet and public are always in debate. They address their public directly in speech patterns their audience understands.

In the current stage of development of Caribbean poetry, deep connections to the rhythms of the people abound. These connections would not have been possible were it not for Kamau Brathwaite's innovative work in nation language. Nation language is always evolving. Contemporary poets continue to explore poetry's connection to the vernacular as they capture, in their imaginative worlds, the rhythms of the people. Younger poets like Jean Binta Breeze and Mutaburuka have shattered the boundaries of nation language and added a new dimension of totality to the written word. In their worlds, poetry is not a static commodity dormant on the page. They bring to the written word an involvement of body, sound, and spirit. This total involvement, a relatively new development in Caribbean poetry, is described as "dub poetry." In *Noises in the Blood*, Carolyn Cooper quotes Oku Onuora's definition of dub poetry:

It's dubbing out the little penta-metre and the little high-
falutin business and dubbing in the rootsical, yard, basic
rhythm that I-an-I know. Using the language, using the body.
It also mean to dub out the isms and schisms and to dub con-
sciousness into the people-dem head. That's dub poetry.[12]

The dub poets' peculiar strength is their ability to penetrate
the roots of the culture, to erase particularities and divisions, and
to celebrate, consciously, regional commonalities. That the artic-
ulation of dub is a highly political act is not in question. The poets
make no compromises. Jean Binta Breeze's poem "Ilands" makes
this point clear.[13] The poet is both the spirit and the conscience
of the islands. In her songs, she invokes the gods and presents
the pain of her people:

> I was in the mountains
> singing out the pain
> for there
> I felt the gods
> would hear
> and did   [77]

Recounting the particular history of each island and Guyana in
a grand symphony, the poem culminates in a moment of "know-
ing," a recognition of the Caribbeanness of things and the birth
of identity:

> leewardwinward
> greaterlesser
> we are one
> in the shelter
> after storm

can we now
Caribe
from all our knowing
finally
be born   [84]

Breeze and the new generation of poets emerging from the tra-
dition of self and societal examination established by Brathwaite
and Walcott have a new awareness of self and world. Their con-
sciousness is no longer fragmented, and the identity they claim
finds its expression in their acknowledgment of a Caribbean
cosmos, where the inspiriting forces of Africa are no longer
marginalized but are located at the center of their existence.

The publication of *Confluence*, an anthology of nine St.
Lucian Poets,[14] is an example of the younger poets' move beyond
fragmentation. Kendel Hippolyte, the editor himself a poet, rec-
ognizes that the "sundering questions of race, colonialism,
Caribbean identity, that split society and self in the two previ-
ous decades, are not confronting [younger poets] in the same
way."[15] McDonald Dixon's, "The Middle Passage," celebrates the
integrated self that emerges from the fires of the crossing from
Africa to the New World. Dixon also explores more inclusive
themes. "A Few Lines Written to a Friend Slowly Dying in Vietnam"
captures the familiar pathos of a slow death in an alien land:

Your mother has bought her black shroud;
When you die your soul flies home to God.
To that green-bordered sea, where
pink shells mourn, and the soft tumbling
wave,
Drums your lamentation to the sand.
It is so useless rotting in a foreign land.   [5]

Most striking here is Dixon's reversal of the African myth of the soul's flying home to Africa upon the death of the body. The African homeland is instead firmly located in the Caribbean, where the ritual drums now beat.

Dixon's poem is significant of another trend in the region's new poetry. More and more Caribbean poets are situating themselves at the center of a global political discourse. While the English-speaking Caribbean's groundbreaking writers and poets migrated mainly to England, the current poets also live in Canada and the United States and often commute between the Caribbean and the metropoles. The work of Nourbese Philip, originally from Tobago and now living in Toronto, emerges directly from the Brathwaite tradition in her topographical experimentations.[16] In addition to her experiments with form, she shares the earlier poets' concern with the deteriorating quality of life in the Caribbean and the growing global marginalization of black people. Jane King in a poem, "Intercity Dub, for Jean," pays tribute to the work of Jean Binta Breeze who manages to suggest a future of possibility, in spite of recounting a narrative of desperation:

> And London is a hell
> In many parts.
> But your voice rings true
> From the edge of hell
> Cause the music is the love
> And you sing it so well.[17]

Not only London, but also the postindependent Caribbean, can be described as "the edge of hell." The invasion of Grenada, in 1983, was the actualization of a continuous psychic invasion and a growing Americanization of the region. Kendel Hippolyte, in "Birthright," attacks the collusion between foreign governments and Caribbean politicians and their populations' growing desire for "the good life U.$.A."[18] Melchoir Henry in the same anthology, asks the question: "How come now / the Poets Speak Of / FIRE? (43). The poets must speak of fire, for in the Caribbean both past and present realities are grounded in catastrophe. But the work of the artist is to find redemption, and they do:

> Until
> the fingers of the blood
> assort the images
> the wind remembers
> sifting the long grass
> the womb impulses
> summoning the beast
> In
> a new testament
> the Word[19]

Here Pamela Mordecai acknowledges past connections to an African ancestry even as she affirms a new beginning. In this acknowledgment and affirmation, the Caribbean's contemporary poets owe a debt to Kamau Brathwaite, Derek Walcott, and the poets who preceded them. The earlier poets have, in the words of Derek Walcott, allowed their heirs to "enter the light beyond metaphor." The younger poets in their search for truth and permanence, secure in their ethnic skins, explore the inner world of feeling and rediscover the outer world of the Caribbean, its shifting landscape and challenging reality.

Notes

1. See Geert Lernout's comment, "The ambition of Walcott's poem is clear: the poet measures himself against Homer, Dante, Shakespeare and Joyce," in "Derek Walcott's *Omeros*: The Isle is Full of Voices," *Kunapipi* 14.2 (1992): 90. See also "A Song of Lost Islands," *The Economist* (10 December 1994): 93. Here it is suggested that Brathwaite overemphasizes the Middle Passage experience and, as a result, "millions [of people] remain perversely indifferent."
2. Edward Said, "Figures, Configurations, Transfigurations," From *Commonwealth to Post-Colonial,* ed. Anna Rutherford (Denmark: Dangaroo, 1992) 3.
3. Wilson Harris, "The Fabric of the Imagination," *From Commonwealth to Post-Colonial,* 29.
4. Nanny was a free Ashanti woman whose history has been shrouded in mystery. She played a major role during Jamaica's First Maroon War. See Lucille Mathurin, "A Historical Study of Women in Jamaica from 1655-1844," diss., University of the West Indies, 1974, 101; and Kamau Brathwaite, *Wars of Respect* (Kingston, Jamaica: API, 1977) 15.
5. "Nanny," *Lorna Goodison Selected Poems* (Michigan: Michigan UP, 1992) 69-70.
6. Jean Binta Breeze, "soun de abeng fi nanny," *Riddym Ravings and Other Poems,* ed. Mervyn Morris (London: Race Today, 1988) 45-47.
7. Cynthia James, "On Moaning Ground-Dream One, *Vigil* (Trinidad: Ferguson, 1995) 26.
8. Olive Senior, "Yemoja: Mother of Waters," *Gardening in The Tropics* (Toronto: McClelland & Stewart, 1994) 131.
9. Fred D'Aguiar, "Letter from Mama Dot," *Mama Dot* (London: Chatto, 1985) 20-21.
10. Jean Binta Breeze, *Spring Cleaning* (London: Virago, 1992) 19-22.
11. Lloyd W. Brown, *West Indian Poetry* (London: Heinemann, 1984) 186.
12. Carolyn Cooper, *Noises in the Blood* (London: Macmillan, 1993) 80-81.
13. Jean Binta Breeze, *Spring Cleaning* 77-85.
14. Kendel Hippolyte, *Confluence: Nine St. Lucian Poets,* ed. Kendel Hippolyte (St. Lucia: The Source, 1988).
15. Kendel Hippolyte, preface, *Confluence* i.
16. See Marlene Nourbese Philip, "Discourse on the Logic of Language," *She Tries Her Tongue Her Silence Softly Breaks* (Canada: Ragweed, 1989) 56-59.

17. Jane King, *Confluence* 23.
18. Kendel Hippolyte, *Confluence* 18.
19. Pamela Mordecai, "Poem for Edward Kamau Brathwaite," *Journey Poem* (Jamaica: Sandberry, 1989) 41.

Bibliography

Achebe, Chinua. "The Novelist as Teacher." *Morning Yet on Creation Day*. New York: Anchor, 1976.

Auerbach, Erich. *Mimesis*. New York: Anchor, 1957.

Awolalu, J. Omosade. *Yoruba Beliefs and Sacrificial Rights*. Essex: Longman, 1979.

Bakhtin, M.M. *The Dialogic Imagination*. Trans. Caryl Emerson and Michael Holquist. Austin: U of Texas P, 1981.

Bascom, William. *The Yoruba of Southwestern Nigeria*. Prospect Heights, Illinois: Waveland, 1969.

Benítez-Rojo, Antonio. *The Repeating Island: The Caribbean and the Postmodern Perspective*. Trans. James Maraniss. Durham: Duke UP, 1996.

Benjamin, Walter. "The Storyteller." *Illuminations: Essays and Reflections*. New York: Harcourt, 1968.

Bhabha, Homi. "Of Mimicry and Man: The Ambivalence of Colonial Discourse." *October* 28. 125-133.

Brathwaite, Edward Kamau. *The Arrivants: A New World Trilogy*. London: Oxford UP, 1973.

—. *Barabajan Poems*. Kingston & New York: Savacou North, 1994.

—. *DreamStories*. Essex: Longman, 1994.

—. *Jah Music*. Jamaica: Savacou, 1986.

—. *Mother Poem*. Oxford: Oxford UP, 1977.

—. *Sun Poem*. Oxford: Oxford UP, 1982.

—. *Trench Town Rock*. Providence: Lost Roads, 1994.

—. *Third World Poems*. Essex: Longman, 1983.

——. *Black + Blues.* Habana, Cuba: Casa de las Américas, 1986.

——. *X/Self.* Oxford: Oxford UP, 1987.

——. *The Zea Mexican Diary.* Madison: U of Wisconsin P, 1993.

——. *History of the Voice.* London: New Beacon, 1984.

——. *Wars of Respect: Nanny and Sam Sharpe.* Kingston, Jamaica: API, 1976.

——. "The African Presence in Caribbean Literature." *Roots.* Havana: Casa de las Américas, 1986. 190-258.

——. "Caribbean Culture: Two Paradigms." *Missile and Capsule.* Ed. Jurgen Martini. Bremen: n.p. 1983. 9-54.

——. "Caribbean Man in Time and Space." *Carifesta Forum.* Ed. John Hearne. Jamaica: Institute of Jamaica and Jamaica Journal. 1976. 199-208.

——. "The Love Axe/1." *Bim* 16.61 (June 1977): 53-65.

——. "Gods of the Middle Passage: A Tennament." *Caribbean Review* Vol. XI.4 (1982): 18+.

——. *Folk Culture of the Slaves in Jamaica.* London: New Beacon, 1971.

——. *Contradictory Omens: Cultural Diversity and Integration in the Caribbean.* Mona, Jamaica: Savacou, 1974.

——. "Timehri." *Is Massa Day Dead? Black Moods in the Caribbean.* Ed. Orde Coombs. New York: Anchor, 1974. 29-45.

——. "History, the Caribbean Writer and X/Self." *Crisis and Creativity in the New Literatures in English.* Eds. Geoffrey V. Davis and Hena Maes-Jelinek. Amsterdam: Rodopi, 1990. 23-45.

——. Interview. *Hambone* 9 (Winter 1991): 42-59.

——. "A Post Cautionary Tale of the Helen of Our Wars." *Wasafiri* 22 (Autumn 1995): 69-78.

Breeze, Jean Binta. *Riddym Ravings and Other Poems.* Ed. Mervyn Morris (London: Race Today, 1988).

——. *Spring Cleaning.* London, England: Virago, 1992.

Brown, Stewart, Mervyn Morris and Gordon Rohlehr. Eds. *Voice Print.* Essex: Longman, 1989.

Brown, Stewart. "Spoiler, Walcott's People's Patriot." *Wasafiri* 9 (Winter 1988/1989): 10-14.

Brown, Lloyd. *West Indian Poetry.* London: Heinemann, 1984.

——. "The Revolutionary Dream of Walcott's Makak." *Critics on Caribbean Literature.* Ed. Edward Baugh. New York: St. Martin, 1978. 58-62.

Buell, Frederick. *National Culture and the New Global System.* Baltimore: Johns Hopkins UP, 1994.

Burnett, Paula, ed. *The Penguin Book of Caribbean Verse in English.* Middlesex: Penguin, 1988.

Cameron, Norman. Ed. *Guianese Poetry: 1831-1931.* Georgetown, Guyana: Argosy, 1931.

Caribbean Freedom: Economy and Society from Emancipation to the Present. Eds. Hilary Beckles & Verence Shepherd. London and Jamaica: Currey and Randle, 1993.

Carlyle, Thomas. "Occasional Discourse on the Nigger Question." *English and Other Critical Essays.* New York: Dutton, 1925. 303-333.

Carter, Martin. *Poems of Resistance.* Georgetown: Guyana UP, 1964.

—. *Selected Poems.* Georgetown, Guyana: Demerara, 1989.

Césaire, Aimé. *Discourse on Colonialism.* New York: Monthly Review, 1972.

Chamberlin, J. Edward. *Come Back to Me My Language: Poetry and the West Indies.* Urbana: U of Illinois Press, 1993.

Cooper, Carolyn. *Noises in the Blood.* London: Macmillan, 1993.

Courlander, Harold. *The Drum and the Hoe.* Berkeley: U of California P, 1985.

D'Aguiar, Fred. *Mama Dot.* London: Chatto, 1985.

Daly, Vere, I'. "The Song of Young Guiana." *Guianese Poetry.* Ed. Norman Cameron. Georgetown, Guyana: Argosy, 1931.

Dash, Michael. "Edward Brathwaite." *West Indian Literature.* Ed. Bruce King. Hamden, Ct: Archon, 1979.

—. *Edouard Glissant.* Cambridge: Cambridge UP, 1995.

Dathorne, O.R., ed. *Caribbean Verse.* London: Heinemann, 1967.

Dayan, Joan. "Caribbean Cannibals and Whores." *Raritan* IX:2 Fall (1989): 45-67.

—. "The Beat and the Bawdy." Review of Edward Kamau Brathwaite's *X/Self. The Nation* 9 April 1988: 504-507.

Deren, Maya. *Divine Horsemen: The Living Gods of Haiti.* New York: McPherson, 1991.

Dixon, Melvin. "Rivers Remembering Their Source." *Afro-American Literature.* Ed. Dexter Fisher and Robert B. Stepto. New York: MLA 1979.

Eagleton, Terry. *Nationalism, Irony and Commitment.* Derry, Ireland: Field Day Pamphlet #13, 1988.

—. *The Ideology of the Aesthetic.* Oxford, Blackwell, 1990.

Edwards, Bryan. *The History Civil, and Commercial of the British West Indies.* New York: AMS, 1966.

Edwards, Gary and John Mason. *Black Gods: Orisha Studies in the New World.* New York: Yoruba Theological Archministry, 1985.

Fabre, Michel. "Adam's Task of Giving Things their Name." *New Letters* 41 (Fall 1974): 91-107.

Fanon, Frantz. *The Wretched of the Earth.* England: Penguin, 1967.

Feder, Lillian. *Ancient Myth in Modern Poetry.* Princeton: Princeton UP, 1971.

Figueroa, John, ed. *Caribbean Voices.* New York: Luce, 1973.

Fox, Robert Elliot. "Derek Walcott: History as Dis-Ease." *Callaloo* 27:9.2. (Spring 1986): 331-340.

Froude, James Anthony. *The English in the West Indies or The Bow of Ulysses.* London: Longmans, 1909.

Gates, Henry Louis. *The Signifying Monkey.* New York: Oxford UP, 1988.

Glissant, Edouard. *Caribbean Discourse.* Trans. Michael Dash. Charlottesville: U of Virginia P, 1989.

Goodison, Lorna. *Selected Poems.* Ann Arbor, Michigan: U of Michigan P, 1992.

Griffiths, Gareth. *A Double Exile: African and West Indian Writing Between Two Cultures.* London: Boyars, 1978.

Hamner, Robert D. *Derek Walcott.* Boston: Twayne, 1981.

Harris, Wilson. *Explorations.* Denmark: Dangaroo, 1981.

——. *Eternity to Season.* Guyana: n.p., 1954.

——. "History, Fable and Myth in the Caribbean and the Guyanas." *Caribbean Quarterly* 16.2. (June 1970): 1-33.

——. *The Womb of Space.* (Westport, Conn.: Greenwood, 1983.

Hippolyte, Kendel. Ed. *Confluence: Nine St. Lucian Poets.* St. Lucia: The Source, 1988.

Idowu, E.B. *Olódùmarè: God in Yoruba Belief.* New York: African Islamic Mission, 1988.

Ismond, Patricia. "Another Life: Autobiography as Alternate History." *Journal of West Indian Literature* 4.1 (January 1990): 41-49.

Izevbaye, D.S. "The Exile and the Prodigal: Derek Walcott as West Indian Poet." *Caribbean Quarterly* 26 (March-June 1980): 70-82.

Jahn, Janheinz. *Muntu.* Trans. Marjorie Grene. New York: Grove, 1961.

James, Cynthia. "On Moaning Ground-Dream One." *Vigil* (Trinidad: Ferguson, 1995) 26.

James, C.L.R. *The Black Jacobins.* New York: Vintage, 1963.

——. *Beyond a Boundary.* New York: Pantheon, 1983.

Jameson, Fredric. "Third-World Literature in the Era of Multinational Capitalism." *Social Text* 15 (Fall 1986): 65-88.

Jonas, Joyce. *Anancy in the Great House.* New York: Greenwood, 1990.

Kennedy, Ellen Conroy. Ed. *The Negritude Poets: An Anthology from the French.* New York: Thunder's Mouth, 1989.

Ker, Walter. *Epic and Romance.* New York: Dover, 1957.

Kiple, Kenneth. *The Caribbean Slaves: A Biological History.* London: Cambridge UP, 1984.

Lamming, George. *Season of Adventure.* London: Allison, 1979.

——. *In the Castle of My Skin*. New York: Collier, 1953.

——. *The Pleasures of Exile*. London: Allison, 1984.

——. *Conversations: George Lamming: Essays, Addresses and Interviews*. Eds. Richard Drayton and Andaiye. London: Karia, 1992.

——. *Coming Coming Home: Conversations II: Western Education and the Caribbean Intellectual*. St. Martin: Nehesi, 1995.

Lernout, Geert. "Derek Walcott's *Omeros*: The Isle is Full of Voices." *Kunapipi* 14.2 (1992):

Lewis, Gordon K. "The Caribbean: Colonization and Culture." *Studies on the Left*. Vol.II. I. (1961): 26-42.

——. *The Growth of the Modern West Indies*. New York: Monthly Review, 1968.

Long, Edward. *The History of Jamaica*. Vol. 2. London: 1774.

Lyn, Diana. "The Concept of the Mulatto in some Works of Derek Walcott." *Caribbean Quarterly* 26.1&2 (March-June 1980): 49-67.

Marshall, Paule. "The Making of a Writer: From the Poets in the Kitchen." *Reena and Other Stories*. New York: Feminist, 1983. 1-12.

Maxwell, Marina. "The Awakening of the Drum." *New World*. 5.4. (1971): 39-45.

McKay, Claude. *The Dialect Poetry of Claude McKay*. 2 vols. Salem, New Hampshire: Ayer, 1987.

Memmi, Albert. *The Colonizer and the Colonized*. Boston: Beacon, 1967.

Menezes, Mary Noel. *Scenes from the History of the Portuguese in Guyana*. England: Victoria, 1986.

Métraux, Alfred. *Voodoo in Haiti*. New York: Schocken, 1972.

Mordecai, Pamela. "The Image of the Pebble in Brathwaite's *Arrivants*." "The Caribbean Poem." *Carib* No. 5. Kingston: WIACLALS, 1989. 60-78.

——. *Journey Poem*. Kingston, Jamaica: Sandberry, 1989.

Moretti, Franco. *Modern Epic: The World System from Goethe to García Márquez*. London: Verso, 1996.

Morrison, Toni. "The Site of Memory." *Inventing the Truth*. Ed. William Zinsser. Boston: Houghton, 1987.

Naipaul, V.S. *The Middle Passage*. Middlesex: Penguin, 1969.

——. "Prologue to an Autobiography." *Finding the Center*. New York: Vintage, 1986. 1-72.

Nettleford, Rex. *Inward Stretch Outward Reach: A Voice from the Caribbean*. New York: Caribbean Diaspora Press, 1995.

Ngugi, Wa Thiong'o. *Decolonizing the Mind*. New Hampshire: Heinemann, 1988.

Nicholas, Tracy. *Rastafari.* New York: Anchor, 1979.

Nichols Grace. "Caribbean Women's Prayer." *Caribbean Women Writers.* Ed. Selwyn R. Cudjoe. Wellesley: Calaloux, 1990. 1-3.

Nuley, John W. and Judith Bettelheim. *Caribbean Festival Arts.* Seattle: Washington UP, 1988.

Okpewho, Isidore. *The Epic in Africa.* New York: Columbia UP, 1979.

Owens, Joseph. *Dread: The Rastafarians of Jamaica.* Jamaica: Sangster's, 1976.

Pagnoulle, Christine. "Labyrinth of past/present/future in some of Kamau Brathwaite's recent Poems." *Crisis and Creativity in the New Literatures in English.* Eds. Geoffrey V. Davis and Hena Maes-Jelinek. Amsterdam: Rodopi, 1990. 449-466.

Parry, J.H., and Philip Sherlock. *A Short History of the West Indies.* London: Macmillan, 1971.

Patterson, Orlando. *An Absence of Ruins.* London: Hutchinson, 1967.

—. *The Sociology of Slavery.* New Jersey: Fairleigh Dickinson UP, 1967.

—. *Slavery and Social Death: A Comparative Study.* Cambridge: Harvard UP, 1982.

Philip, Marlene Nourbese. *She Tries Her Tongue Her Silence Softly Breaks.* Charlottetown, P.E.I., Canada: Ragweed, 1989.

Price, Richard. Ed. *Maroon Societies.* Baltimore: Johns Hopkins UP, 1979.

Ramchand, Kenneth and Cecil Gray. *West Indian Poetry.* Essex: Longman, 1989.

Rigaud, Milo. *Secrets of Voodoo.* New York: Arco, 1969.

Rodney, Walter. *How Europe Underdeveloped Africa.* London: Bogle L'Overture, 1972.

—. *A History of the Guianese Working People, 1881-1905.* Baltimore: Johns Hopkins UP, 1981.

Rohlehr, Gordon. "Song of the Skeleton: Flowers of the Harmattan." Interdepartmental Conference in English. University of the West Indies, St. Thomas W.I. 1985.

—. *Calypso & Society in Pre-Independence Trinidad.* Port of Spain, Trinidad: Rohlehr, 1990.

—. "Dream Journeys," *World Literature Today.* Autumn (1994): 765-774.

—. "The Problem of the Problem of Form: The Idea of an Aesthetic Continuum and Aesthetic-Code Switching in West Indian Literature." *The Shape of That Hurt.* Trinidad: Longman, 1992. 1-65.

—. "West Indian Poetry: Some Problems of Assessment." *Bim* 14.55 (July-Dec. 1972): 134-144.

——. *Pathfinder: Black Awakening in the* Arrivants *of Edward Kamau Brathwaite.* Port of Spain, Trinidad: Rohlehr, 1981.

Rutherford, Anna. Ed. *From Commonwealth to Post-Colonial.* Denmark: Dangaroo, 1992.

Said, Edward. *The World, the Text and the Critic.* Cambridge, Massachusetts: Harvard UP, 1983.

Samaniego, Filoteo. "Naming Things in a New World." *Diogenes* (Summer 1979): 90-109.

Seaga, Edward. *Revival Cults in Jamaica.* Jamaica Journal Reprint Vol. 3 No. 2 (June 1969): Kingston, Jamaica: Jamaica Institute 1982.

Senior, Olive. *Gardening in the Tropics.* Toronto: McClelland & Stewart, 1994.

Seymour, A.J. *The Guiana Book.* Guiana: Argosy, 1948.

——. *The Making of Guyanese Literature.* Guyana: n.p., 1978.

Simmons, Harold. "Notes on Folklore in St. Lucia." *Iouanaloa.* Ed. Kamau Brathwaite. St. Lucia: 1963. 41-49.

Skidelsky, "A Song of Lost Islands." *The Economist* 10 December 1994: 93.

Taylor, Patrick, *The Narrative of Liberation.* Ithaca: Cornell UP, 1989.

The Art of Kamau Brathwaite. Ed. Stewart Brown. Plantin, Wales: Cromwell, 1995.

The Art of Derek Walcott. Cardiff, Wales: Seren, 1991.

Thomas, J.J. *Froudacity: West Indian Fables by James Anthony Froude.* London: New Beacon, 1969.

Thompson, Robert Farris. *Flash of the Spirit.* New York: Vintage, 1983.

Trollope, Anthony. *The West Indies and the Spanish Main.* New York: Hippocrene, 1985.

Uhrbach, Jan. "A Note on Language and Naming in *Dream on Monkey Mountain.*" *Callaloo* 29:9.4 (Fall 1986): 578-582.

Vendler, Helen. "Poet of Two Worlds." *The New York Review.* 4 March 1982.

Walcott, Derek. *25 Poems.* Bridgetown, Barbados: Advocate, 1949.

——. "The Antilles: Fragments of Epic Memory." *The Nobel Lecture.* New York: Farrar, 1970.

——. *In a Green Night.* London: Cape, 1969.

——. *The Castaway.* London: Cape, 1969.

——. *The Gulf.* New York: Farrar, 1970.

——. *Sea Grapes.* New York: Farrar, 1976.

——. *The Star-Apple Kingdom.* London: Cape, 1980.

——. *The Fortunate Traveller.* New York: Farrar, 1980.

——. *Another Life.* Washington: Three Continents, 1982.

——. *Midsummer.* London: Faber, 1984.

——. *Collected Poems.* New York: Farrar, 1986.

——. *The Arkansas Testament.* New York: Farrar, 1987.

——. *Omeros.* New York: Farrar, 1990.

——. *Dream on Monkey Mountain and Other Plays.* New York: Noonday, 1989.

——. Interview. By Melvyn Bragg. *The South Bank Show.* London Weekend Television. 2 Nov. 1988.

——. *Bookmark.* With Lewis Lapman. Channel 31. 14 Feb. 1991.

——. "The Muse of History." *Is Massa Day Dead? Black Moods in the Caribbean.* Ed. Orde Coombs. New York: Anchor, 1974.

——. "The Caribbean: Culture or Mimicry." *Journal of Interamerican Studies and World Affairs* 16.1 (Feb. 1974): 3-13.

——. "Caligula's Horse." *Kunapipi* X1.1 (1989): 138-150.

——. Address. Medgar Evers Black Writers Conference. New York, 26 March 1988.

——. Interview with Lewis Lapman. *Thirteen Live.* PBS, New York. 14 Feb. 1991.

——. Interview. *Callaloo* 34:11.1 (Winter 1988): 80-89.

Walmsley, Anne. "Dimensions of Song." *Bim* 13 (July-Dec. 1970): 152-167.

Warner, Keith. *Kaiso! The Trinidad Calypso.* Washington: Three Continents, 1985.

Warner-Lewis, Maureen. *Notes to Masks.* Benin: Ethiope, 1977.

Williams, Eric. *Capitalism and Slavery.* New York: Putnam, 1966.

——. *From Columbus to Castro.* New York: Vintage, 1984.

Williams, Francis. "A Double Exile." *Voices in Exile.* Eds. Jean D'Costa and Barbara Lalla. Tuscaloosa: U of Alabama P, 1989. 9-12.

Wright, Philip. Ed. *Lady Nugent's Journal.* Jamaica: Institute of Jamaica, 1966.

Index

Permissions
Acknowledgements

For permission to reprint quotations from works by the poets mentioned in this book, grateful acknowledgement is made to the following:

Reprinted by kind permission from Ayer Company Publishers, Inc., North Stratford, NH. Excerpt from Claude McKay's "Bumming," 1987.

Reprinted by permission of Addison Wesley Longman Ltd. Excerpts from "Manchile" and "Kingston in the Kingdom of this World" from *Third World Poems* by Kamau Brathwaite, 1983.

Reprinted by kind permission of Louise Bennett. Excerpts from "Back to Africa" and "Independance" from *The Penguin Book of Caribbean Verse in English*, 1988.

Reprinted by kind permission of Kamau Brathwaite. Excerpts from "Alpha," "Hex," "Nametracks," and "Mid/Life" from *Mother Poem*, Oxford University Press, 1977.

Reprinted by kind permission of Kamau Brathwaite. Excerpts from "Red Rising," "Yellow Minnim," "The Crossing," "Noom, "Clips," and "Son" from *Sun Poem*, Oxford University Press, 1982.